MFA HIGHLIGHTS european painting and sculpture before 1800

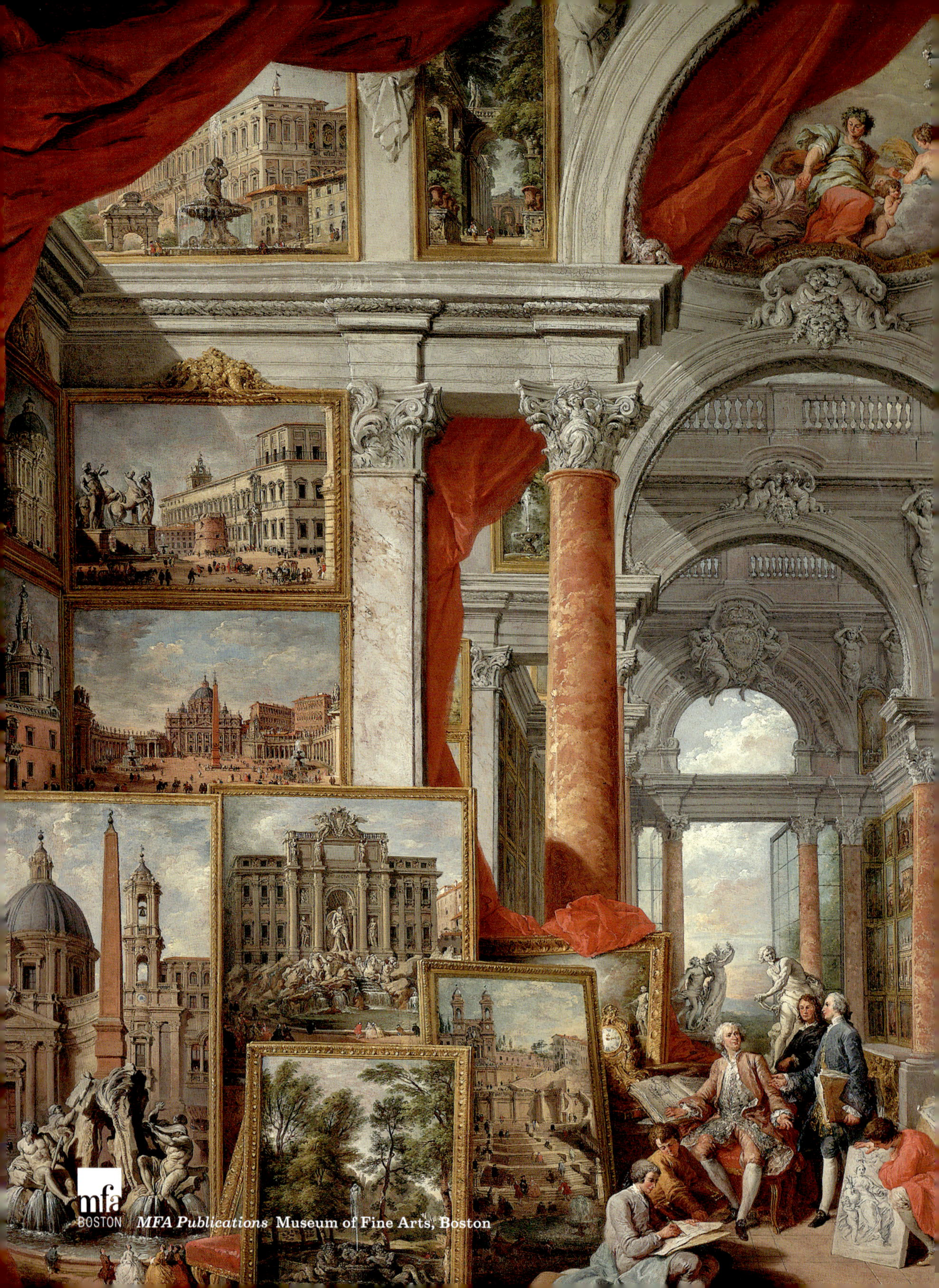
mfa
BOSTON
MFA Publications Museum of Fine Arts, Boston

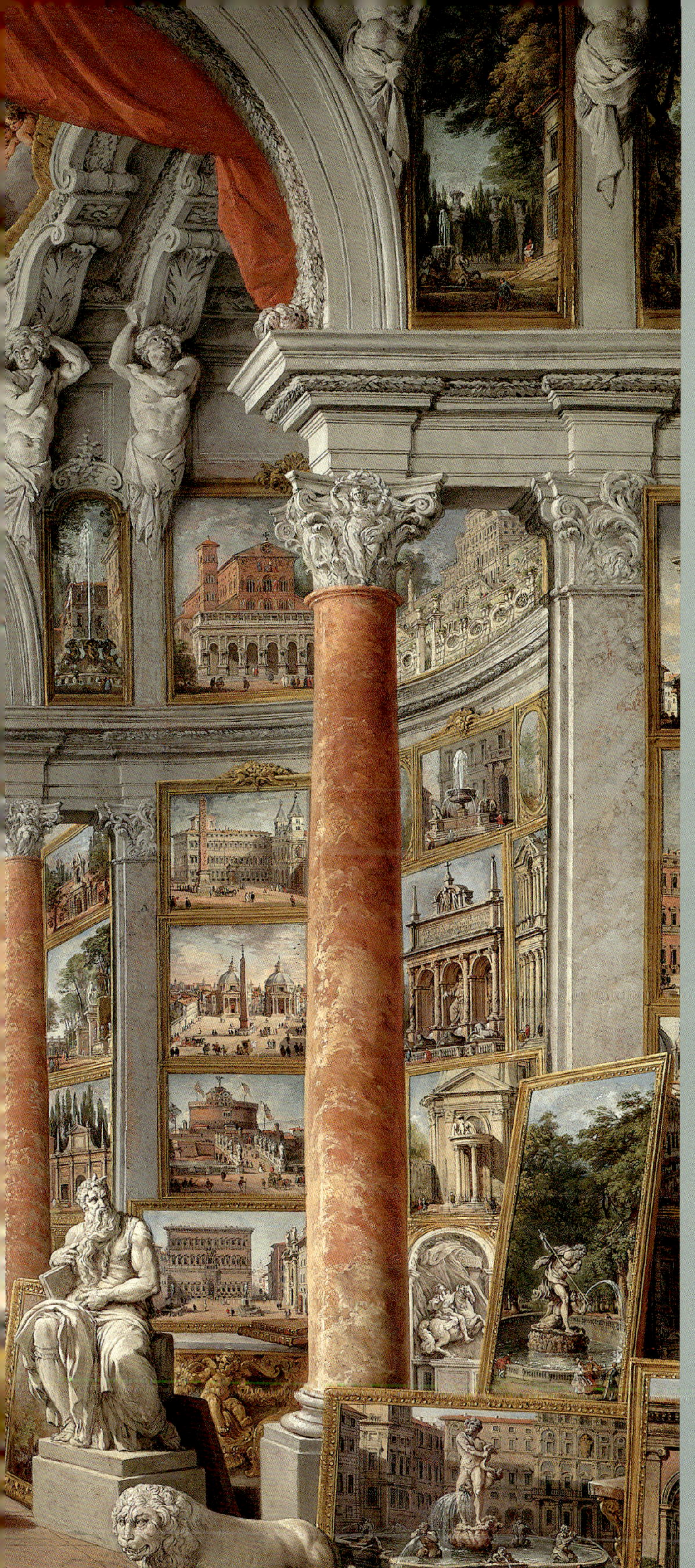

MFA HIGHLIGHTS european painting and sculpture before 1800

Frederick Ilchman, Ronni Baer, Marietta Cambareri, Courtney Leigh Harris, Katie Hanson, and Anna C. Knaap

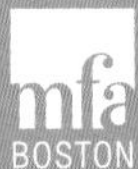

MFA PUBLICATIONS
Museum of Fine Arts, Boston
465 Huntington Avenue
Boston, Massachusetts 02115
www.mfa.org/publications

Support for this publication was provided by the Anne Poulet European Decorative Arts and Sculpture Publication Fund and the Ann and William Elfers Publications Fund at the Museum of Fine Arts, Boston.

ISBN 978-0-87846-878-2
Library of Congress Control Number: 2020945823

While the objects in this publication necessarily represent only a small portion of the MFA's holdings, the Museum is proud to be a leader within the American museum community in sharing the objects in its collection via its website. Currently, information about approximately 400,000 objects is available to the public worldwide. To learn more about the MFA's collections, including provenance, publication, and exhibition history, kindly visit www.mfa.org/collections.

For a complete listing of MFA publications, please contact the publisher at the above address, or call 617 369 4233.

Illustrations in this book were photographed by the Imaging Studios, Museum of Fine Arts, Boston, except where otherwise noted.

Editing and production by Hope Stockton
Copyedited by Dianne Woo
Proofread by Kathryn Blatt
Production assistance by Jessica Altholz Eber and John Woolf
Designed by Christopher DiPietro
Typeset by Frances Presti-Fazio
Printed on 150 gsm Gardamatte
Printed and bound at Verona Libri, Verona, Italy

Distributed in the United States of America and Canada by
ARTBOOK | D.A.P.
75 Broad Street, Suite 630
New York, New York 10004
www.artbook.com

Distributed outside the United States of America and Canada by
Thames & Hudson, Ltd.
181A High Holborn
London WC1V 7QX
www.thamesandhudson.com

FIRST EDITION
Printed and bound in Italy
This book was printed on acid-free paper.

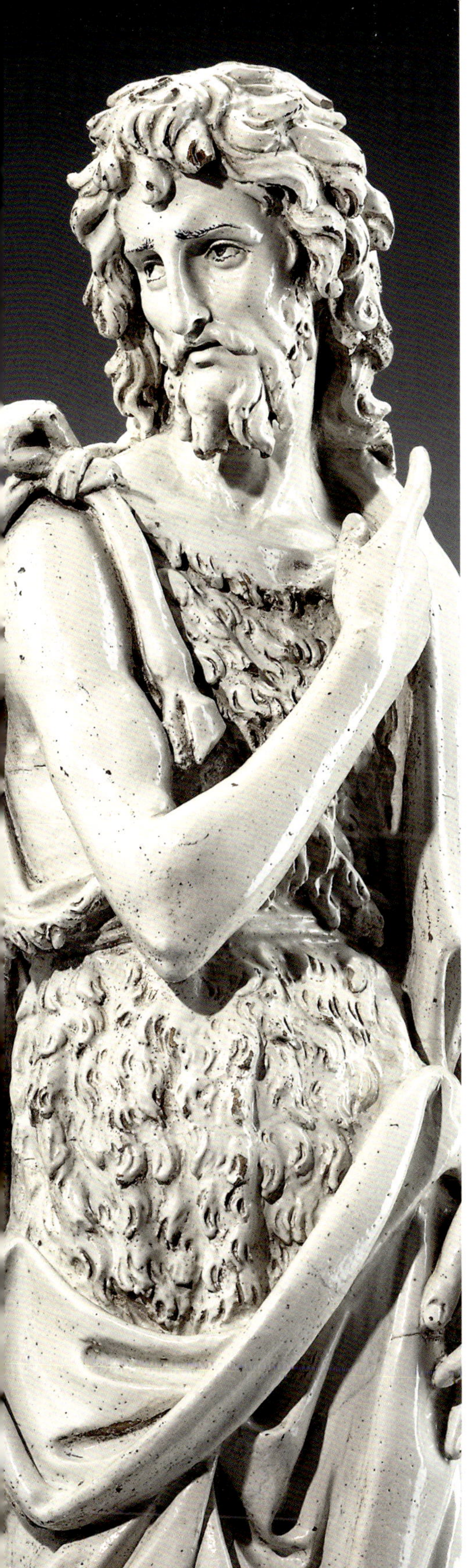

Contents

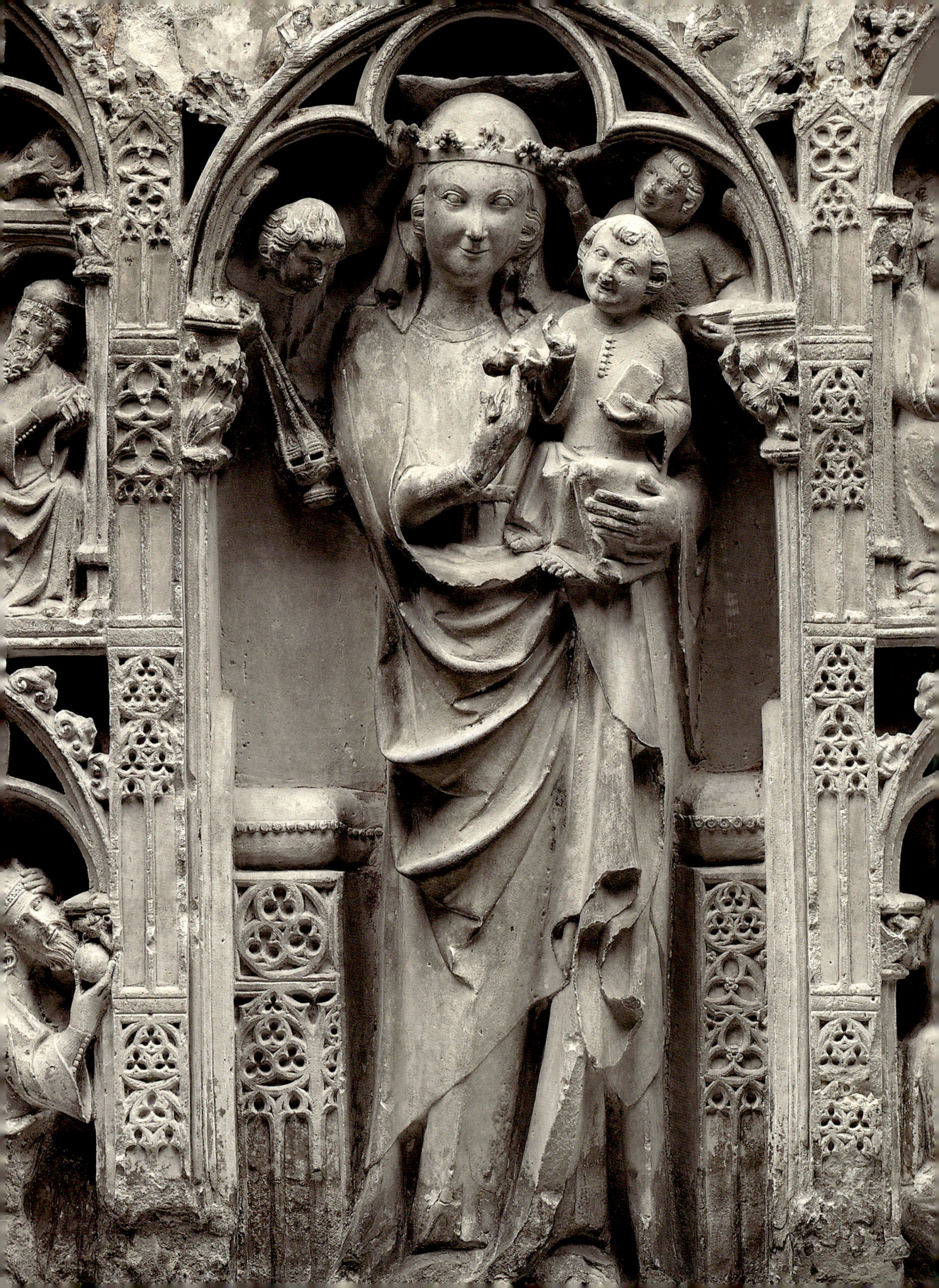

Director's Foreword

In 1870, the founders of the Museum of Fine Arts, Boston, aspired to establish an encyclopedic institution for the study of world cultures, envisioning a universally admired collection of European painting and sculpture at its center. In the Museum's first decades, a small but growing group of masterworks came to be displayed alongside copies of Renaissance paintings and plaster cast reproductions of European sculpture. As the collection grew, key works donated by collectors and acquired by the museum helped to realize the founders' vision. Curatorial research, ties to Boston's great teaching institutions, and dedication to state-of-the-art standards of conservation further enhanced the collection.

This volume presents paintings and sculpture from the collection of the MFA made during the years 1000–1800, when European cities such as Florence, Venice, Madrid, Amsterdam, London, and Paris were hubs of artistic and cultural exchange. It was a time when historical and religious transformations from the creation of Medieval empires to the Renaissance, Reformation, and Enlightenment produced gloriously inventive works of art in a dazzling variety of styles, techniques, and materials. Today, the art of Europe at the MFA takes its place within a broad encyclopedic collection that seeks to highlight and connect cultures and artists from around the globe. It is a pleasure to share this volume with you, filled with the evidence of studied learning and exuberance of the pleasures of contemplation. Support for this publication was provided by the Anne Poulet European Decorative Arts and Sculpture Publication Fund and the Ann and William Elfers Publications Fund at the Museum of Fine Arts, Boston.

Matthew Teitelbaum
Ann and Graham Gund Director
Museum of Fine Arts, Boston

Acknowledgments

This book, like the deep European collection itself, has benefitted from the dedication of generations of donors and staff who came before us. For the paintings side, Frederick Ilchman and Ronni Baer would like to thank the paintings team, current and past, in the Art of Europe. Katie Hanson, Associate Curator, Paintings, and Anna C. Knaap, Curatorial Research Fellow, took on the writing of entries in addition to their regular duties. Of former staff, John Hawley and Claire Whitner made a particular difference, undertaking research on the collection and drafting entries incorporated in other texts. A group of energetic paintings interns, including Gabriella Davies, Ella Mints, and above all Julia M. Vázquez helped us in the final stretch. Marietta Cambareri wrote entries on paintings as well. Close collaboration between curatorial and conservation departments at the Museum has permitted many insights into the creation of these paintings and sculptures as well as their current condition; Matthew Siegal, as chair of conservation, has enthusiastically promoted this partnership with curators across the institution. Special thanks in Paintings Conservation are due to Rhona MacBeth, Head of Paintings Conservation and Eijk and Rose-Marie van Otterloo Conservator of Paintings, Jean Woodward, and Lydia Vagts, Cunningham Associate Conservator of Paintings. Andrew Haines was unfailingly helpful, and always reminded us that every painting offers a great excuse to think about picture frames.

On the sculpture side, Marietta Cambareri and Courtney Harris thank the graduate research interns who contributed to our understanding of the works in this volume: Shirin Fozi, Heidi Gearhart, Carolyn Twomey, and, in particular, Elisa Foster, who reviewed the medieval and Renaissance sculptures, making significant contributions reflected in many entries. We thank our present and former colleagues in Objects Conservation and Research Science for their work on these sculptures, especially Pamela Hatchfield, Robert P. and Carol T. Henderson Head of Objects Conservation; Abigail Hykin; Flavia Perugini; Richard Newman; and Michelle Derrick, Schorr Family Associate Research Scientist as well as Rika Smith McNally. We are especially grateful to Michael Gould, whose photographs of our sculptures are works of art in themselves. Greg Heins and Maggie Loh helped make this photography possible, almost never an easy task when it comes to sculpture, along with our Facilities and Collections Care colleagues, especially Lisa Ceccarini.

The authors would like to thank our Art of Europe colleagues past and present, especially the late Tracey Albainy, former Russell B. and Andrée Beauchamp Stearns Senior Curator of Decorative Arts and Sculpture; George T.M. Shackelford, former Arthur K. Solomon Curator of Modern Art and Chair, Art of Europe; Thomas Michie, Russell B. and Andrée Beauchamp Stearns Senior Curator Emeritus of Decorative Arts and Sculpture, Art of Europe; Victoria Reed, Monica S. Sadler Curator of Provenance; Simona Di Nepi, Charles and Lynn Schusterman Curator of Judaica; and Christopher Newth. Mary Feenan Nelson and Cara Wolahan helped shepherd the process. We thank our co-authors in the volume, for a long, winding, and mostly happy collaboration.

Both the past and current Ann and Graham Gund Directors, Malcolm Rogers and Matthew Teitelbaum, have supported robust curatorial activity at the Museum. Katie Getchell spearheaded the Highlights series to draw attention to the breadth and depth of the collection and abundant new research. Finally, we wish to recognize our colleagues in Publications, former and current, including Mark Polizzotti, Emiko K. Usui, and Debra LaKind, all champions of the printed book. We are especially grateful to editor Hope Stockton, whose tenacious dedication to the volume, and careful editing of the texts, assured its publication.

Frederick Ilchman
Chair and Mrs. Russell W. Baker Curator of Paintings, Art of Europe

Ronni Baer
Allen R. Adler, Class of 1967, Distinguished Curator and Lecturer at the Princeton University Art Museum
Former *William and Ann Elfers Senior Curator of Paintings*

Marietta Cambareri
Senior Curator of European Sculpture and Jetskalina H. Phillips Curator of Judaica

Courtney Leigh Harris
Curatorial Research Fellow, Art of Europe

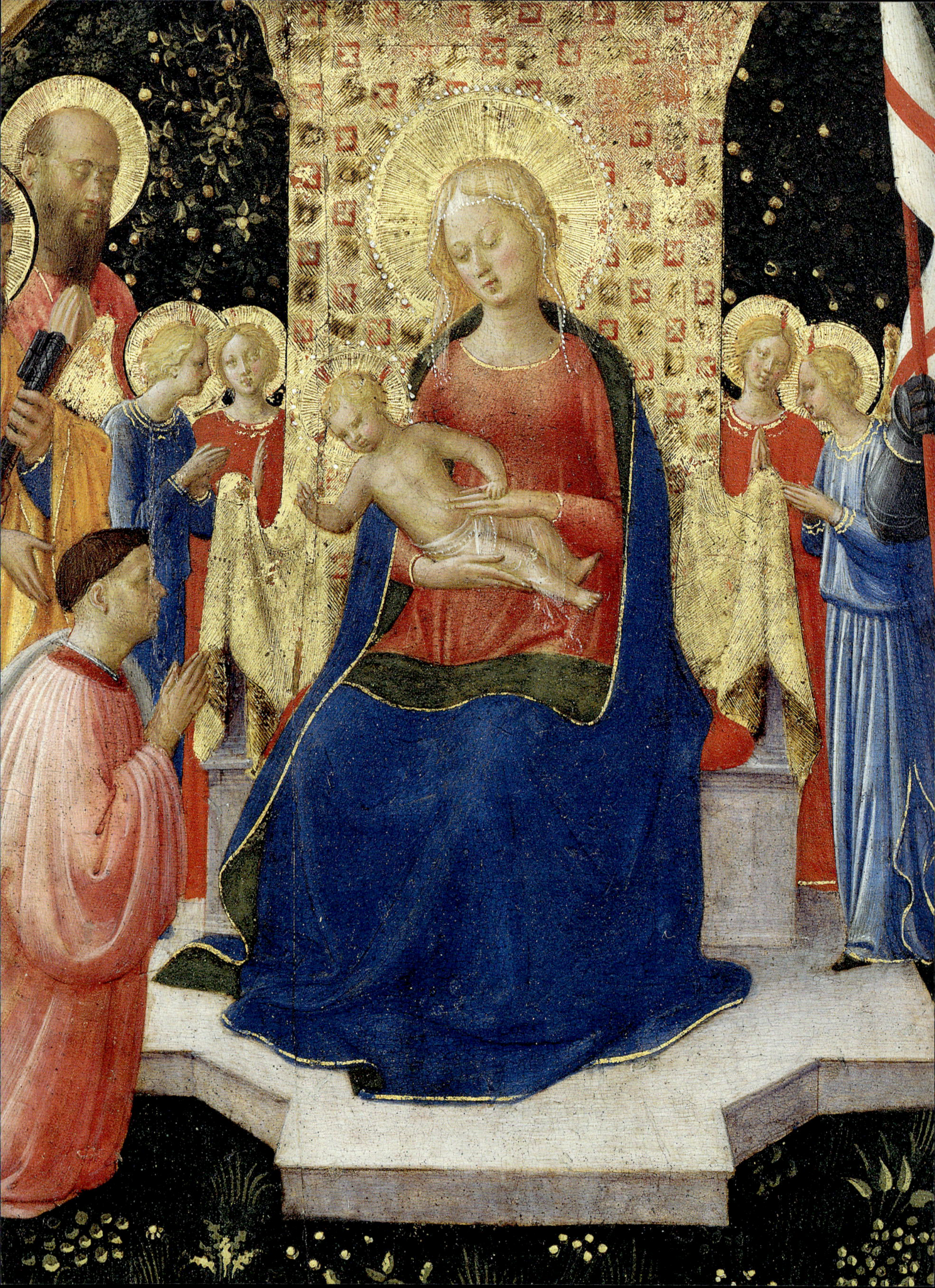

Old Masters, New Mastery

Frederick Ilchman

The paintings and sculptures in this book were produced from about 1000 to 1800, the High Middle Ages to the Enlightenment of the late eighteenth century. All were made in Europe, geographically defined as western Eurasia bordered by the Mediterranean Sea and the Atlantic and Arctic Oceans. Modern notions of art and artists, the art market, as well as the births of art history and the art museum as an institution, all trace their origins to Europe in these centuries. Indeed, the concepts of painting and sculpture—the fundamental and most recognizable forms of art across the globe even today—were transformed in this period, establishing a tradition that continues to inspire artists.

The story begins much earlier, with two overlapping phenomena that determined the course of subsequent European painting and sculpture: the art of classical antiquity, that is, ancient Greece and Rome, and the institution of the Roman Catholic Church. The simplicity of Greek architecture and art, emphasizing harmony, balance, and proportional treatment of the human body, established a canon of aesthetics deemed "classical." Think of the colonnaded architecture of the Parthenon, constructed in Athens from 447 to 432 BC, or the reliefs—sculpture whose forms project from the background—seen in the frieze of a procession on horseback that once decorated this building. Think of statues (sculptures in the round) such as idealized Greek athletes known from copies by Roman carvers. The Parthenon is a structural marvel, with each vertical column and horizontal lintel placed in careful mathematical relationship with the other elements of the building. Similarly, the sculptural frieze in low relief proclaims the beauty of the human body and the agency of the individual with the dynamic poses of horses and riders propelling the narrative forward. While relief sculpture excels at storytelling, independent statues can be admired from multiple angles. Many classical sculptures show powerful male nudes with proportions regarded as exemplary at the time that they were made and still influential today. The subject often stands at rest, his weight on his right leg with the left leg trailing, generating a sinuous curve. The gently asymmetrical pose, called contrapposto ("counterpoise"), is simultaneously graceful and embodies potential movement. The calm precision of these buildings and sculptures developed in Greece and later spread throughout the Roman Empire, offering a standard for European cultures in subsequent eras.

At its greatest extent, in the early second century, the Roman Empire encompassed most of Western Europe and surrounded the entire Mediterranean Sea. In the fourth century, Christianity was adopted enthusiastically, and the Catholic Church made the visual arts central to its communication strategy. Christians promoted saints, individuals officially recognized for outstanding holiness, by constructing churches and commissioning artworks dedicated to them. In the fifth century, the disintegration of the Roman Empire launched the medieval era, which lasted for nearly a millennium, only ending with the Renaissance in the fifteenth and sixteenth centuries.

Nevertheless, the classical world had a lasting influence and nowhere more so than in the Roman Empire's thorough embrace of Christianity. As a result, this faith was pervasive in the Middle Ages and remains influential today. Although divided into many smaller kingdoms, the inhabitants of medieval Europe began to think of themselves as a broader community of Christians, and Europe as Christendom, in opposition to the Muslims of the Middle East and North Africa. Directed by the pope in Rome, Christianity permeated daily life. The king of England in the late ninth century, Alfred the Great, declared that kings succeed when three different kinds of subjects thrive: those who pray, those who fight, and those who work. Placing priests and monks first, before warriors or artisans and farmers, was deliberate. Through prayer, clerics could battle unseen adversaries, such as the devil, considered far more menacing than enemy troops. Ensuring that God and his representatives, especially the saints and the Virgin Mary, favored a king and his subjects was a vital task; those who led the spiritual fight were revered.

Consequently a great deal of medieval art and architecture was Christian in subject matter and devotional in function. Doctrine held that financial contributions to Catholic institutions, including charity for the poor and the funding of construction of churches, would hasten the journey of one's soul to heaven. Donations thus flowed to religious organizations. Although castles still capture the public imagination and inform our picture of medieval Europe, it is revealing that many thousands of castles have fallen into ruin or disappeared, while a similar number of churches and cathedrals remain standing seven hundred or even a thousand years after their construction. Gunpowder and improvements in cannonry rendered medieval castles obsolete by the sixteenth century, yet the vitality of Christianity and the beauty of its architecture meant that churches and cathedrals have been cherished down to the present.

During the Middle Ages, churches were constructed first in the Romanesque style (meaning "of the Romans"). Flourishing in the eleventh century, this style superficially recalls the forms of ancient Roman architecture, employing semicircular arches but with squatter proportions. Sculpture and painting produced in this era prized the expressive potential of the human body, with exaggerated features, rather than the naturalistic proportions found in classical art. The successive style, known as Gothic, began in Northern France in the late twelfth century and dominated European art through the fourteenth and even into the fifteenth centuries. It featured pointed arches and attenuated proportions. Columns composed of base, shaft, and capital—employed in Romanesque architecture (and of course classical architecture)—were now conspicuously stretched to emphasize soaring verticality. This taste can be seen in architectural forms from windows in buildings to picture frames as well as most painting in the fourteenth century, where human figures are typically lithe, even dainty.

Many sculptures were made for churches, ornamenting architectural forms such as doorways or tombs. Entire walls were painted with pigments mixed in fresh plaster (hence the term fresco), creating a durable image when the plaster dried. Each church possessed at least one altar, a table for the celebration of the Mass; paintings on wood or sculptures in stone decorated the front of the altar or served as a focal point behind it. In the medieval period, art was also made for elite private homes, much of it religious to encourage private devotion. The forms of domestic art resembled miniature versions of works created for churches. Artists employed gold leaf to create shimmering backgrounds for their paintings. Secular subjects were very rare, but slowly increased in popularity over time.

A surge in production of religious art was just one indication of a new urban character. Political stability and population growth fostered thriving commerce across Europe. New religious movements, particularly the Franciscans and Dominicans, emerged in the bustling towns of the early thirteenth century and grew dramatically in the next. Unlike existing orders of monks, who renounced material concerns to live in seclusion, the new mendicant (begging) orders emphasized living within urban communities and preaching to large publics. To this day some of the largest structures in any given Italian or Spanish town remain a Franciscan or Dominican church built in the thirteenth or fourteenth century. The decoration of these substantial buildings could take generations; sometimes the painters were themselves members of these orders, such as Fra Angelico or Fra Carnevale.

In the first half of the fifteenth century, a massive shift occurred in Italy as writers, rulers, and artists began to see their time as a renaissance, a rebirth of the culture of ancient Greece and Rome. Classical languages and literature were revived. The most visible break happened with art and architecture, as classicizing buildings and art eclipsed Gothic style. Florentine artists took the lead and made the human body the primary vehicle of expression. The sculptures of Donatello and paintings of Masaccio evoked the art of ancient Greece and Rome with sturdy figures and graceful contrapposto. Sculptures and paintings of classical subjects were in great demand, and occasionally indistinguishable from their ancient prototypes. Central to the achievement of the Renaissance, however, was the merging of Christian subject matter with classical forms, creating a new kind of religious art. The Virgin Mary, for example, was shown with the features and poise of a Roman goddess. In the years around 1500, the unclothed figure was deeply admired, and even allowed in religious art for certain male subjects, such as the crucified or dead Christ. Although classical style was revived most enthusiastically in areas with abundant examples of surviving classical statuary and buildings such as Italy, Renaissance innovations spread throughout Europe. Italian artists placed their figures in settings with fanciful classical architecture and chessboard floors. These elements were central to linear perspective, which employed grids of lines converging on a vanishing point to convey the illusion of depth on a flat surface. Perspective became ubiquitous in Italian painting in the later fifteenth century, and this mathematical approach to space paralleled new technologies in other realms, such as printing, advanced artillery, and mechanical clocks.

Renaissance culture celebrated ingenuity. An artist who could succeed in many realms was regarded as a *uomo universale* (universal man), what is now known as a Renaissance man. The ultimate such figure was Leonardo da Vinci, today best known for his paintings and anatomical drawings. In about 1482 he wrote a letter to Ludovico Sforza, ruler of Milan, angling for a job. Leonardo boasts of his inventions for all manner of siege engines, devices for tunneling, cannons, and catapults, and only lists his skills as an architect, a sculptor, and a painter at the end, almost as an afterthought.

Art became prized for the skill and personal style of its maker, rather than the value of the materials. For example, sculpture historically has derived prestige from using expensive media, with marble and bronze consistently more exalted than clay or wood. Innovative sculpture by Donatello and his contemporaries, however, elevated modest substances, including fired and glazed clay, to great acclaim, a shift from prizing materials themselves to valuing what a creator could do with them. Similarly, whereas fourteenth-century painters routinely employed gold for backgrounds and highlights, by 1435, the Italian architect Leon Battista Alberti claimed in *On Painting* that using gold in a picture did not endow the work with majesty; instead "there is more admiration and praise for the painter who imitates the rays of gold with colors."

Art became self-conscious. Artists inserted self-portraits in their compositions and began to produce independent self-portraits. The greatest artists explored the creative act itself. Active in Brussels, Rogier van der Weyden maintained the Netherlandish predilection for observed detail but added claims for the power of painting. His *Saint Luke Drawing the Virgin* shows—within the setting of a contemporary interior in a Netherlandish town—a painter executing a preparatory drawing on paper in order to paint the first image of the Virgin and Child (see p. 86). As he created this painting, Rogier revised the artist's face many times, and ultimately depicted a specific physiognomy, likely a self-portrait. Thus Rogier identifies with Luke, the patron saint of painters, and invokes painting's divine function.

In the sixteenth century, writing about art emerged as its own literary genre. Giorgio Vasari's *Lives of the Most Excellent Painters, Sculptors, and Architects*, published in Florence in 1550 and revised in 1568, compiled the biographies of prominent artists from the thirteenth century until his day. This foundational work of art history coined the term Renaissance to describe this period. Vasari maintained that *disegno*—meaning both a physical drawing on paper and the ability to capture the essence of form by rendering three dimensions convincingly on a flat surface—was the practice that united the three other arts: painting, sculpture, and architecture. He asserted that mastery of *disegno* was a prerequisite for success in any of them. Some Renaissance artists excelled in two of the three (Raphael and Vasari himself were both painters and architects) and a few, such as Leonardo and Michelangelo, pursued all three. Even if fluency in more than one art was a feature of the age, intellectuals enjoyed debates about the relative merits of one over the other, known as the *paragone* ("comparison"). In Baldassare Castiglione's dialogue *The Courtier* (1528), characters dispute whether sculpture or painting is the superior art form. Painting wins the argument since sculpture is unable to reproduce the colors in nature and thus cannot convey "the color of blond hair, the gleam of weapons, the darkness of night, a tempest at sea, thunder and lightning, a city in conflagration, or the break of rosy dawn with its rays of gold and red."

Within Italy, some cities formed distinct aesthetic preferences and published treatises championing their painting style. Critics in Rome and Florence extolled the sculptural contours and smooth brushstrokes, indicative of good *disegno*, of painters such as Raphael or Rosso Fiorentino, who typically painted glossy pictures on wooden panels. Meanwhile in Venice a fondness for loose and expressive brushwork developed, exploiting the textured surface of canvas supports. Venetian critics praised Titian and Jacopo Tintoretto, artists who privileged coloring—that is, the layering of textured brushstrokes—over line. Despite many advocates and competing approaches, the prestige that painting enjoys today was long in coming. During the Renaissance, paintings from even the most famous artists cost only a fraction of woven tapestries, marble cladding on a building, or bronze church bells. The basic costs of materials and labor still counted for more than an artist's skill or reputation.

In addition to new kinds of conversations and publications about art, people changed their physical relationship to art, most significantly by living with it. Beginning in the later fifteenth century, for the first time in European history, paintings and sculptures were commonly found not only in churches and palaces but also in private homes. Upper-middle-class houses in cities like Florence, Venice, Brussels, or Bruges were filled with objects admired for their beauty, not solely as aids to religious devotion. Art was collected and displayed in dedicated spaces, like a *studiolo* or study, usually alongside books. Aristocrats and scholars kept particularly fine collections in a *kunstkammer*, a cabinet of curiosities, which celebrated the wonders made by nature and humans, and almost always included ancient art.

Beginning in 1517, the Protestant Reformation split Europe between Martin Luther and his followers and those loyal to the Catholic Church. Northern Europe became Protestant and Southern Europe remained Catholic. No single country or monarch dominated the continent politically, yet in the seventeenth century, Catholic Rome solidified its place as the capital of European art. Rome offered unparalleled opportunities for artists to decorate churches and palaces. Classical statuary was regularly unearthed, finding willing buyers, and the ruins of ancient structures provoked awe. In the years around 1600, the painter Caravaggio dominated the Roman scene with a new style based on tightly rendered human figures, illuminated as if by spotlights, creating marked juxtapositions of light and darkness, or chiaroscuro. The classical poise and harmony of Renaissance art was replaced by an emphasis on violence and drama and compositions with strong diagonals. After studying Caravaggio's works firsthand in Rome, painters working elsewhere in Italy, such as Guercino and Jusepe de Ribera, and in Flanders, including Peter Paul Rubens and Theodoor van Loon, disseminated this style across Europe.

Many of the most influential art patrons were princes of the church in Rome. The patronage of the pope and cardinals put many artists of the Baroque age on the map, including Caravaggio and Gian Lorenzo Bernini. Working for these clients helped launch the careers of young foreigners or offered additional accolades for established artists, such as Diego Velázquez, who traveled to Italy in 1649 to acquire antiquities and Renaissance paintings for his employer, King Philip IV of Spain. The highlight of the journey, however, was a stay in Rome where Velázquez painted portraits, including that of the pope, and was hailed by his artist peers. A collection of ancient Roman statuary was de rigueur in a palazzo in Rome, inspiring contemporary sculptors to surpass these classical works. Another development—a long gallery for displaying paintings—became influential across Europe, a precursor to the public art museum. Beginning in the seventeenth century, Rome was a destination not only for artists, but for sightseers. The city was the eagerly anticipated terminus of the Grand Tour, where Northern European aristocrats traveled to Italy to acquire good taste and costly souvenirs. Guidebooks proliferated, as did prints to be collected in personal albums. A new category of painting, the *capriccio*, depicted architectural fantasies. An example such as Pannini's *Picture Gallery with Views of Modern Rome* (see pp. 172–73) offers a meta-commentary about picture galleries and art collecting.

By the seventeenth century, the break with the Catholic Church galvanized by the Reformation had given rise to a completely different art market in the Netherlands, one reflecting prosperity created by global trade, scientific discoveries and inventions, and widespread literacy. Rather than relying on ecclesiastical or aristocratic commissions, still the norm in Italy and other Catholic countries, Dutch artists produced paintings on spec for a thriving middle class. By the middle of the century, some two-thirds of the population of the city of Delft possessed paintings, averaging eleven per household. The Dutch market for pictures featured an unprecedented range of subject matter—portraits, still life, episodes from daily life, landscapes, seascapes, religious narratives, and more—and painters generally specialized in one category. The variety of subjects embraced by the French Impressionists two centuries later, for example, is a consequence of these Dutch innovations.

Artists up through the eighteenth century are often called Old Masters. The term evokes a historical period distant from the current one as well as acknowledges a technical mastery. These paintings and sculptures were made to last. But the concept of master also encompasses teacher; nearly all artists before the nineteenth century were trained by apprenticing to an established master. At about twelve years old, a boy (or more rarely a girl) would begin a course of study by drawing after sculpture or copying drawings and prints, eventually copying paintings or sculptures. Pupils would help the business function efficiently by cleaning the workspace, preparing materials such as grinding pigments and mixing paints, and ultimately executing portions of a work under the master's supervision. Successful artists relied upon this division of labor, trusting trained assistants to fulfill large portions of a painting or sculpture, particularly the early stages, and make replicas of compositions in particular demand. Needless to say, sophisticated collectors were wary of purchasing studio copies when they could afford works entirely by the master. In 1618, Rubens tried to reassure an English collector by clarifying which available paintings were by his hand, which were begun by an assistant and then touched up by him so that it "would pass as an original," and which relied upon a specialist for certain sections, such as the landscape. At its best, the workshop system produced a remarkably consistent product; determining which portions of a work were created by the master and which by pupils remains a preoccupation of art historians today.

Supplementing this system, Royal Academies were established in Paris in 1648, The Hague in 1682, Madrid in 1744, and London in 1748 to train artists, promote art, and collect suitable models. Not surprisingly, these institutions looked to the past to ensure high standards going forward. Frequent disagreements occurred in formulating a syllabus. Recalling the sixteenth-century disputes between Florentine *disegno* and Venetian coloring, members of the French Royal Academy in the 1670s debated the same aesthetic poles—whether to privilege classicizing contour or expressive brushwork—and divided themselves into *Poussinistes* or *Rubenistes*, champions of the styles of Nicolas Poussin or Rubens, respectively. Well into the eighteenth century, with the emergence of Antoine Watteau and the young François Boucher, standard-bearers for the Rococo style, the rich brushstrokes of Rubens seem to have prevailed.

Innovations in art were rivaled by dramatic changes in thought known as the Enlightenment, which exalted reason and science. Secular learning and art depicting secular subject matter grew in importance. Intellectuals believed everything could be known, categorized, and counted. Perhaps the most famous Enlightenment achievement was the publication in France of the *Encyclopédie* (1751–72), a storehouse of human knowledge in twenty-eight volumes. This same educational impulse led to the founding of public art museums, including the British Museum in London (1753) and the Musée du Louvre in Paris (1793). Within a few years, the Louvre became greatly enriched with treasures from across Europe, thanks to the conquests of a young art-savvy general, Napoleon Bonaparte. In the years around 1800, the predominant style in Europe was Neoclassicism, yet another revival of classical art, fueled by revived esteem for the ancients and the yearning of rulers like Napoleon to emulate their Roman forebears.

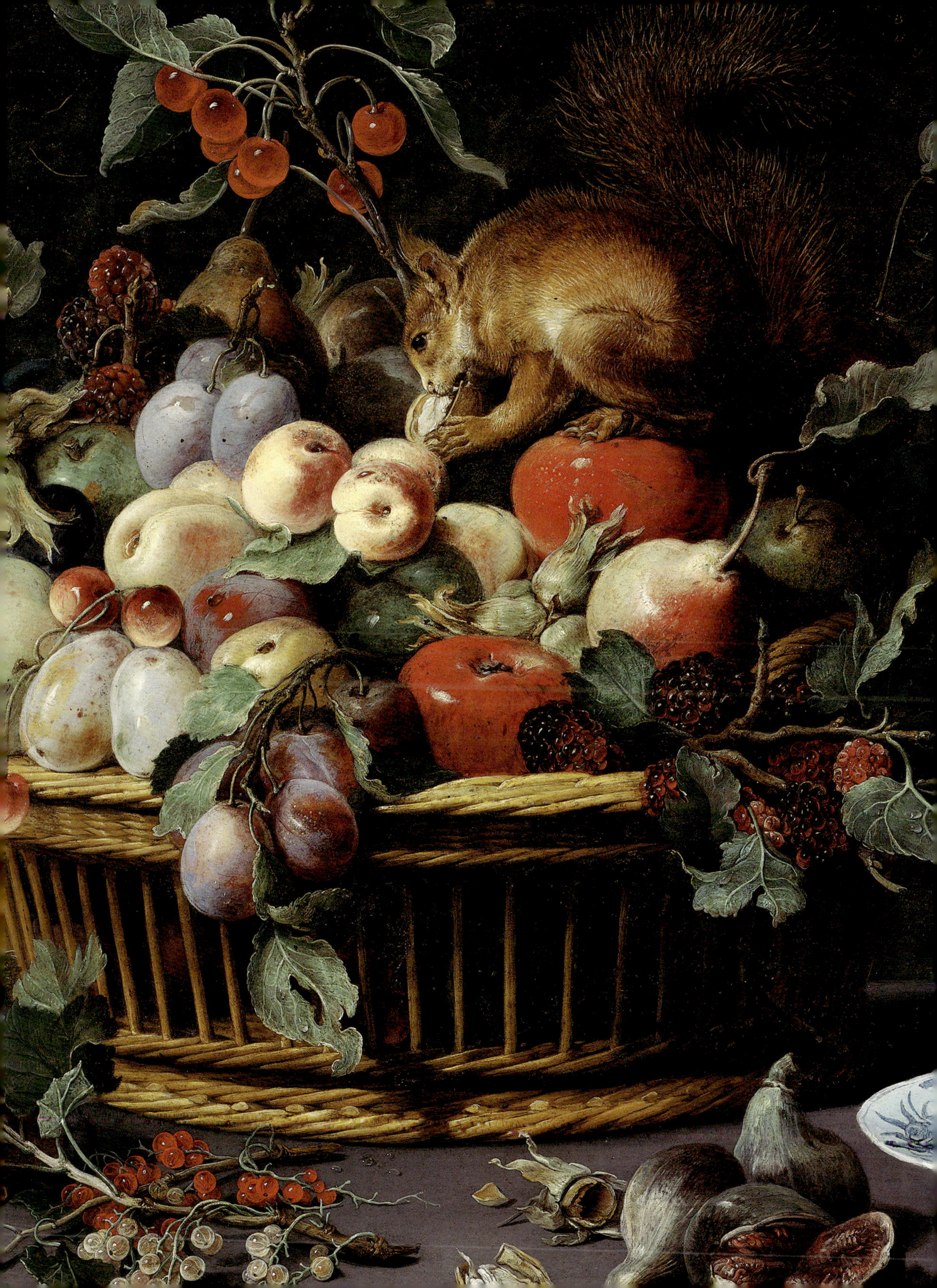

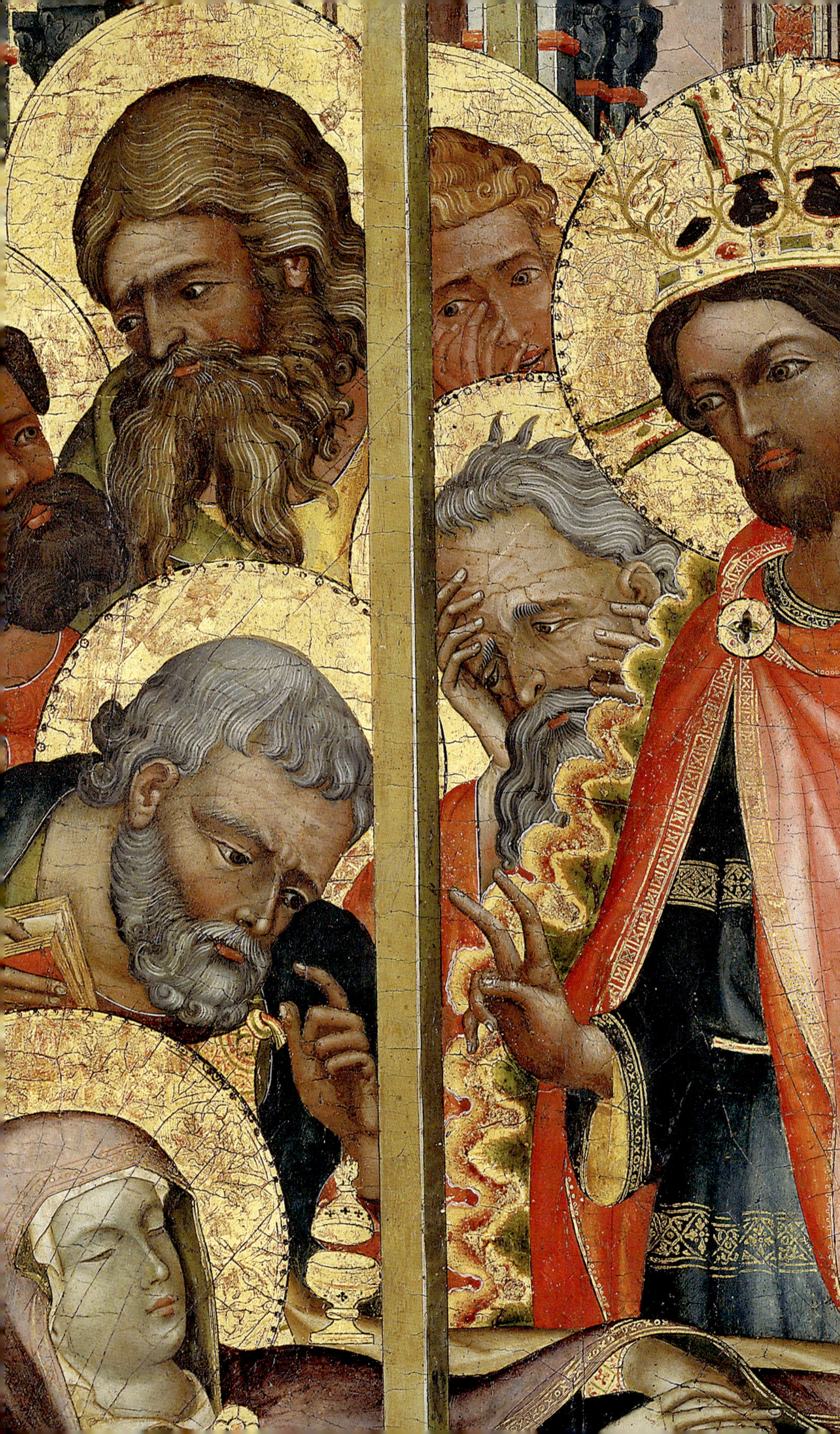

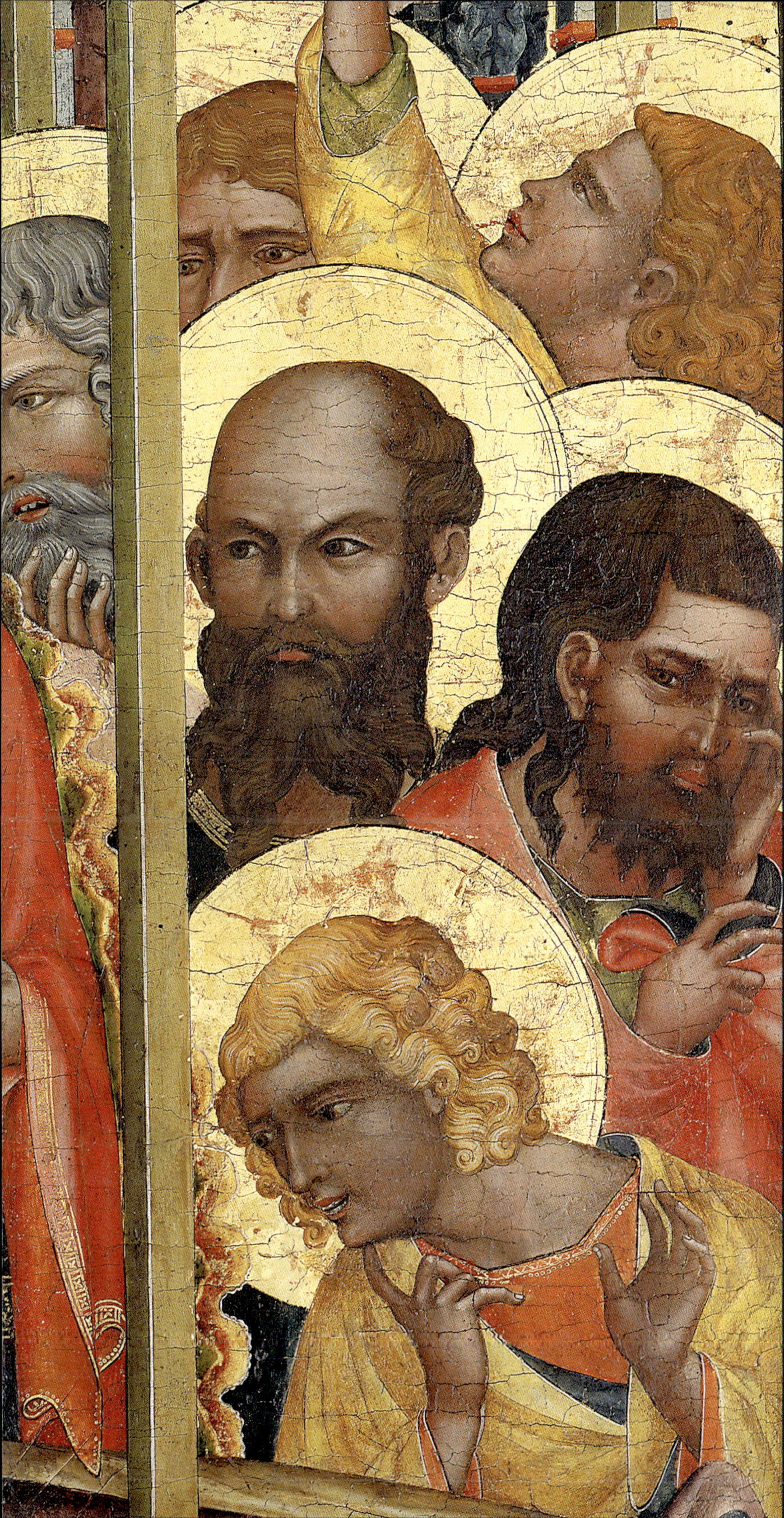

1 MEDIEVAL EUROPE

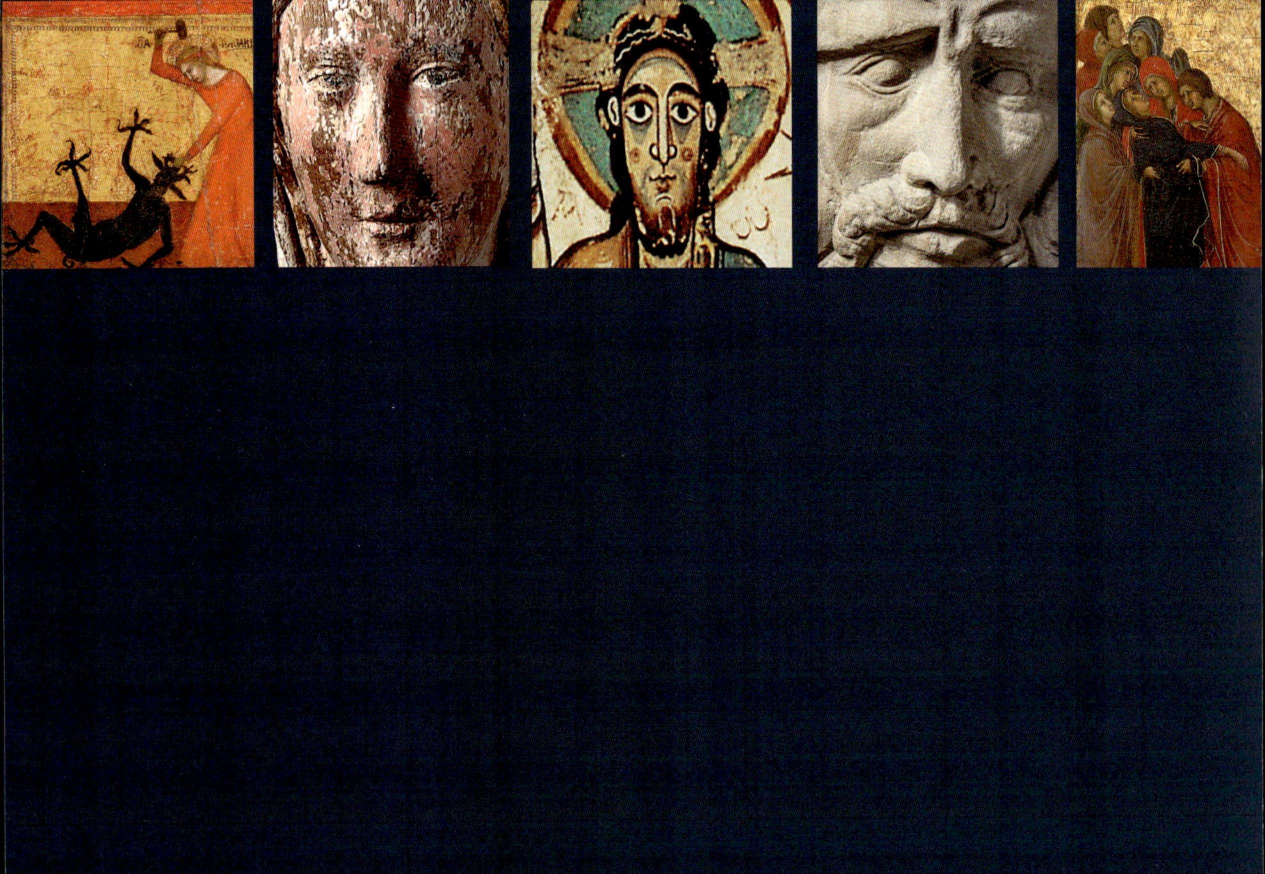

Medieval Europe

The period dating roughly between 500 and 1500 in Europe has come to be known as the medieval era, because it was long considered a bridge between the classical world and the so-called modern era. These centuries were a time of remarkable change and interchange. While there was no unified sense of Europe as a whole in this period, individual states began to take recognizable shape, and the continent emerged as a center of power and a nexus for global trade. Christianity became the dominant faith with the Papacy, located in Rome, assuming spiritual and temporal power that was felt throughout Europe.

Though the economy was driven primarily by agriculture, the growth of cities changed the way people in Europe lived and worshipped. City-states grew in power in Italy; universities were established in several European cities, attracting scholars and students; Paris became a center of artistic, intellectual, and religious culture for France and beyond. Shifts of power and extensive trade routes across land and sea brought interactions with people from Africa, Asia, and even the Americas, some of them peaceful, others leading to war and strife. Trade led to interchange of ideas as well as goods, and this sharing of resources and commodities, materials, techniques, and scientific discoveries is all reflected in the works of art created during this time.

Although Christianity dominated, the Ottoman Empire and the growth of Islam, as well as the presence of Jews in many cities and towns, contributed to a complex interweaving of cultures and faiths, creating shifting alliances, antagonisms, and perceptions across the centuries. Pilgrimage and crusade also brought Europeans far beyond the confines of their own cities and towns. But movement also spread disease, adding devastating plagues to natural disasters like flood and famine that continued to threaten lives.

Art became part of the civic fabric as new buildings both sacred and secular were decorated inside and out. For a population that was mostly illiterate, images joined the spoken word to help instruct and engage the faithful in their religion and their culture. The millennial year 1000, the rough date of the earliest work of art considered in this book, can be seen as a watershed year. By this point, the Holy Roman Empire was centered in Germany under the rule of the Ottonian emperors, who saw themselves as heirs to ancient Rome and inspired a revival of ancient artistic styles and techniques. As a result, the prevailing artistic style throughout Europe in the eleventh and twelfth centuries is described as Romanesque. Many churches and monasteries were built in towns and in the countryside, often becoming local centers of religious and civic life. According to one eleventh-century writer, Europe seemed to be "covering itself in a mantle of white churches." As building techniques developed that allowed churches to reach for the skies, and brilliantly colored windows transformed church interiors into glistening, jewel-like spaces, the Romanesque style developed into the Gothic style in the thirteenth and fourteenth centuries.

The power of art to inspire devotion and to help, or sometimes even hinder, viewers on their spiritual journey meant that it played a crucial role in the religious life of the period. Art could illustrate biblical narratives, support ritual practice, and bolster the messages of preachers, as sculpture decorated pulpits and facades, and paintings covered walls and were set upon altars. New empathetic devotional practices encouraged individuals to pray and to contemplate the stories of Jesus, his mother Mary, and the saints and apostles by imagining that they themselves were present at specific scenes. This personal approach created a demand for private devotional art. Manuscripts enlivened by painted illuminations as well as small paintings and sculptures were made for use in the home.

The works of art created in the medieval period capture a time of innovation, exchange, violence, slavery, illness, pilgrimage, crusade, science, education, the centrality of faith, civic and national identity and pride, fear of the other, and embrace of the varieties of human experience.

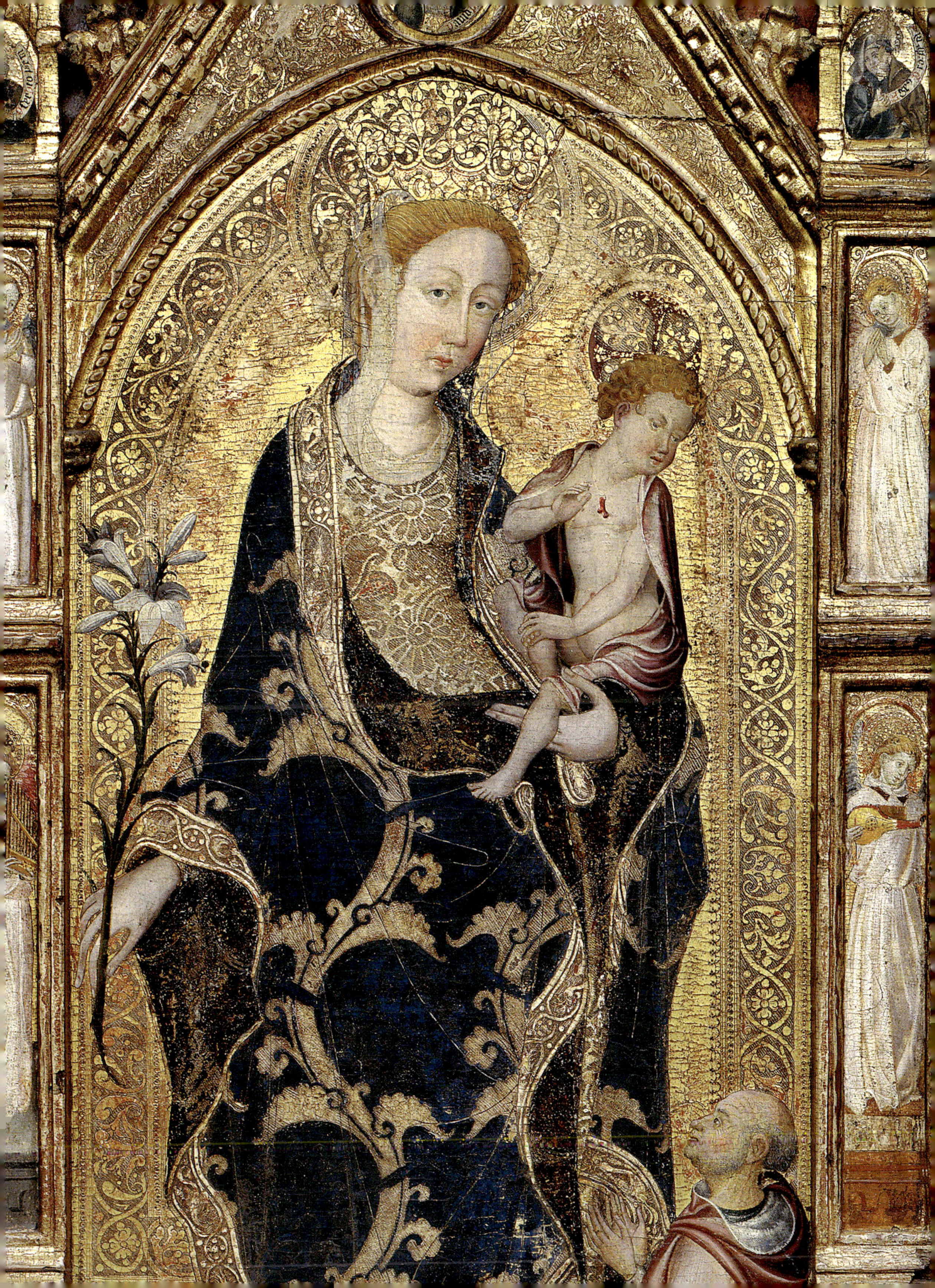

Christ in Majesty with Symbols of the Four Evangelists

Spanish (Catalan), 1150–1200

This fresco originally decorated the apse of Santa Maria de Mur, a small church in the foothills of the Spanish Pyrenees. Painted directly onto the plastered walls, it remained until 1919, when craftsmen covered its surface with adhesive-covered cotton muslin and carefully separated the paint layers from the wall in sections.

More than twenty feet high, the fresco is composed of three horizontal registers. The top register shows Jesus Christ, enthroned and holding a book with the inscription "I am the way, the truth, and the life; no man cometh unto the Father but by me." He is surrounded by the symbols of the four Evangelists—the lion, for Mark; the angel, for Matthew; the eagle, for John; and the ox, for Luke—whose heads are turned toward him. In the next register, the twelve apostles stand among three windows. The lowest register, heavily damaged at some point, depicts episodes from the Bible, including the Visitation, the Nativity, and the Annunciation to the Shepherds.

The artist used thick outlines and a large scale to create the imposing figure of Christ and transformed drapery into decorative geometric patterns that are typical of Romanesque painting and sculpture. The work's solemn tone would have been reinforced by the flickering candlelight inside the chapel and the liturgical rituals taking place below.

Fresco secco transferred to plaster and wood
H. 645 cm (254 in.)
Maria Antoinette Evans Fund 21.1285

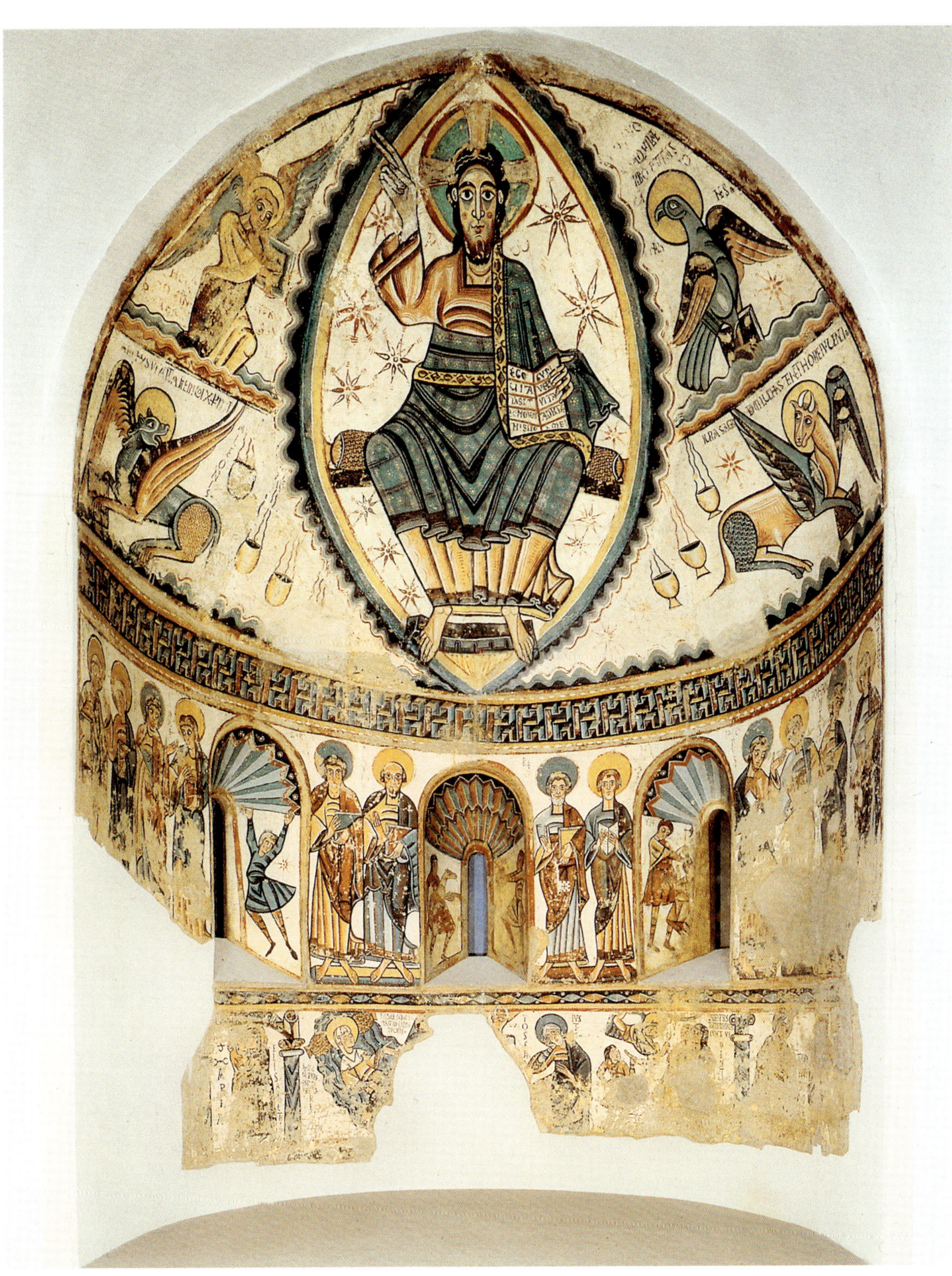

Crucified Christ

Southern German or Austrian (diocese of Salzburg, possibly Bad Reichenhall), early 11th century, with subsequent alterations

This is one of the oldest large-scale wood sculptures of the crucified Christ to survive from Northern Europe. The figure was originally attached to a cross and would have hung over the high altar in a church. Its impressive, larger-than-life-size scale would have created a sense of immediacy as well as reinforced the message of the Mass being conducted below.

Another sculpture of the crucified Christ, commissioned around 970 by Gero, archbishop of Cologne, and preserved at Cologne Cathedral, provides an important point of reference. Similar in scale and both carved of wood, these works depict Jesus dead on the cross, as opposed to earlier Crucifixion images that showed him alive as if triumphant over death. They mark a transition to imagery that stressed the pathos of Jesus's death, a new approach that sought to evoke empathy in the devotee. Recent technical studies of this *Crucified Christ* have revealed that in the centuries after its creation, several campaigns of subtle alterations were carried out. These served to emphasize more and more the sorrowful quality of the work by re-carving and repainting certain details. Previously, the piece was dated to between 1050 and 1100, but the alterations indicate the sculpture was likely made even earlier, probably in the first decades of the 11th century.

Wood (willow) with paint
H. (from base to top of head) 175 cm (68 7/8 in.),
w. 154 cm (60 5/8 in.)
1951 Purchase Fund 51.1405

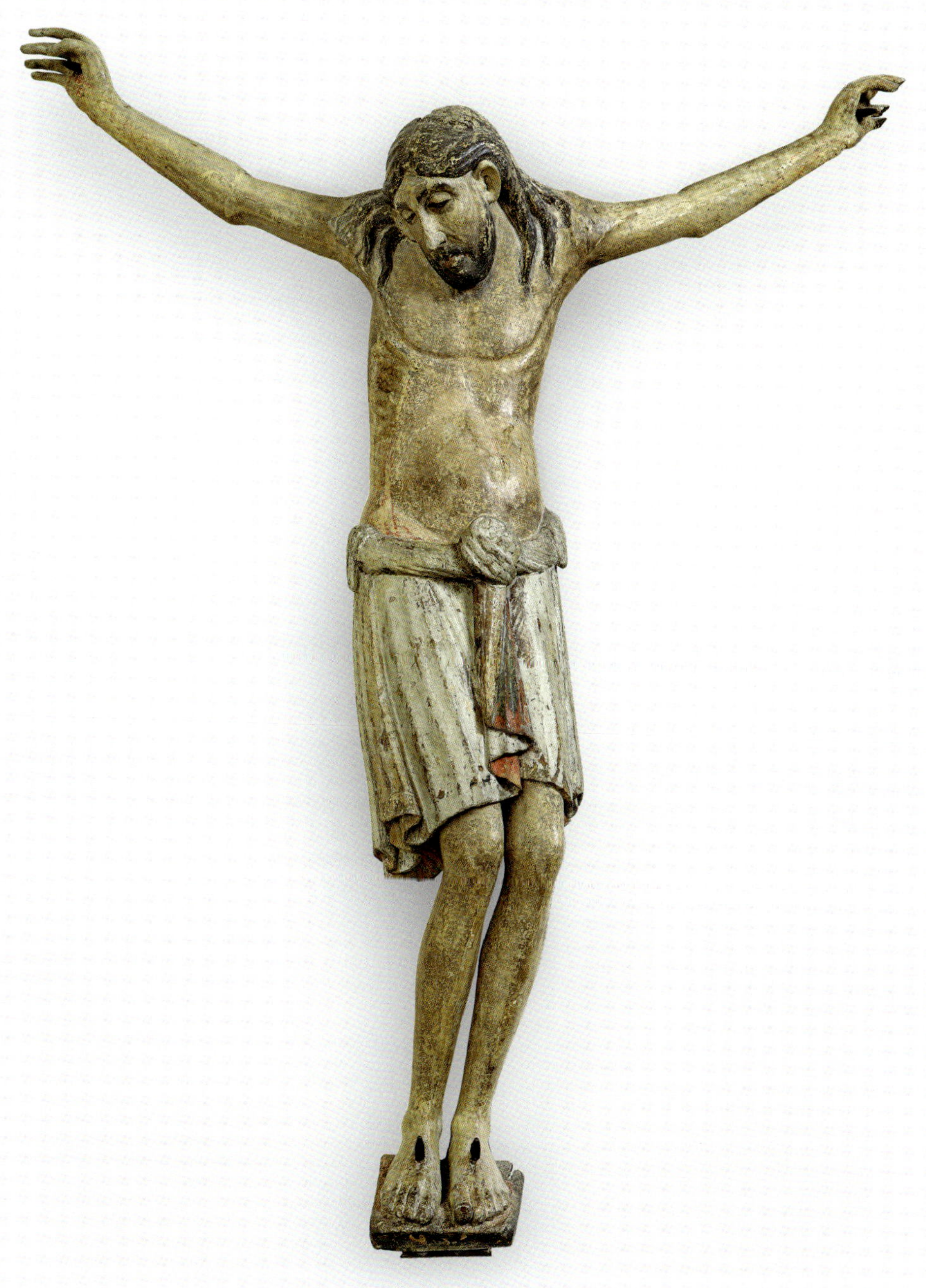

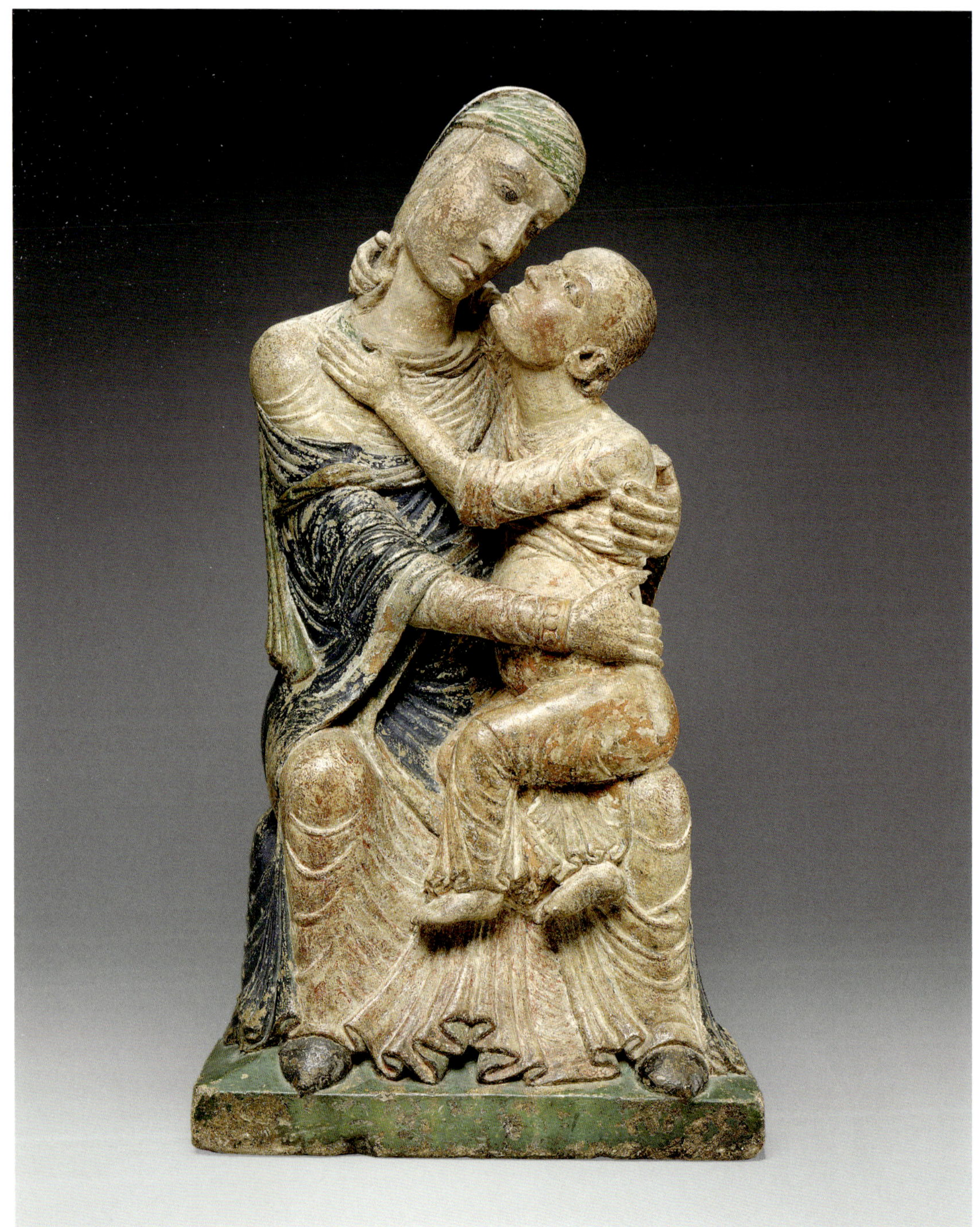

Virgin and Child

Italian (Lombardy or Emilia-Romagna), 1125–50

Mary sits with Jesus on her lap. The figures embrace, bending their heads so that their gazes meet, almost as if they are about to kiss. They share similar physiognomies and expressions, from the elongated shape of their heads to their downturned lips. Though this image represents a mother with her infant son, the baby Jesus has been given the proportions of a small man. Mary's complicated drapery wraps around her head, shoulders, and arms, spreading across her legs in linear patterns and culminating in sharp folds at the hem of the garment. While the idiosyncratic representation of the figures and their draperies allows us to localize and date this statue, the artist is as yet unidentified and the original setting remains only speculative. The work may have decorated an altar in the parish church of Castell'Arquato, not far from the town of Piacenza in Emilia-Romagna. It was probably carved in the second quarter of the twelfth century.

The sculpture likely stood upon an altar. By emphasizing the familial relationship between Jesus and the Virgin Mary, it conveys the notion that Jesus, though a deity, took on human form, a central doctrine of the Christian faith known as the Incarnation. Their intimate embrace embodies the human love between mother and son. It can be seen as an allegory of the love of Christ for his Church, because the Virgin Mary is often presented as a type of the Church itself. Finally, this embrace may also reflect the allegorical interpretation of the biblical Song of Songs, a love poem about a bride and groom, as the love between Christ and his people.

Limestone with paint

74 x 40 x 22 cm (29⅛ x 15¾ x 8⅝ in.)

Maria Antoinette Evans Fund 57.583

Virgin and Child

French (Soissons?), 1210–25

This polychrome wood sculpture of the crowned Madonna shows her as both Queen of Heaven and the Seat of Wisdom (*sedes sapientiae*), a reference to her as the vessel for the Christ Child. Mary is seated on a throne, holding the Christ Child on her lap; the pair face the viewer in similar frontal positions. At the time of its acquisition in 1959, this sculpture had been whitewashed. Careful cleaning revealed the current polychromy and gilding. The polychromy on these sculptures rarely survives because of the fragility of the materials. While it is likely that the paint and gilding are from a later date, they may reflect or record the original decoration of the sculpture.

The tall, columnar shape of the figures, along with the strong linear cuts and quality of the drapery, reflects contemporary styles in stone statuary. In particular, this work relates to monumental sculptures made for the exterior of cathedrals in the Île-de-France under Philippe Auguste (r. 1180–1223) such as those at Chartres and Laon. This sculpture is associated with Soissons, a district northeast of Paris, based on the supple, slender form of the Virgin's body and her small, delicate head.

The figures are not carved fully in the round, so it is likely that this group might have been placed on an altar dedicated to the Virgin. The piece is hollowed out at the back, as is often the case with wood sculpture. There is also a small slot in the back of the head that could have been used to hold a relic.

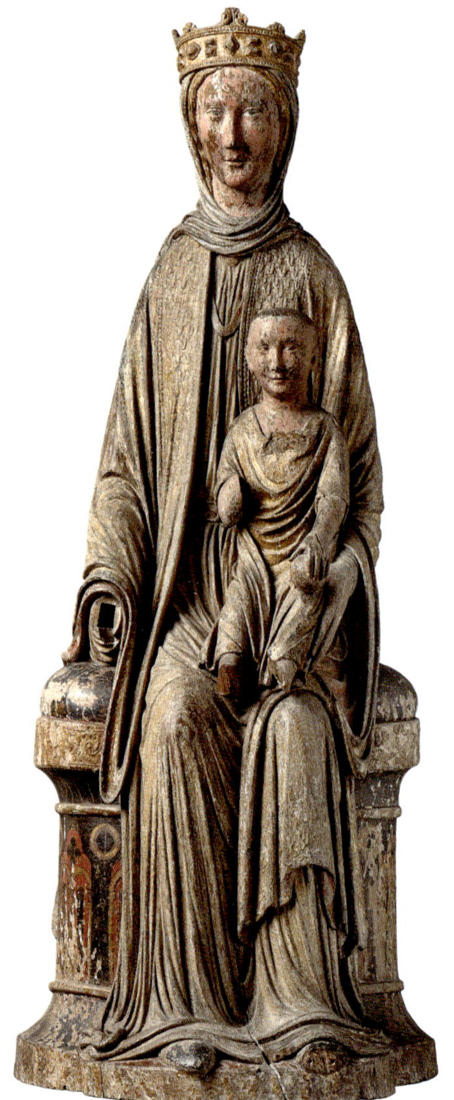

Wood with polychromy and gilding

154.9 x 53.3 x 45.1 cm (61 x 21 x 17¾ in.)

William Francis Warden Fund 59.701

Head of a prophet

French (Strasbourg), about 1300

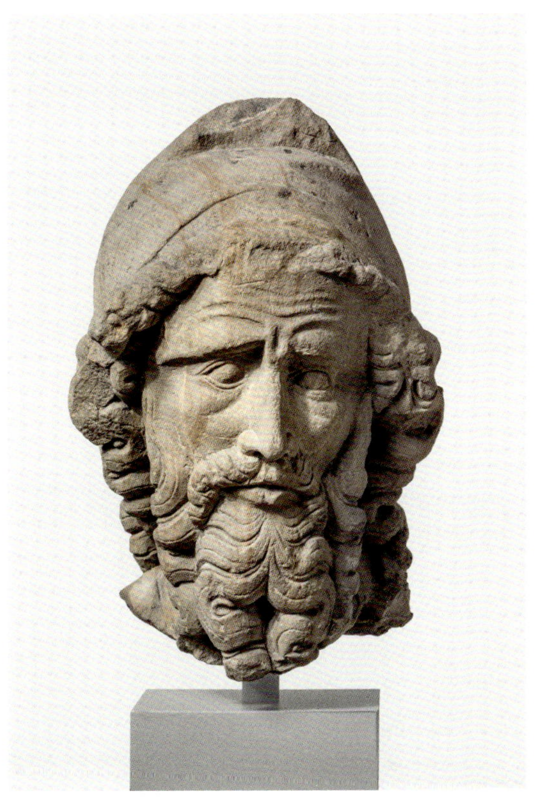

With a deep, furrowed brow and thickly curled beard, this figure wears a pointed hat—a traditional signifier of an Old Testament prophet in both monumental sculptures and illuminated manuscripts. The fragmentary state of this work, with only the head of a larger figure surviving, makes it impossible to determine whether the prophet held an attribute, such as a scroll, which might have allowed for a more specific identification. With his lips slightly parted, he seems on the verge of speaking his prophecy.

The features of this face, with the stylized lines forming the beard and mustache, seem most closely related to sculptures that survive at the cathedral in Strasbourg. The sandstone of which it is made also links it with this center of production. Strasbourg Cathedral was designed during the Romanesque period but redesigned in the newer Gothic style toward the end of the thirteenth century. Strasbourg's location in the Upper Rhineland made it an important artistic center, combining French and German styles and traditions.

In the late eighteenth century, during the French Revolution, many sculptures were removed from church facades and interiors and destroyed, including those at Strasbourg, which may account for the fragmentary nature of this piece.

Sandstone

36.5 x 23.5 x 25.4 cm (14 3/8 x 9 1/4 x 10 in.)

William E. Nickerson Fund 56.506

Saint Peter as Pope

French (possibly Lorraine), third quarter of the 14th century

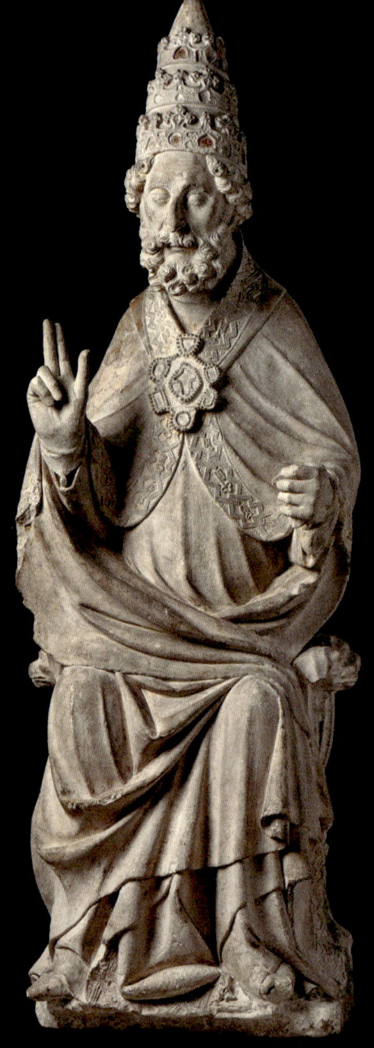

The apostle Peter is considered the first pope, as he was called on by Jesus to be the foundation of the church. He is shown here in papal ceremonial dress, his triple-crowned tiara signifying his spiritual and temporal authority. The sculpture was likely once painted, and his crown and the clasp of his stole, or cope, originally would have been encrusted with jewels. Peter sits on a folding stool with dogs' heads carved on the finials at the front. This type of stool has deep roots in ancient furniture design and further signals Peter's authority. He blesses with his right hand and would once have held the identifying attribute of the keys of heaven in his left hand.

This imposing sculpture would have asserted papal authority and primacy by making clear the connection between the historical Saint Peter and the current pope. The triple-crowned tiara came into use when, between 1309 and 1376, the papacy was based in Avignon, France, rather than in Rome. Because the papacy was understood to be so firmly rooted in Rome, it is not surprising to find works like this made in France, stressing the notion that papal authority was manifest in the person of the pope himself as successor to Saint Peter, not localized in the Vatican in Rome. A saying coined in the thirteenth century conveys this: "Wherever the pope is, there is Rome."

Limestone with traces of paint
H. 152.5 cm (60 in.)
1948 Purchase Fund 48.265

Retable of the Virgin

Spanish (Anglesola, Province of Lérida, Catalonia), about 1320

The Virgin Mary stands in the central niche of this altarpiece, holding the infant Jesus and flanked by angels, one of whom places a crown on her head. Surrounding her are narrative scenes from the life of Christ, beginning at the top left with the Annunciation and continuing with scenes of his birth and infancy, including the Adoration of the Magi and the Presentation in the Temple. This sculpture was made for the parish church in the town of Anglesola in Catalonia, Spain. It was carved from a single slab of limestone and was at one time painted. This type of altarpiece, known as a retable, was popular in Catalonia in the fourteenth century. Stone retables of this kind, which directly echoed the horizontal shape of the altar table, may have stood upon or been set directly onto the front face of the altar table. In later years, tall painted altarpieces composed of numerous wood panels replaced such sculptures, making this a rare surviving example of Spanish medieval church decoration in stone.

The Virgin and Christ Child in the central niche play an unusual dual role. On the one hand, the two figures relate to the liturgy taking place on the altar, and the angel swinging a censer next to Mary mirrors the use of incense during the Mass. On the other hand, Mary and Jesus are participants in the carved narrative, receiving the gifts and prayers of the three kings as part of the Adoration of the Magi scene carved in two panels at the lower left.

Limestone with traces of paint
H. 106.7 cm (42 in.)
Gift of Mrs. Walter Scott Fitz, Edward Jackson Holmes, John Nicholas Brown and Purchase: Marie Antoinette Evans Fund
24.149

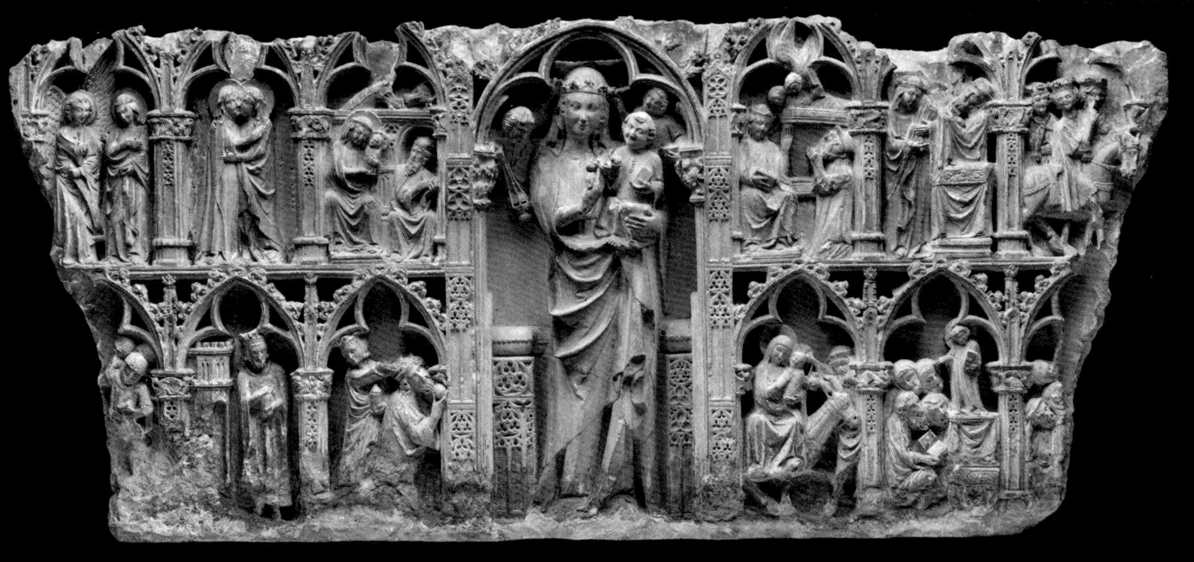

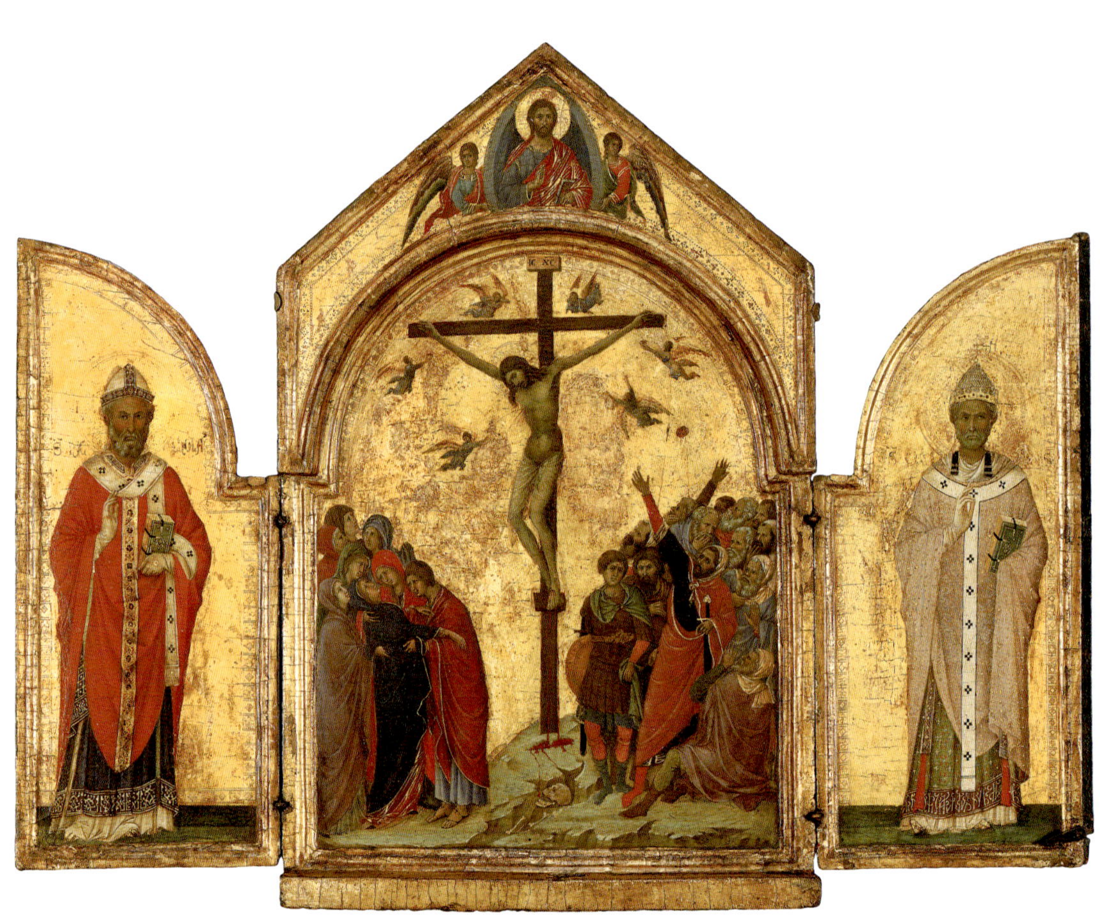

Duccio di Buoninsegna
Italian (Sienese), active in 1278, died by 1319
The Crucifixion; the Redeemer with Angels; Saint Nicholas; Saint Clement, 1311–18

Tempera on panel
H. 61 cm (24 in.)
Grant Walker and Charles Potter Kling Funds 45.880

In the years around 1300, Duccio di Buoninsegna transformed European painting, bringing an unprecedented refinement to the arts of Tuscany. He remains renowned for his delicacy of execution and his persuasive and lively storytelling. Both qualities are evident in this portable painting. Today it is among the greatest Sienese works—and one of the best preserved—outside Europe.

This is a triptych, a work composed of three panels hinged in a manner that allows the two outer panels, or wings, to be closed to protect the painted surfaces. The subjects of the wings offer clues to the work's patron, while the central panel contains the main narrative of the Crucifixion. On the central panel's left side, below the cross, grief-stricken followers of Jesus minister to the Virgin Mary, whose body is limp as she gazes up at her dying son. Whereas these mourners coalesce in their sorrow, on the right side a much larger group of bystanders explodes outward in either bewilderment or disbelief. The soldier in red, a centurion who has converted at this instant, gestures toward Christ. Immediately to the left of his black sleeve, a nearly hidden face emerges. Might this be a self-portrait of the assistant who collaborated with Duccio on this painting?

The figures on the wings are particularly elegant and were certainly done by the master himself. These saints point to Niccolò da Prato (about 1250–1321), a high-ranking papal representative, as the patron of the work. Nicholas, shown on the left wing, was his name saint, and Clement, on the right, was one of the first popes. Niccolò also probably commissioned a triptych by Duccio of nearly identical construction now at the National Gallery, London, with wings featuring Saint Dominic and Saint Aurea. Niccolò was a Dominican friar and the cardinal bishop of both Ostia and Velletri, whose patron saints were Aurea and Clement, respectively.

Attributed to Arnolfo di Cambio

Italian, active from 1265, died 1302

Caryatid group of a deacon and two acolytes, 1265–68

This caryatid group, a trio of supporting figures that surround a column, was once part of the Arca di San Domenico in Bologna. The Arca, constructed between 1265 and 1268, was a tomb built to house the body of Saint Dominic, founder of the Dominican order. Although Saint Dominic had died in Bologna in the early thirteenth century, the construction of the tomb reflects a systematic effort in the 1260s to promote the Dominican order through the building of new churches and sites dedicated to the saint. The design for the tomb is traditionally attributed to Nicola Pisano, the leading Italian sculptor of his day, who had recently completed a prominent commission for the pulpit of the baptistery in Pisa. Nicola drew inspiration for the decoration of the tomb from pulpits—an appropriate source given the Dominican order's focus on preaching.

Most scholars agree that two members of the Pisano workshop, Lapo di Ricevuto and Arnolfo di Cambio, sculpted the individual components of the tomb. Attributed to Arnolfo, the three figures of this group all relate to the liturgy: the figure with a sash over one arm is a deacon who is carrying a pillow for the missal, and the other two figures are acolytes, one holding a water pitcher and the other a pyx (a container for the consecrated host). The detailed depictions of these attributes may suggest that Arnolfo based them on actual objects, possibly those owned by the church. This caryatid group, along with others surviving in the Museo Nazionale del Bargello, Florence, and the Victoria and Albert Museum, London, would have supported a large sarcophagus decorated in the *all'antica* style, incorporating references to ancient sarcophagi. Intended to be viewed in the round, the tomb's decoration and unique design would influence Italian tomb architecture for generations.

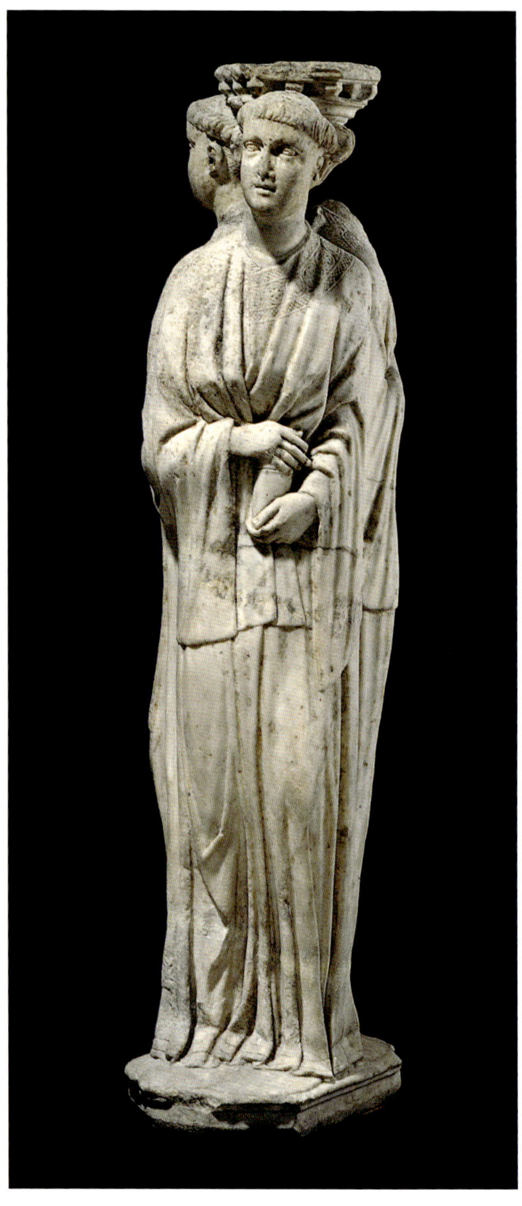

Marble

102.9 x 29.2 x 21 cm (40½ x 11½ x 8¼ in.)

Juliana Cheney Edwards Collection 47.1290

Attributed to Tino di Camaino
Italian, about 1280–1337
Head of a saint or prophet, about 1320–25

Recent scholarship has convincingly tied this fragmentary head of a saint or prophet to the sculptor Tino di Camaino. Given that Tino was active in so many centers throughout Italy, it is challenging to firmly identify works as his. He trained in Siena but also spent time in Pisa, where his style drew closer to that of Nicola Pisano. One of his better-documented commissions was sculpture for the exterior of the baptistery in Florence. It is possible that this head might be among that group of works, some of which are now in the Museo dell'Opera del Duomo in Florence. The treatment of the hair and beard, with its deep drill work, relates to a surviving head of John the Baptist from the Florence Baptistery. The visible drill marks are evidence of Tino's craftsmanship. The artist's time in Florence in the 1320s coincided with a transition in the medium from the sharper, more angular forms of earlier work by sculptors such as Arnolfo di Cambio to a softer, lyrical style showing the influence of the French Gothic.

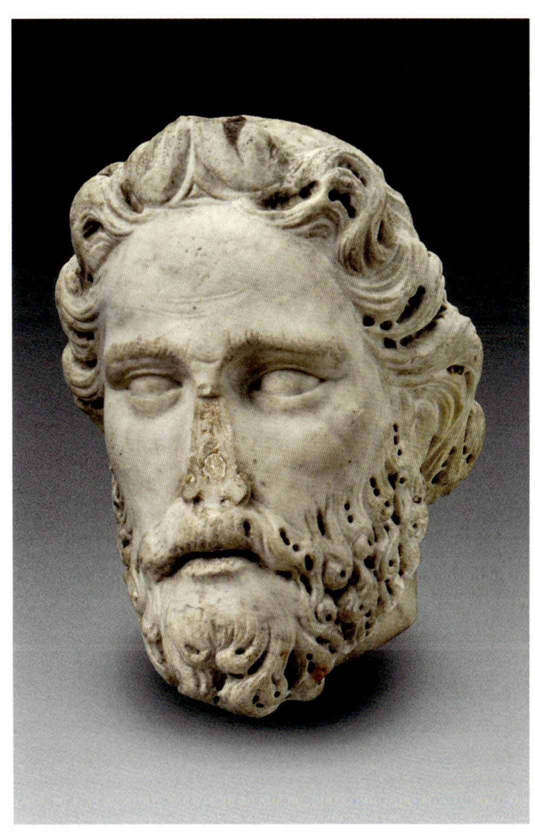

The boldly carved features and contrasting surfaces between soft skin and rougher hair would have made this sculpture legible from a distance, further strengthening the argument that it would have been installed on the exterior of a building. Despite the broken nose, this sculpture is in good condition overall, indicating that if it was indeed outdoors, it might have been protected from the elements.

Marble
33 x 24.1 x 27.9 cm (13 x 9½ x 11 in.)
Charles Amos Cummings Fund 47.1447

"Barna da Siena"

Italian (Sienese), active about 1330–50

The Mystic Marriage of Saint Catherine, about 1340

In his *Lives of the Most Excellent Painters, Sculptors, and Architects*, Giorgio Vasari discussed a painter named "Berna," whose identity remains a mystery. This painting is one of the works usually associated with this artist, now referred to as "Barna da Siena."

Catherine of Alexandria was renowned for her intellect, beauty, and devotion to Christianity and suffered martyrdom for her beliefs. According to legend, she experienced a mystical vision in which she was betrothed to Jesus.

Paintings of the scene typically show Jesus as a baby placing a ring on Catherine's finger, but here Jesus is shown as a grown man. Catherine stands alongside him in what resembles an actual marriage ceremony. At their feet, Jesus is shown as a child standing between his mother and grandmother. This domestic scene would resonate with women who nurtured their children and taught them about life and faith. Along the bottom are three scenes: At center, an archangel oversees a ritual act of peace as two men, dressed in contrasting colors and having laid down their arms, embrace and kiss. At left, Saint Margaret slays a demon, holding him by the horns and beating him with a hammer, a vivid demonstration of the power of good over evil. At right, Saint Michael fights a dragon. The inscription, which translates as "Arigo di Neri Arighetti had this painting made," suggests a votive offering celebrating the peace illustrated in the painting.

By stressing the roles of women, family, the home, devotional experience, and civic ritual at a time when factionalism regularly flared up, the painting conveys the idea that female role models such as Mary and the saints could influence behavior and, with angelic help, engender peace and civic harmony.

Tempera on panel

138.7 x 111.1 cm (54⅝ x 43¾ in.)

Sarah Wyman Whitman Fund 15.1145

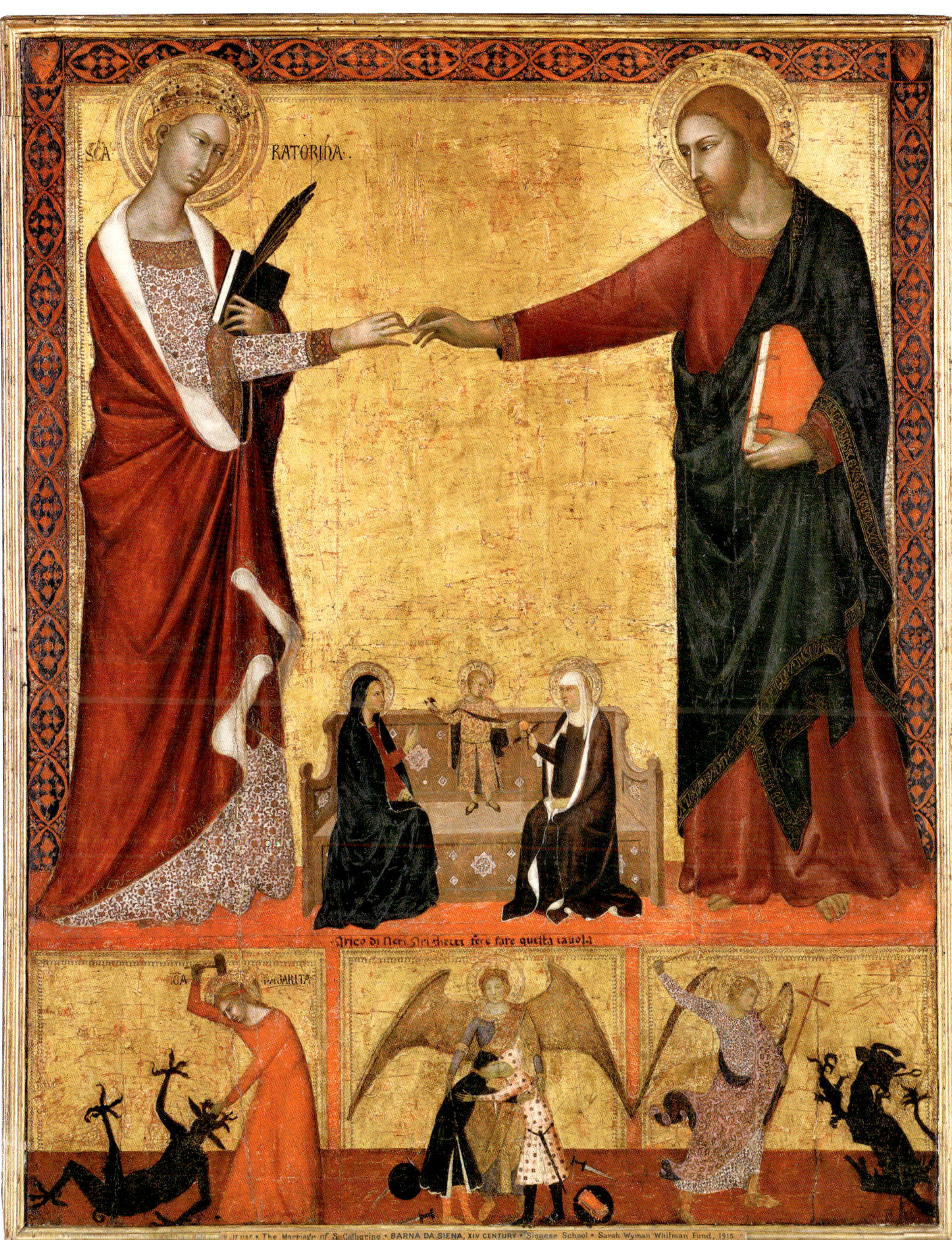
SCA KATORINA
The Marriage of S. Catherine • BARNA DA SIENA, XIV CENTURY • Sienese School • Sarah Wyman Whitman Fund, 1915

Master of the Urbino Coronation

Italian (Riminese), active about 1340–80

The Crucifixion, 1360s

This monumental work is one of only a few detached frescoes from this period and of this size in an American museum. The term *fresco* describes a painting made in fresh plaster applied to a wall or ceiling. As the plaster dries, the work bonds to the wall, creating a durable image distinctive for its saturated earth tones and matte finish. This *Crucifixion* was converted into a portable painting in the mid-nineteenth century. It began life, however, some five hundred years earlier, on the wall of a church in the Italian city of Fabriano.

The unidentified artist is named for a painting in the same style now in a museum in Urbino. Deeply influenced by the Florentine painter Giotto, the Master of the Urbino Coronation is distinguished by a predilection for imposing, substantial bodies. Whereas Duccio di Buoninsegna's *Crucifixion* (see pp. 36–37) is a masterpiece of delicacy, this version is heavy with emotion conveyed through telling details. Here, the Virgin Mary slumps into the arms of two concerned attendants, her hair uncovered and loose, a sign of her feeling of helplessness. The attendant on her left, in pale purple, catches Mary's head in her hand, trying to preserve the dignity of the dying Christ's mother. Next to her, a young man in green and red—John the Evangelist—looks directly out, drawing the viewer into the story. He gestures toward the kneeling Mary Magdalene, weeping at Jesus's feet, as if to identify her as an exemplary mourner. On the right, a man in yellow turns his back to the cross as he claims possession of Jesus's red robe, arguing with another figure, now fully deteriorated on the fresco. Above, angels perform a panoply of despair, rending their garments or raising their arms in grief. The angel closest to Jesus winces as he catches his blood in a bowl.

Fresco transferred to canvas

337.8 x 275.6 cm (133 x 108½ in.)

Augustus Hemenway Fund 40.91

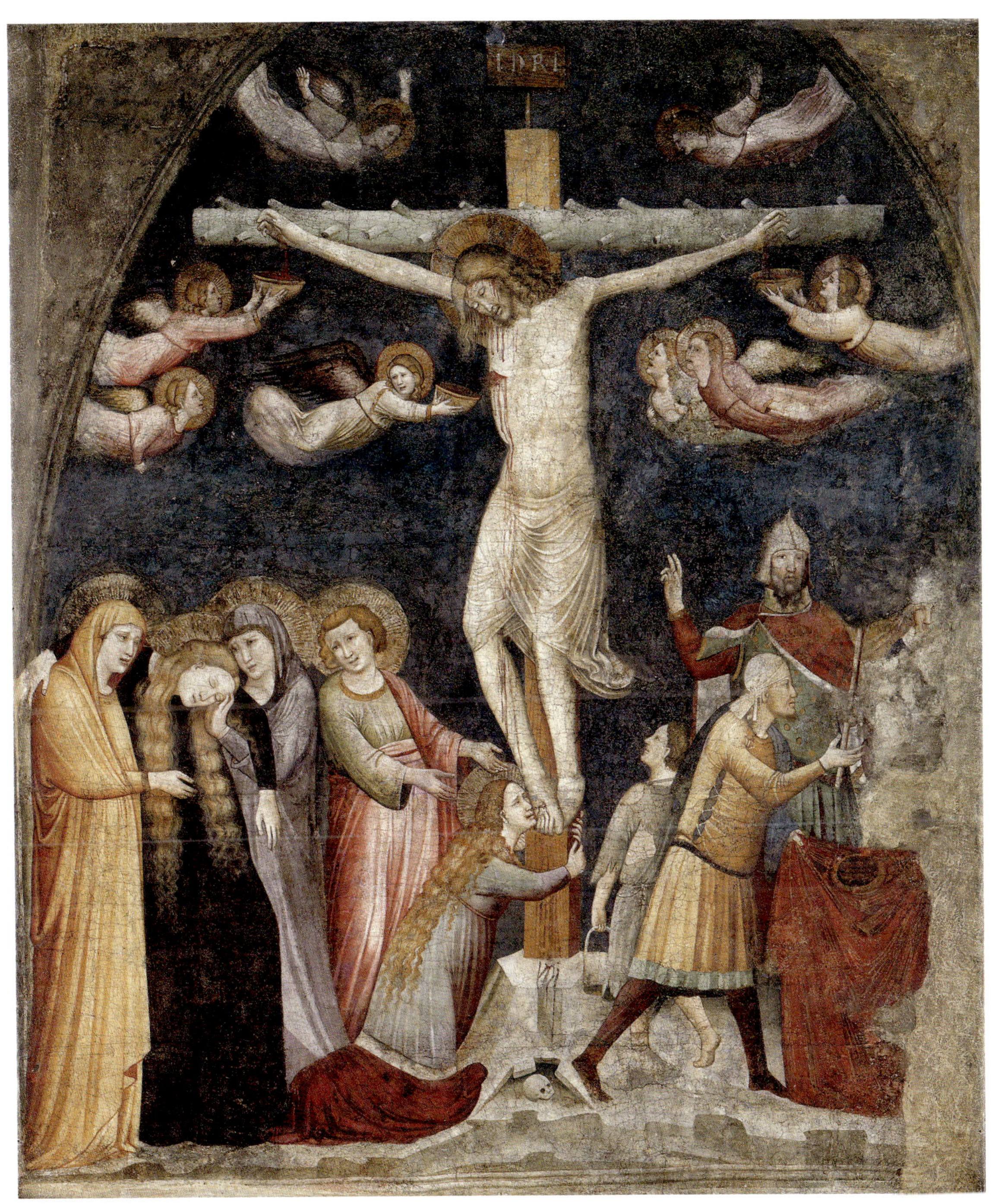

Dormition of the Virgin

Bohemian, about 1350–60

This panel, which probably originally formed part of a larger altarpiece, is one of only a handful of similar surviving works from the reign of Charles IV, Holy Roman Emperor (1316–1378, r. 1355–78). Its subject is the death of the Virgin Mary and the subsequent assumption of her body to heaven. Jesus appears midpanel, his right hand extended toward his mother in a gesture of blessing, his left hand holding an effigy of Mary's soul. Behind these central figures, situated in a sumptuous Gothic interior, stand the twelve apostles, their faces conveying a wide range of emotions.

The artist included three smaller figures in the foreground along the bottom of the panel. The two veiled female figures probably represent professional mourners, while the tonsured male figure is a Benedictine or Augustinian monk kneeling in prayer. It has been suggested that he is Beneš Krabice of Veitmile (d. 1375), a canon of St. Vitus Cathedral in Prague and chronicler of Charles IV. Around 1420, his family acquired Košátky Castle, near Mladá Boleslav, where this painting was rediscovered in the early twentieth century.

In the fourteenth century, Bohemia, and particularly its capital, Prague, was the artistic and intellectual center of the Holy Roman Empire. This cosmopolitan environment ensured that local artistic production was influenced by foreign—especially Italian—stylistic developments. The expressive faces of the mourning apostles, the undulating folds of the various fabrics, and the background architecture that lends structure to the composition all find parallels in contemporary Italian painting. At the top right, the youthful apostle extending his arm upward seems to be the artist's own invention, however. His action alludes to the moment of stillness during the Mass of the Dead announced by the ringing of a bell.

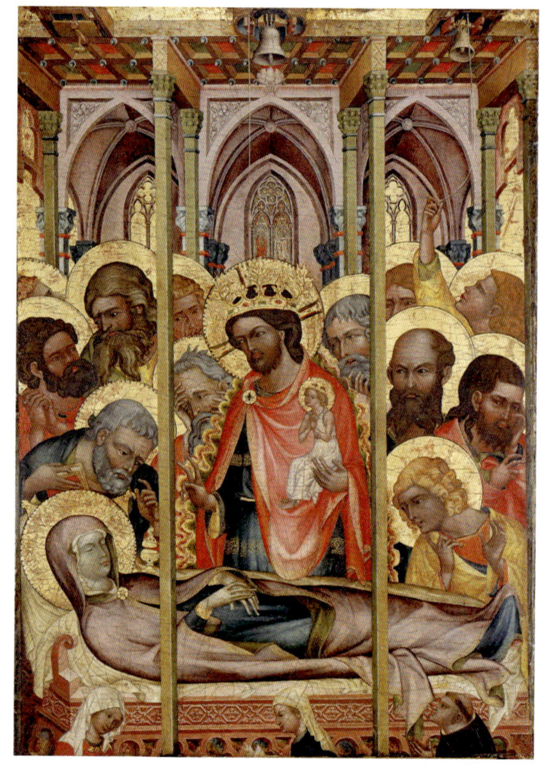

Tempera on panel
100 x 71.1 cm (39⅜ x 28 in.)
William Francis Warden Fund, Seth K. Sweetser Fund, The Henry C. and Martha B. Angell Collection, Juliana Cheney Edwards Collection, Gift of Martin Brimmer, and Gift of Reverend and Mrs. Frederick Frothingham, by exchange
50.2716

Bosom of Abraham Trinity

English, about 1420–50

This alabaster sculpture combines two themes that usually appear separately in medieval art: the Trinity and the notion of being held to the bosom of the biblical patriarch Abraham. This unusual combination stresses mercy and salvation and appears almost exclusively in English art of the period. Here, God the Father is represented seated, supporting a cross with the crucified body of Christ between his legs, while the Holy Spirit is symbolized by a dove painted above Jesus's head. Close to God the Father's chest, a piece of cloth contains a group of figures representing souls seeking safety and salvation, imagery derived from the Gospel parable about Lazarus, a poor man who sought refuge in the Bosom of Abraham. Of the nine figures, two can be identified by their headgear as a king wearing a crown and a bishop wearing a miter. God the Father looks at his viewers with compassion as he blesses them with his right hand.

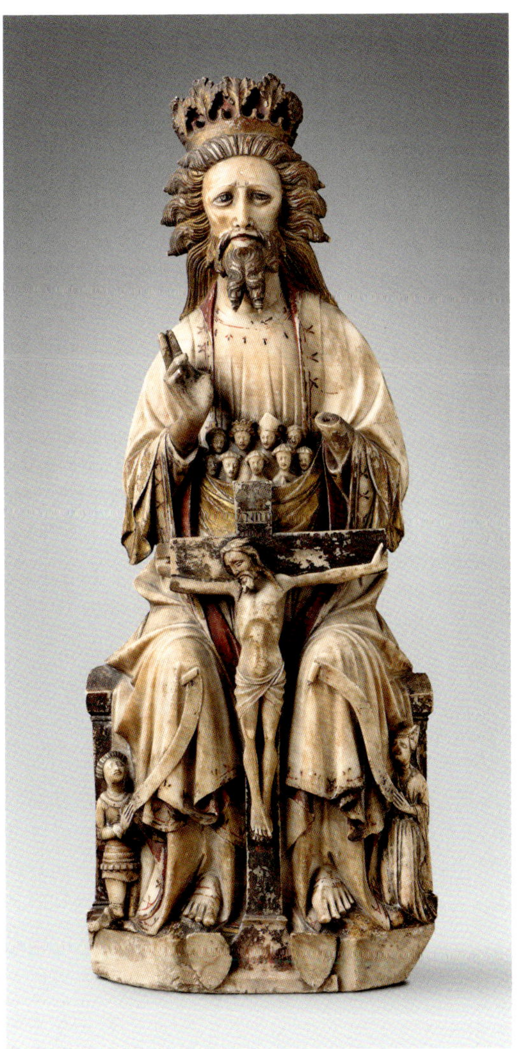

The *Bosom of Abraham Trinity* is a large, well-preserved, and particularly elaborate example of painted alabaster sculpture, which was produced in large quantities in the region of Nottingham. It is further distinguished by the two small donors who kneel at either side of Abraham's feet and hold scrolls that would have communicated their prayers to the Trinity. The small shields at the base of the sculpture would have been at one time decorated with coats of arms, likely representing the donors' families, making this an intriguingly personalized example of English alabaster carving. The work probably originally decorated the altar in a church or chapel.

Alabaster with paint and traces of gilding

95.9 x 38.1 x 12.7 cm (37¾ x 15 x 5 in.)

Decorative Arts Special Fund 27.852

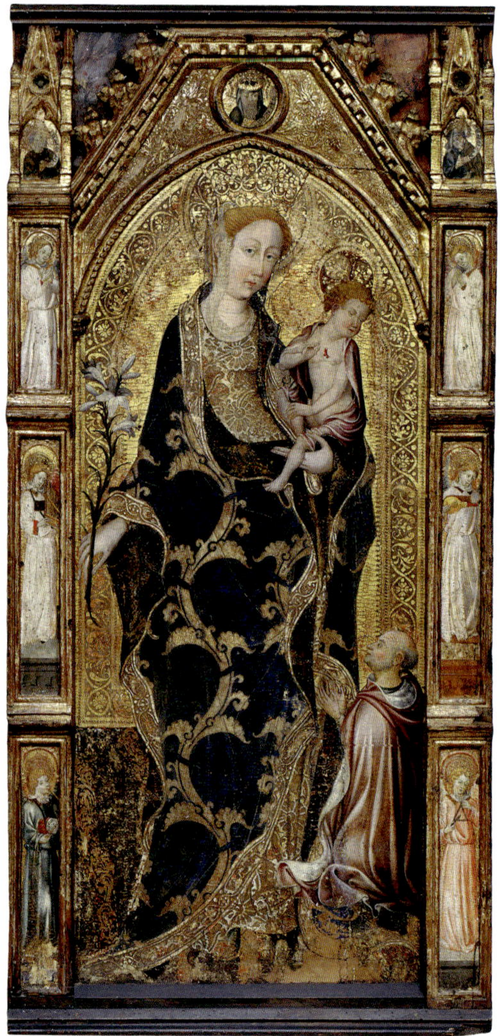

Gonçal Peris

Spanish (Valencian), active first quarter of the 15th century

Virgin and Child Enthroned with Cardinal Alonso Borja (Borgia)

Gonçal Peris worked in the International Gothic style, an elegant manner of painting celebrating surface decoration and lavishly patterned foliage and textiles. As the head of a productive workshop, Peris received many commissions from the clergy of Valencia and Barcelona. This tall panel was originally the center section of a larger altarpiece that was commissioned by Cardinal Alonso Borgia, possibly for the collegiate church of Xàtiva in Spain.

In this work, the elongated figure of the Virgin Mary is dressed in a long, flowing cloak with an undulating border. Tilting her head delicately, she gazes out at the viewer. The young Jesus wears a piece of coral around his neck, a talisman to ward off evil, and blesses the kneeling donor on the lower right whose pink cloak identifies him as a cardinal in the Catholic Church. His furrowed brow gives him the individualized features of a portrait, especially when compared with Mary's idealized visage. Flanking the Virgin are rectangular compartments containing music-making angels, and the top of the frame shows small bust-length depictions of the prophets David, Hosea, and Ezekiel.

The golden background reinforces the painting's precious character. Using a technique called punchwork, the artist tooled the gold surfaces of the halos, the central arch, and Mary's crown and mantle with a metal stamp to create slightly three-dimensional decorative patterns. The refined forms and overall opulence would have been enhanced by the candlelight, incense, and liturgical sounds of the painting's original setting, further inspiring the worshipper.

Tempera on panel

155.9 x 77.4 cm (61⅜ x 30½ in.)

Maria Antoinette Evans Fund 29.1129

Virgin and Child on the Crescent Moon

Austrian, about 1440–50

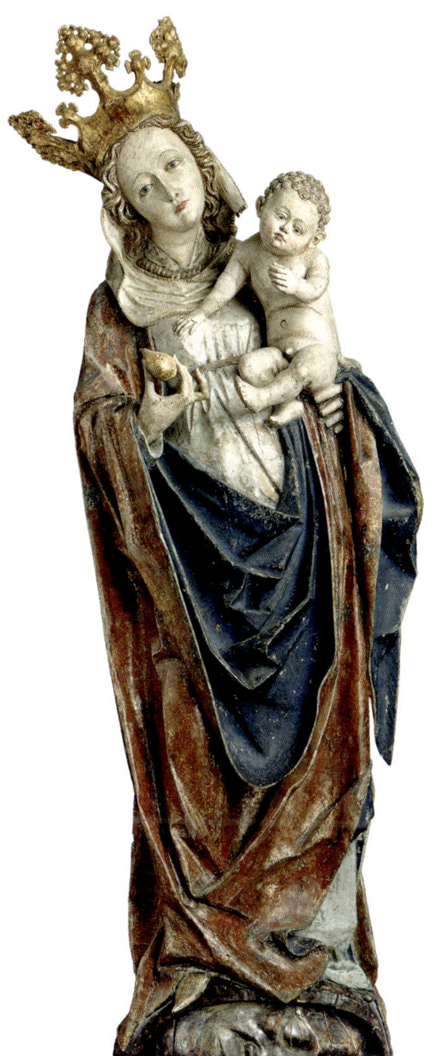

Carved from a single piece of poplar, this polychrome sculpture perfectly represents the style of the *schöne Madonnen* (beautiful Madonnas) especially prominent in Germany and Austria in the first half of the fifteenth century. The blond-haired, exquisitely dressed Virgin stands in an elegant, swaying position, the Christ Child resting on her hip. Instead of looking at his mother, he reaches with one hand for the fruit she holds—a symbol of the Passion—and gestures with his other hand toward the viewer.

This sculpture likely came from a church dedicated to the Virgin Mary in Krenstetten, Lower Austria, where it might have stood alone as a singular devotional sculpture or on an altar as part of a more elaborate (now lost) altarpiece. The Virgin stands atop a crescent moon with a face beneath. Conservation research indicates that this face may be a modern addition. The image of the Virgin standing on a crescent moon, known as *mondsichelmadonna*, can be associated not only with the Immaculate Conception but also with the Woman of the Apocalypse from the book of Revelation. In the early fifteenth century, a revival of the Marian cult would have made such an image—intentionally ambiguous and with many possible interpretations by worshippers—appropriate.

The unidentified artist of this graceful and colorful sculpture likely knew the work of Jakob Kaschauer, one of the most important sculptors in the German-speaking world in the middle of the fifteenth century. Kaschauer's influence can be seen in the gently swayed shape of the Virgin, who stands in pronounced contrapposto while cradling a lively, active child. The drapery of the Virgin's cloak is both soft and angular, particularly in the deep U-shaped fold at her waist, showing the influence of both the earlier International style and the growing focus on realism in Gothic art.

Poplar with polychromy

176.5 x 55.9 x 30.5 cm (69½ x 22 x 12 in.)

Centennial Purchase Fund 65.1354

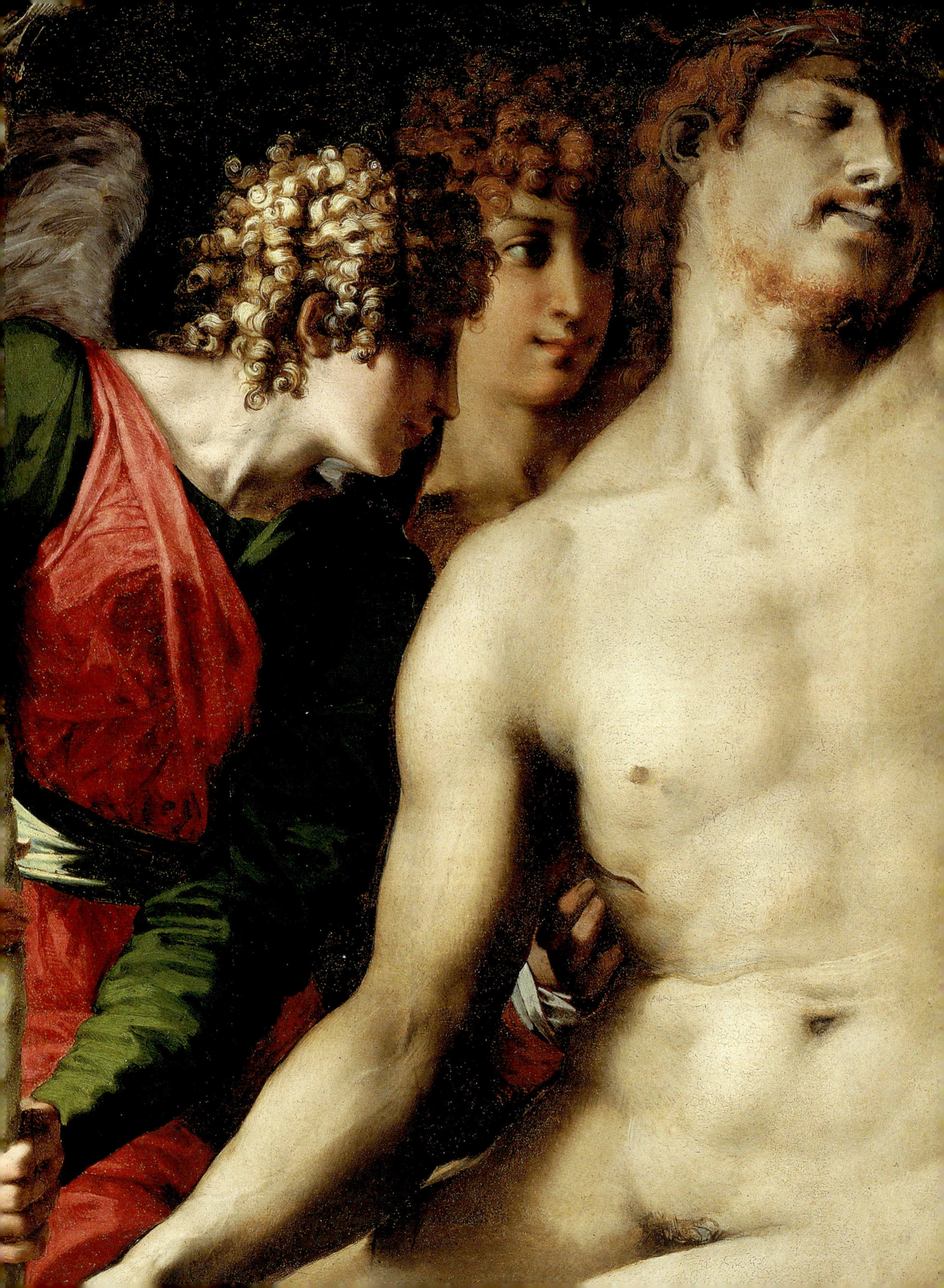

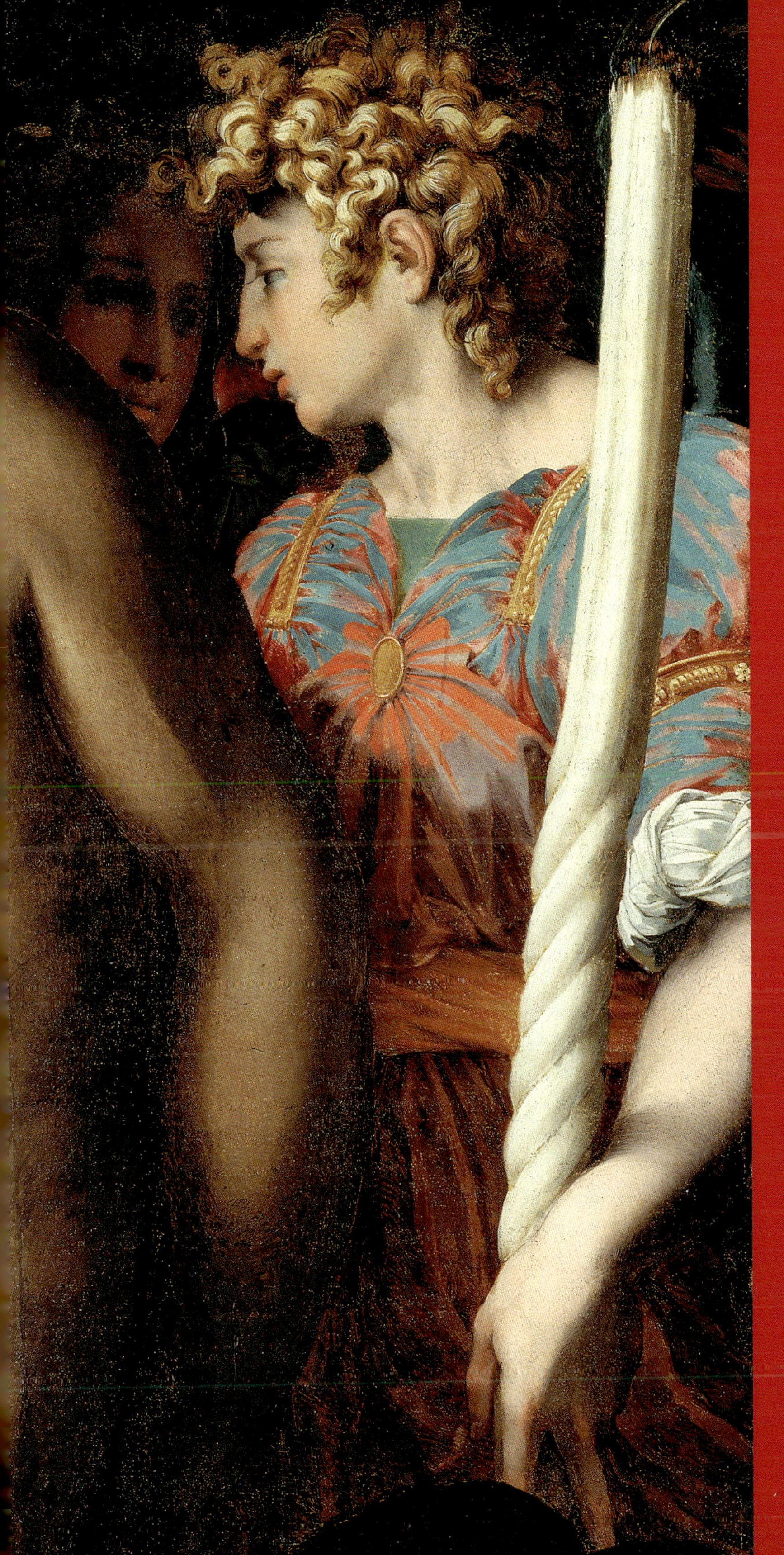

2 THE RENAISSANCE IN ITALY

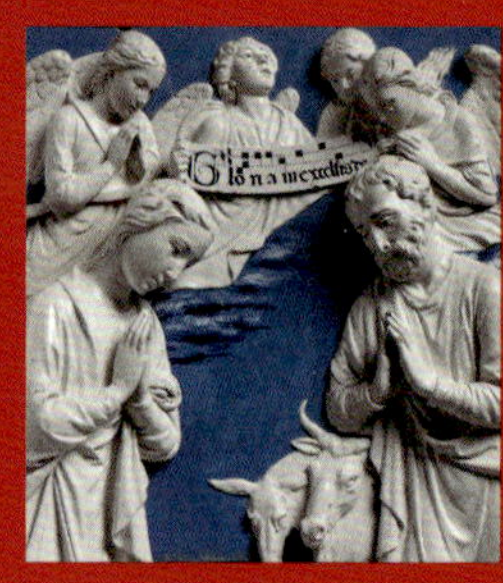
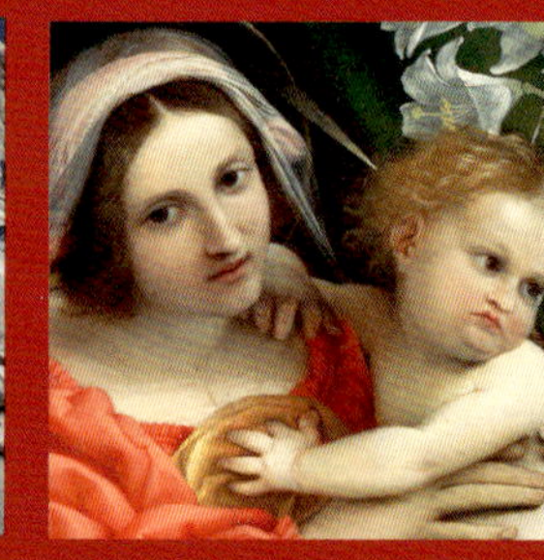
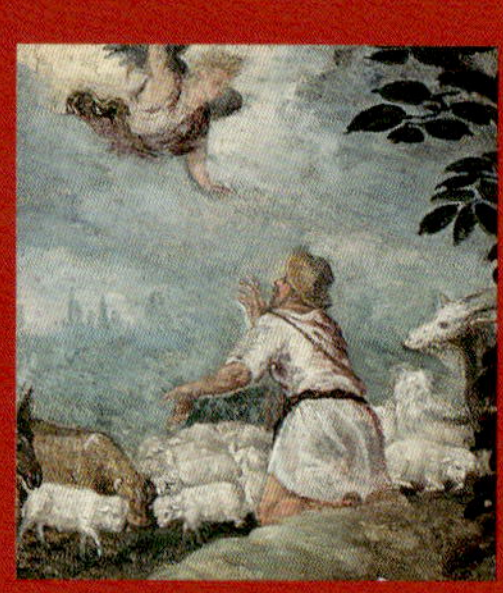
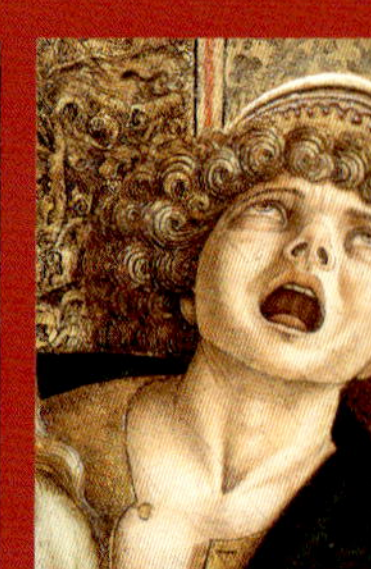

The Renaissance in Italy

Italians in the fifteenth and sixteenth centuries characterized their era as a rebirth or revival of the culture of ancient Greece and Rome. Across the peninsula, intellectuals from aristocrats to clerics enthusiastically embraced the study of classical languages, literature, and philosophy. Ancient texts were copied, annotated, and shared, and new ones were created using these as templates. Rulers aspired to the ideal of the Renaissance man, whose military prowess was equaled by his deep knowledge of ancient literature and his *sprezzatura*, the effortlessness with which he conducted his life. This cultural reawakening—a dramatic rupture with the medieval era—was particularly striking in the visual arts. Starting in the early 1400s, and especially in Florence, painters, sculptors, and architects rejected the conventions of medieval art in favor of classical forms, thus reclaiming the gravitas of antiquity.

It is often argued that there were earlier "renaissances" in Europe, and that there was plenty of continuity of thought across the centuries. Moreover, the influence of the Catholic Church and the importance of faith in daily life were as present in 1500 as they were three hundred years prior. Yet the visual evidence makes clear that something dramatic happened in the 1400s. Suddenly architects embraced the careful proportions and forms of ancient Roman buildings: rounded arches, columns surmounted by capitals, and so on. This inspiration came from the many examples, both ruined and intact, of classical architecture found throughout Italy. When painters began to render homage to ancient art, it is not surprising that they emphasized architectural settings, complete with Roman triumphal arches, pediments, and columns. Clothing worn in paintings and sculptures began to resemble Greek and Roman togas. The patterns of drapery folds found in earlier periods of Italian art, whether bold and corrugated in Romanesque art or delicate with meandering hems in Gothic, quickly looked old-fashioned. Whereas clothing always expresses the priorities of its time, in the Renaissance, artists could prove they were forward thinking by recalling the classical past.

In the fifteenth century, thinkers revived the adage of the ancient Greek philosopher Protagoras, "Man is the measure of all things," which made the human being, rather than God or philosophy, the basis for understanding. Not surprisingly, the primary vehicle of Renaissance painting and sculpture was the human figure, and the nude one at that. Although the near-naked bodies of Christ and male saints had a long legacy in medieval art, by the later 1400s Italian artists created works that rivaled ancient sculptures in their heroic forms, simultaneously natural and perfect. The unclothed body, reminiscent of the confident nudes of Periclean Athens, was celebrated rather than seen as shameful in the years around 1500.

Such conspicuous achievement brought new status to the work of art and to the artist. It also irrevocably changed the relationship between artist and client. Artists cultivated signature styles and market niches, burnishing their reputations. In turn, patrons began to think about art in new and more discerning ways, often as collectors rather than commissioners. The aristocrat Isabella d'Este of Mantua (and very likely the patron of the *Bust of Cleopatra* on p. 73) exemplified a new attitude, that of a voracious collector who coveted specific artists. For instance, she wrote to Leonardo da Vinci in Florence in 1504, expressing her desire for a work by his hand. Evidently the artist himself was more important to her than any particular subject matter. Such a mindset would have been uncommon a century earlier, and unheard of during the Middle Ages. A few years later, in 1510, Isabella wrote to her agent in Venice to acquire a painting recently created by Giorgione. Rather than commissioning a new work, she sought one that already existed, demonstrating the beginnings of the secondary market as it exists today. Sadly for Isabella, she was unable to obtain either her Leonardo or her Giorgione. Now, for the first time in a thousand years, the most sought-after artists could have the upper hand.

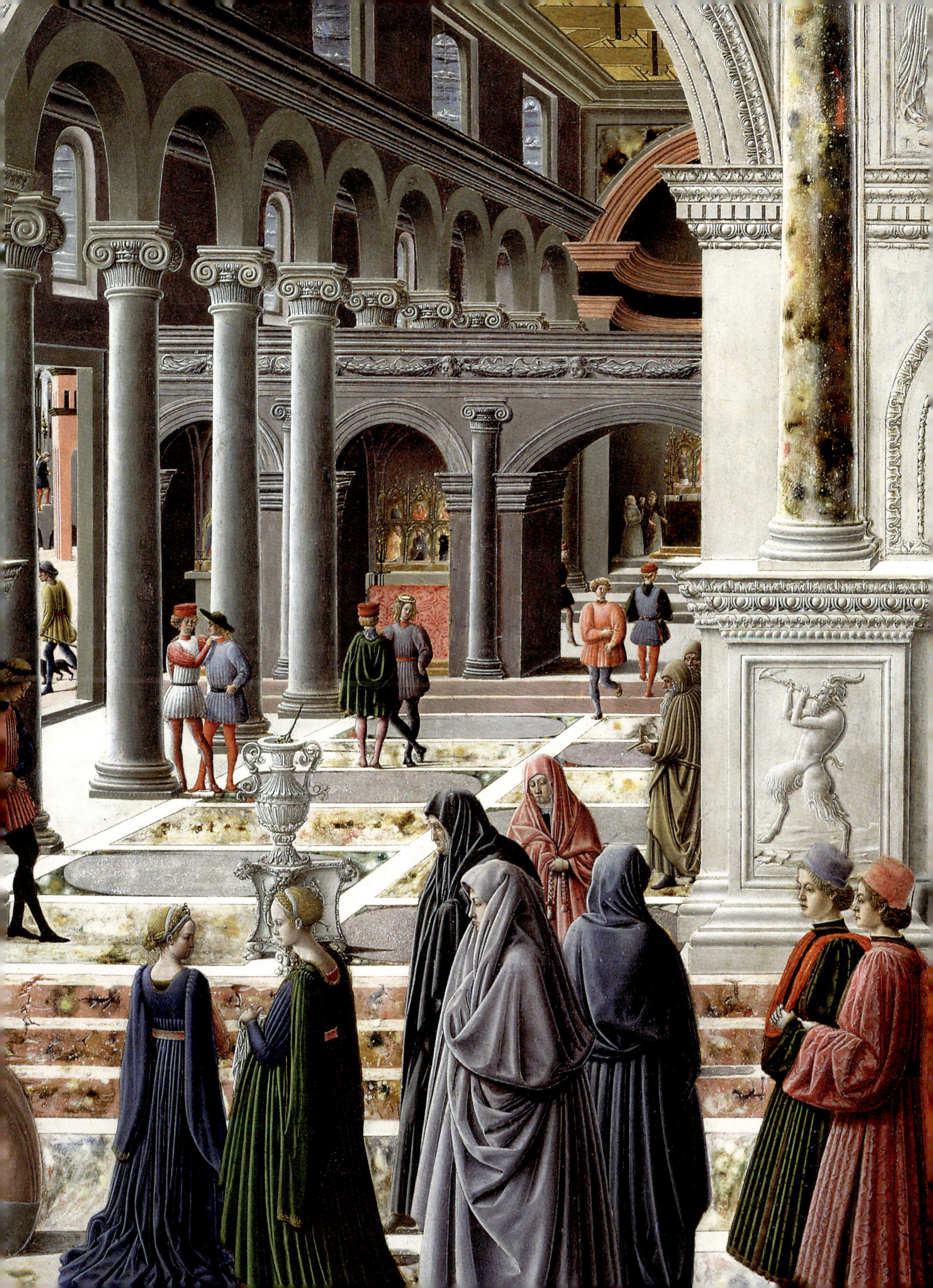

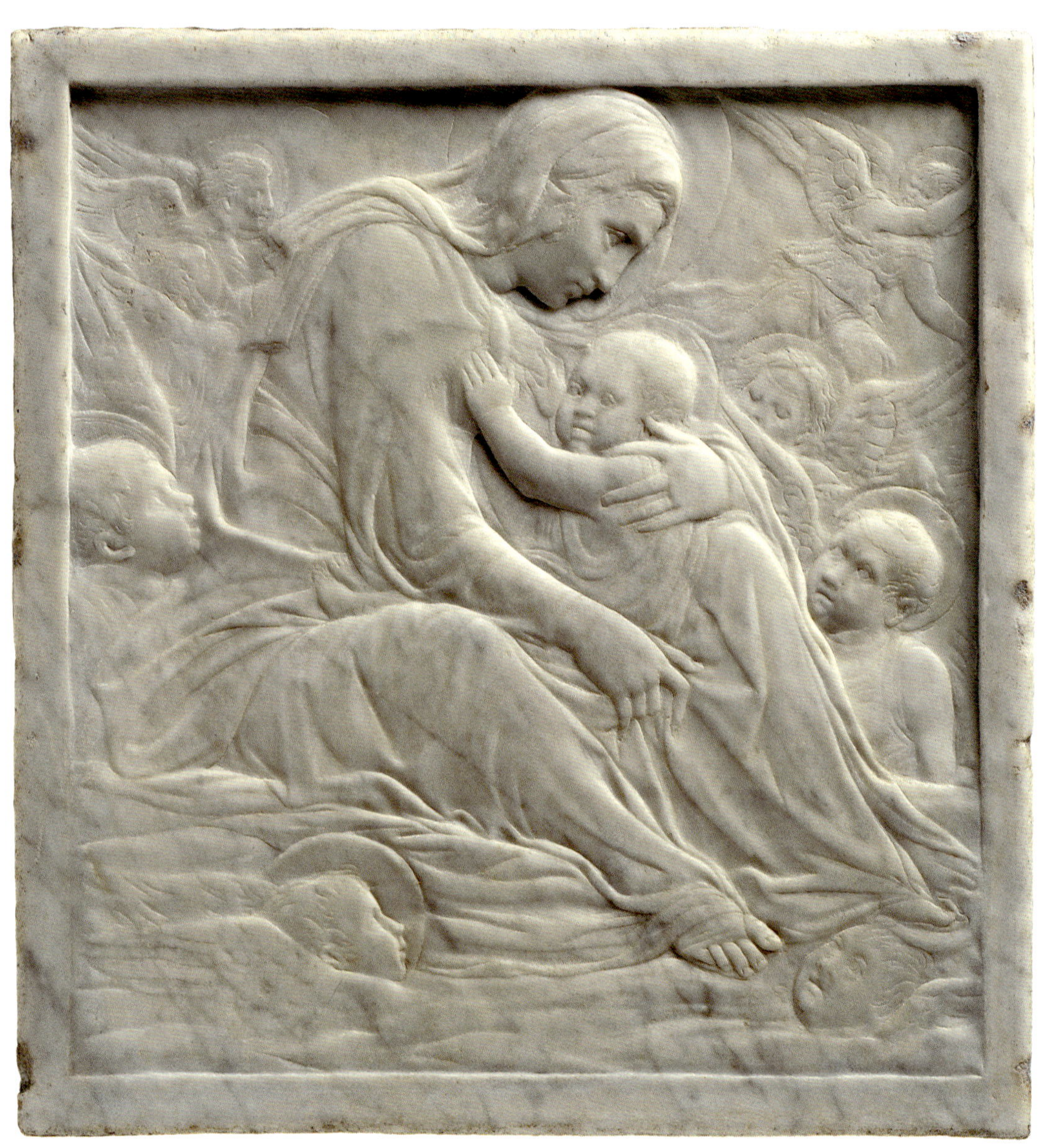

Donatello
Italian (Florentine), 1386–1466
Madonna of the Clouds, about 1425–35

Donatello was one of the artistic geniuses of the Italian Renaissance. Acknowledged in his own day as an exemplar of creative ingenuity, he worked in nearly every sculptural medium, including marble, bronze, terracotta, and stucco. This marble relief of the Virgin and Child is carved using a technique of Donatello's own invention, known in Italian as *rilievo schiacciato* (flattened relief). The sculptor worked with great subtlety, carving only minimally into the stone to create a sense of depth and atmosphere, like drawing on the face of a slab of marble. Donatello's sensitivity to his materials is evident in the way he laid out the composition in concert with the characteristic gray graining of Carrara marble, flowing from the upper left to the lower right here. Cleverly, Donatello ensured that the overall patterns of the figures and their drapery follow this same directional pull.

The relief is as innovative in its subject matter as it is in its technique. The image of Mary sitting humbly on the ground with the baby Jesus on her lap appears in Italian art from the fourteenth century and is often called the Madonna of Humility. But Donatello sets his Virgin in the clouds, surrounded by animated flying angels. Thus she becomes Queen of Heaven, another type for the Virgin. The top of the frame seems almost to press down on Mary's head, causing her to bend closer toward the Christ Child. Her bold profile and the way she appears to look off into the distance create a sense of foreboding, as if she is already aware of the sad fate that awaits her child. She pulls him in close, the fingers of her left hand pressing urgently into the flesh of his upper arm. He reaches out to her with both arms, hands on her chest, and looks out at the viewer. This creative approach to material, technique, subject matter, and expressive content characterizes Donatello's brilliant artistry.

Marble
33.1 x 32 cm (13 x 12⅝ in.)
Gift of Quincy Adams Shaw through Quincy Adams Shaw, Jr. and Mrs. Marian Shaw Haughton 17.1470

Fra Angelico

Italian (Florentine), about 1395–1400 to 1455

Virgin and Child Enthroned with Saints Peter, Paul, and George, Four Angels, and a Donor, about 1446–49

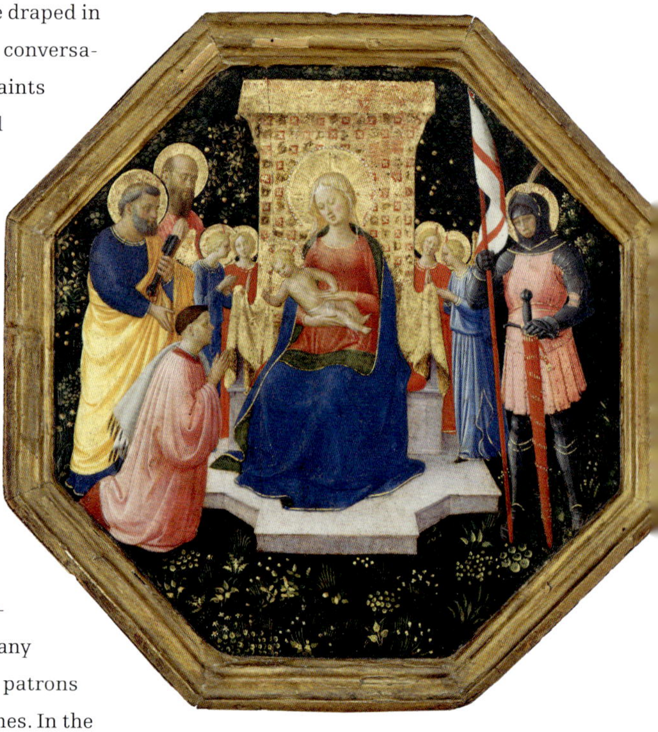

An elegant entourage is gathered around a throne draped in golden cloth. Pairs of boyish angels, engrossed in conversation, stand on each side. At left are two bearded saints identifiable as Peter, dressed in blue and gold and holding the keys to heaven, and Paul, in red beside him. Their counterpart on the right, meeting our gaze, wears a suit of armor with a pink tabard. The banner he carries bearing a red cross implies he is Saint George. Yet the seated mother only has eyes for her baby. Ten figures are in this scene, and all but one has a golden halo, marking them as holy. Fra Angelico, a Dominican friar and the maker of this painting, was himself revered as a holy man. Contemporaries praised the purity of his art and faith, and he was canonized in 1982.

At the center, the infant Jesus twists in the Virgin Mary's arms to bless the kneeling donor. In many paintings, the saints depicted were chosen by the patrons to reflect a special devotion or even their own names. In the works of Duccio di Buoninsegna (see pp. 36–37) and Lorenzo Lotto (see p. 67), for example, the saints stand in for the person who commissioned the work. Fra Angelico, by contrast, here included a portrait of the donor himself, whose name remains unknown. Richly saturated colors, particularly ultramarine blue created with lapis lazuli, play off details in gold, suggesting the client spared no expense.

The unusual octagonal format may allude to a specific function. Originally the picture was double-sided, with the head of Jesus Christ on the verso. It has been proposed that this was used as a pax, an image kissed by believers during the Catholic Mass.

Tempera on panel

24.9 x 24.8 cm (9¾ x 9¾ in.)

Gift of Mrs. Walter Scott Fitz 14.416

Luca della Robbia

Italian (Florentine), 1399 or 1400–1482

Nativity with Gloria in Excelsis Deo, about 1470

Luca della Robbia's signature technique of glazed terracotta enlivens this scene of the Nativity with bright colors and shiny surfaces. Considered by his contemporaries to be one of the most ingenious artists of his time, Luca was credited with the invention of this method of adding color, brilliance, and permanence to sculptures modeled in clay. Luca's family workshop produced glazed terracottas for nearly a century, but the recipes for his glazes remained such closely guarded secrets that they still are not fully understood to this day.

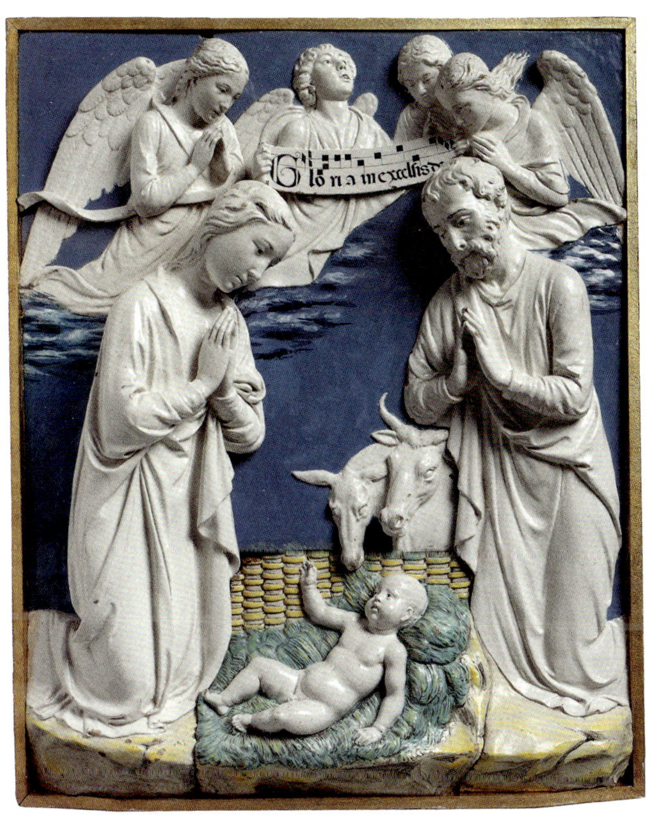

Glazed terracotta

88.9 × 73.7 × 20 cm (35 × 29 × 7⅞ in.)

Gift of Quincy Adams Shaw through Quincy Adams Shaw, Jr., and Mrs. Marian Shaw Haughton 17.1463

Here, the bright white of the figures stands out against the deep, shiny blue of the sky. Luca added naturalistic details, such as the green tufts of hay on which the infant Jesus lies and the yellow fence beyond which stand the ox and the ass. Mary and Joseph kneel in adoration, and Jesus lifts his right hand in blessing. Above, angels fly through the clouds and sing the hymn "Gloria in excelsis Deo," as indicated by the staff of musical notes. The relief was made in sections, probably to ensure safe firing in the kiln. It likely served as an altarpiece in a small chapel, perhaps in a church or a private home, where it would encourage devotees to emulate Mary and Joseph in kneeling and praying as well as joining the angels in song.

Bartolomeo Vivarini

Italian (Venetian), active about 1440, died after 1500

Virgin and the Dead Christ with the Ascension and Saints Benedict, Andrew, George, Scholastica, Jerome, Gregory, Mary Magdalen, and Christopher, 1485

Made for a monastic church on the island of Rab, then part of the Venetian empire but today part of Croatia, this altarpiece weaves together sculpture, wood carving, and painting. Much of the elaborate Gothic frame is original, and its openwork, spires, and crockets create an impressive presence and give a sense of the impact the work would have had in its original setting above an altar. The central niche contains a carved and painted relief sculpture of the *Pietà*, a devotional image of the dead Jesus on the lap of his mother Mary. Directly above is the Ascension of Christ, witnessed by Mary and the Apostles. Both scenes illustrate key tenets of the Christian faith, directly related to the liturgy celebrated on the altar below. The saints on either side include members of the Benedictine order to which the monastery adhered, and foster a sense of community among the viewers of the altarpiece.

Although it is unknown who carved the sculpture and frame, Bartolomeo probably painted the relief himself. His signature takes a typical Venetian form and is set on a fictive piece of paper, "attached" to the base of the sculpture. Written in Latin, the inscription FACTVM VENETIIS PER BARTOLOMEUM VIVARINVM DE MVRIANO PINXT 1485 (Made in Venice by Bartolomeo Vivarini of Murano, he painted it, 1485) provides a wealth of information. It includes the Vivarini family's origins in Murano, where they were glassmakers, and establishes Bartolomeo as part of a prestigious Venetian artistic heritage. Just as today the words "Made in Italy" carry the promise of excellence, the phrase "Made in Venice" here does the same. By saying that he painted it, there is a further guarantee of quality, serving to reassure patrons who were located far from Venice itself.

Carved and painted wood, tempera and oil on panel, gilding

236.1 x 198 cm (93 x 78 in.)

Gift of Quincy Adams Shaw 01.4.1-10

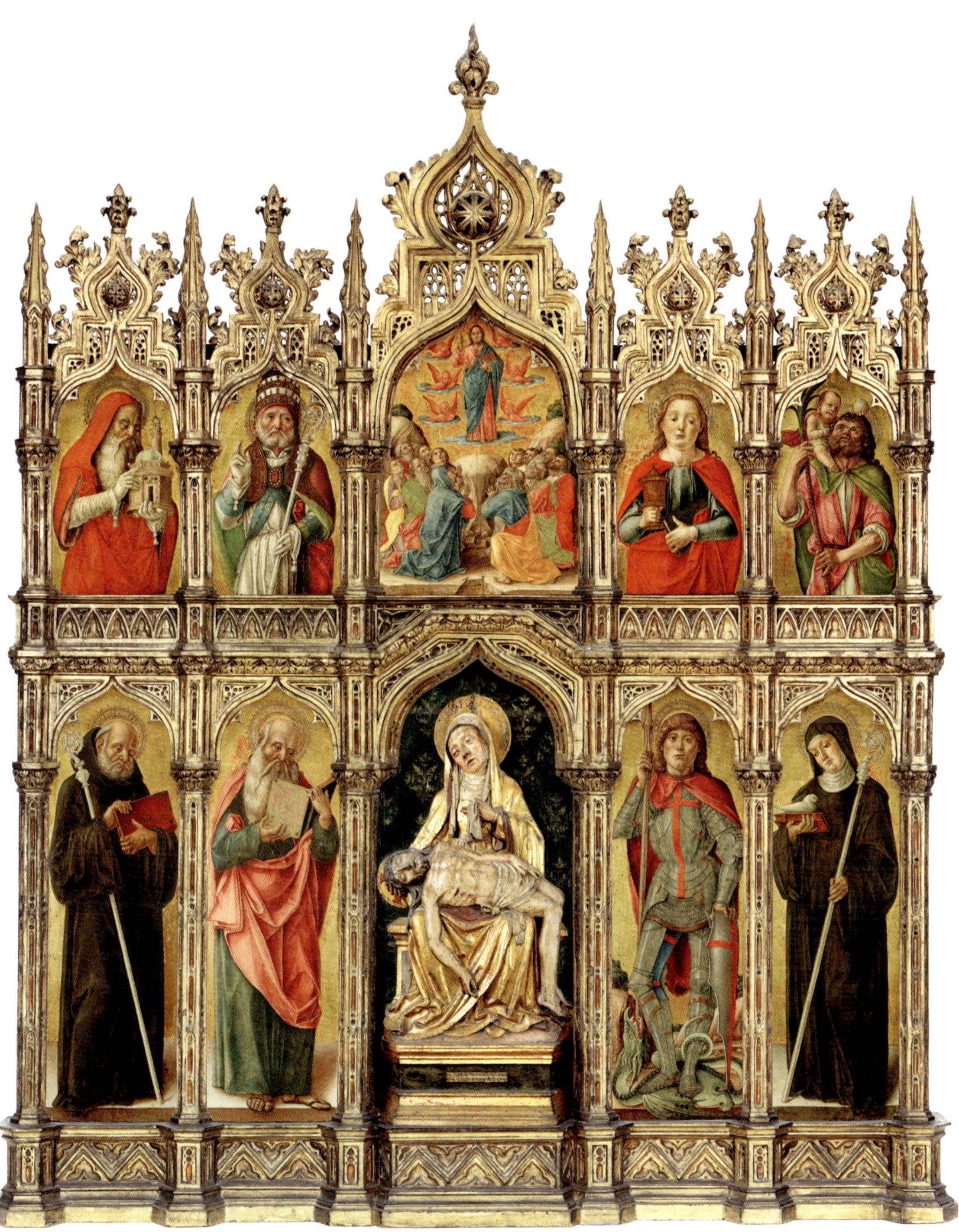

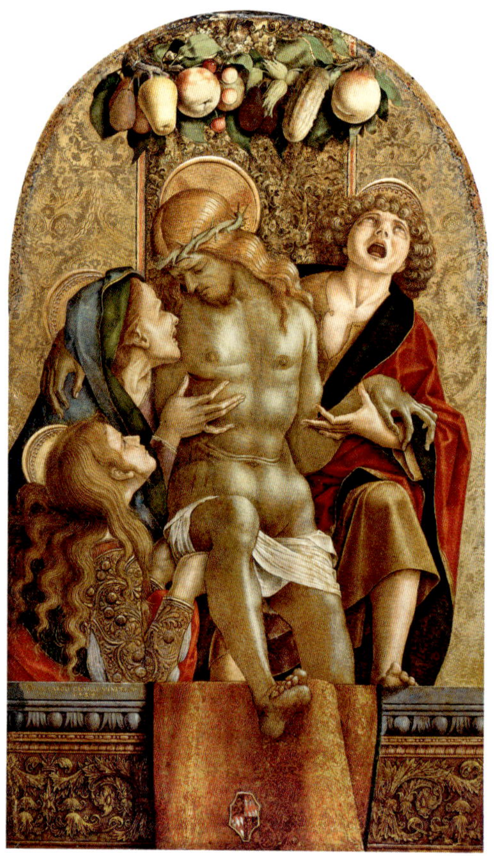

Carlo Crivelli
Italian (Venetian), about 1430–35 to about 1495
Lamentation over the Dead Christ, 1485

Carlo Crivelli was born in Venice but spent most of his career in the Marches, a central Italian region along the Adriatic coast. There, he developed a particular style of painting that combines intensely expressive figures with a highly ornamented surface. This work displays these characteristics as well as Crivelli's attention to naturalistic detail, especially in the drapery and the garland of fruit above the figures. The abundance of gilding and the decorative motifs create rich surface patterns, yet the focus is on the emotionalism of the scene.

The dead body of Christ is supported by Mary Magdalene, the Virgin Mary, and John the Evangelist, all interwoven through touch, gaze, and pose. The viewer is encouraged to experience the scene as if present, entering from below and, like Mary Magdalene, looking up toward Christ. The eye then moves to the Virgin Mary, who touches the wound in Christ's side as if measuring it between her thumb and forefinger, and looks searchingly into his downturned face. At center, Jesus is both static and animated; his right leg extends over the parapet and into the viewer's space. John holds Jesus's left arm, emphasizing the contrast between living and dying flesh. He lifts his head in despair, opens his mouth wide, and wails. Vividly alive and sweet in contrast to the scene below, the lush arrangement of fruit tops the painting and serves to remind the viewer that Christ will be resurrected. The painting may have been made as part of an altarpiece or as a private devotional image. In either setting, it would take viewers on a journey into this sorrowful event, functioning, like contemporary written treatises and sermons, as a spiritual guide.

Tempera on panel
88.3 x 53 cm (34¾ x 20⅞ in.)
Anonymous Gift and Julia Bradford Huntington James Fund
02.4

Bartolomeo Bellano
Italian (Paduan), 1437–1496/7
Virgin and Child with Two Angels, about 1460–70

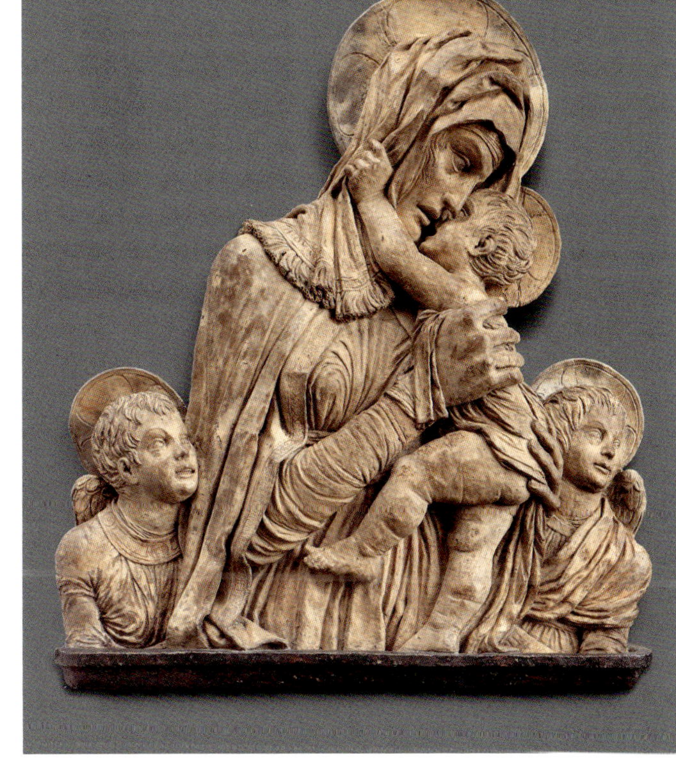

This composition of the Madonna with the young Christ Child derives from earlier examples by the Florentine sculptor Donatello, such as the *Madonna of the Clouds* (see pp. 54–55). Bartolomeo Bellano originally came from Padua, where he likely worked with Donatello in the artist's workshop in the 1440s and 1450s before joining Donatello on his return to Florence.

The Virgin's sharply delineated profile and long face give the work a melancholy feeling that contrasts with the playful pose of the Christ Child, who kicks out with his foot and grabs at his mother's veil. Intensity of emotion between figures is a hallmark of Donatello's work. Here, in Bellano's sculpture, the Virgin embraces her son so tightly that their bodies become almost one triangular shape.

It is possible that the halos surrounding the heads of the four figures are not original to the composition as the clay seems to be different and they all are attached with iron staples. The sculpture must also be imagined with colorful paint and gilding on the surface, some remnants of which still survive. Though the relief is not very deep, Bellano achieves a high level of detail in the figures' clothing and features. The Virgin's draped garments have fine details, including the delicately carved trim and the tassels on her veil.

Terracotta with traces of paint and gilding
78.7 x 67.3 x 11.4 cm (31 x 26 ½ x 4 ½ in.)
Gift of Quincy Adams Shaw through Quincy Adams Shaw, Jr., and Mrs. Marian Shaw Haughton
17.1462

Fra Carnevale (Bartolomeo di Giovanni Corradini)

Italian (Marchigian), active by 1445, died in 1484

Presentation of the Virgin in the Temple (?), about 1467

At first glance, this painting seems to sum up Italian Renaissance art by presenting a Christian story—that of Mary as a toddler brought by her parents to the temple in Jerusalem—in classical guise. The architecture and relief carvings evoke the triumphal arches of ancient Rome, while the pictorial depth created by the chessboard-pattern paving displays the linear perspective championed by Renaissance artists. Upon reflection, however, the painting is enigmatic, with unusual juxtapositions of pagan and Christian imagery, such as the relief of a classical satyr blowing an aulos, or pipe, at lower right and the relief depicting the Gospel episode of the Virgin Mary and Elizabeth, both pregnant, greeting each other at upper left. Equally jarring is the contrast of the church's more contemporary architecture with its old-fashioned altarpieces, such as the Gothic polyptychs in gold frames. The precise subject is elusive. Although traditionally identified as the Presentation of the Virgin in the Temple, the girl in blue in the foreground is much older than Mary is normally depicted, and she does not climb the temple steps, nor is she greeted by the high priest. Furthermore, no one bears a halo.

In 1467, Fra Carnevale, both a Dominican friar and a painter like Fra Angelico (see p. 56), was paid to create an altarpiece for the Church of Santa Maria della Bella in Urbino. This panel is believed to be part of that altarpiece; the repainted area at top indicates the shape of the original frame. A similar painting (now at the Metropolitan Museum of Art) depicts the Birth of the Virgin Mary in an equally elaborate setting. The two panels were part of the same ensemble, although they are unlike any Italian altarpiece of the period. Nevertheless, scholars agree on the remarkable condition of this painting, which allows astonishing details—including the lit candles before the altars—to be visible more than five hundred years after its creation.

Oil and tempera on panel

146.4 x 96.5 cm (57⅝ x 38 in.)

Charles Potter Kling Fund 37.108

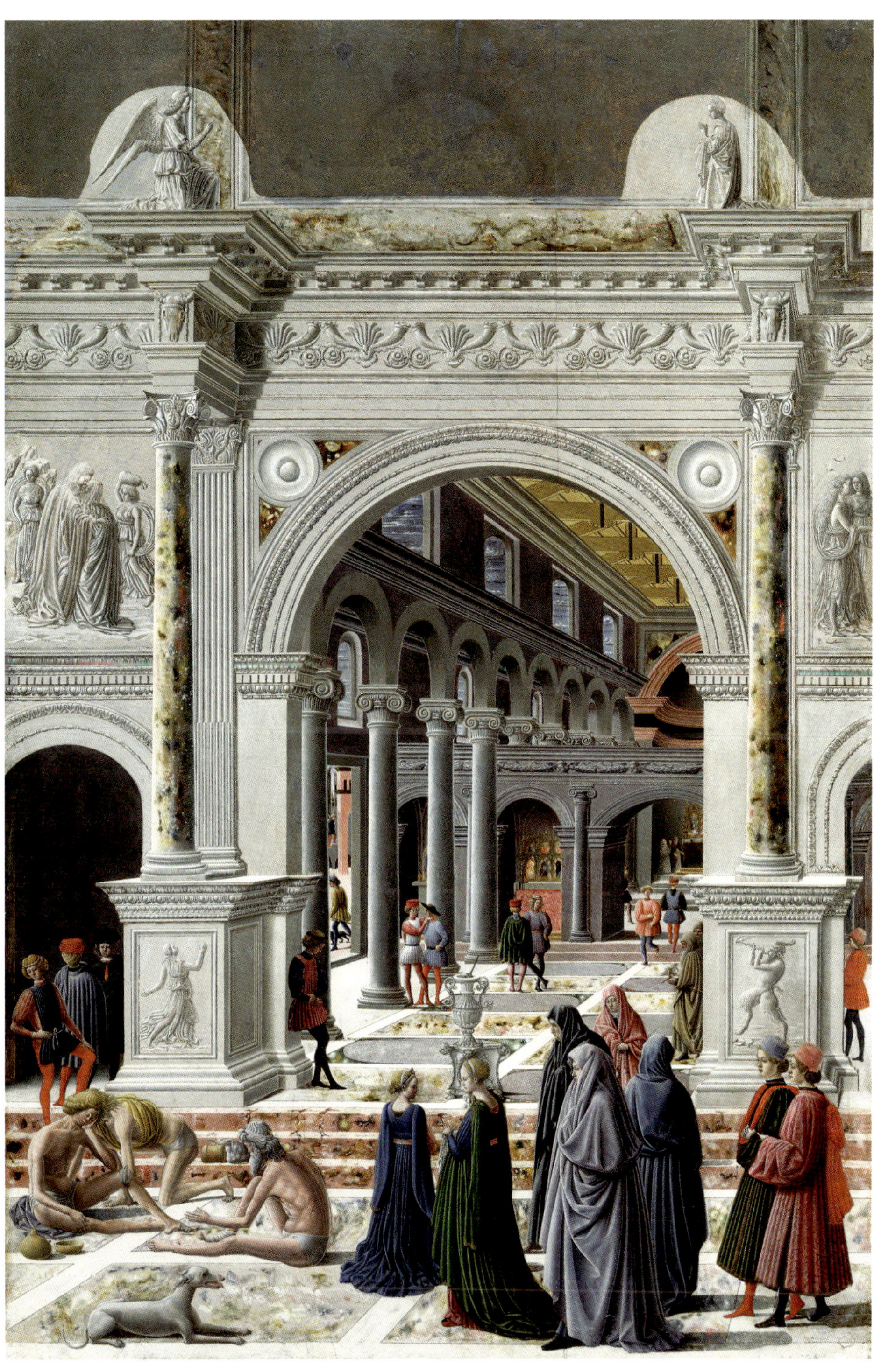

Mino da Fiesole

Italian, 1429–1484

***Roman Emperor (Julius Caesar?)*,**

around 1455

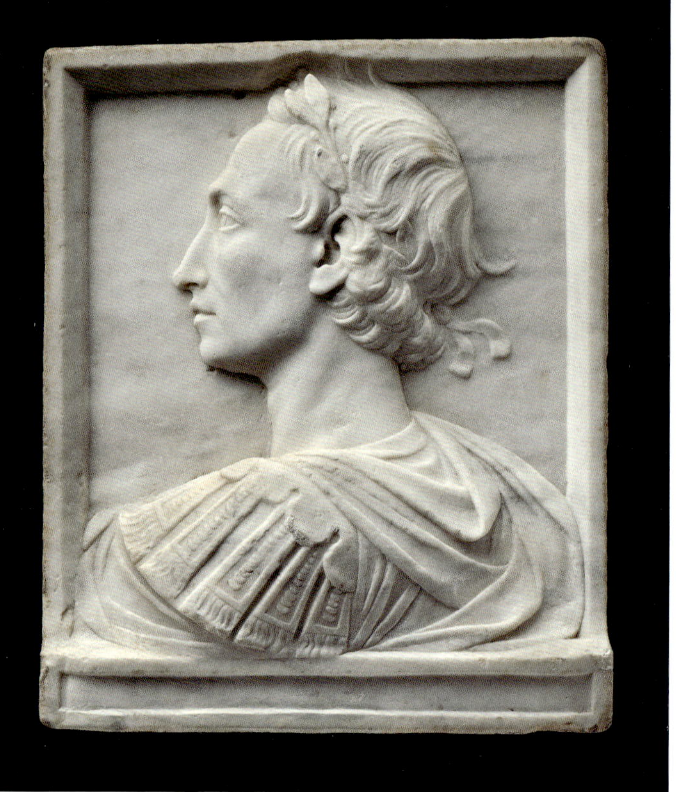

Florence during the fifteenth century experienced a revival of interest in ancient Roman and Greek history and art. Artists such as Mino da Fiesole found success in depicting their contemporary Florentines in the style of Roman portraiture, for example, Mino's portrait bust in the round of the leading Florentine Piero de' Medici.

This marble relief, presenting a man crowned with laurel leaves, clearly portrays a Roman emperor, likely Julius Caesar on the basis of similarity to surviving ancient images of the ruler found on busts, coins, and medals. His face is shown in profile and his shoulder, turned at an angle, breaks through the plane of the surrounding border toward the viewer, animating the pose. The neck shows hints of muscle beneath the surface, further enhancing the active form of the work. The fine, intricate carving of the hair contrasts with the smooth skin. With its soft skin and delicate lips, this is clearly an idealized depiction rather than a real one. Even the pure quality of the marble underscores the dignified nature of the relief.

While this work does not bear an identifying inscription, Mino sculpted portraits of Roman emperors that do. Other reliefs of emperors made in Florence around this time formed part of the architectural decoration on the exterior of buildings. This piece, however, is in very good condition, indicating that it was displayed indoors, most likely in a wealthy patron's private study, or *studiolo*.

Marble

40 x 34 x 7.6 cm (15¾ x 13⅜ x 3 in.)

Gift of Quincy Adams Shaw through Quincy Adams Shaw, Jr., and Mrs. Marian Shaw Haughton 17.1471

Bust of a woman
Italian (possibly Montelupo)
about 1490–1500

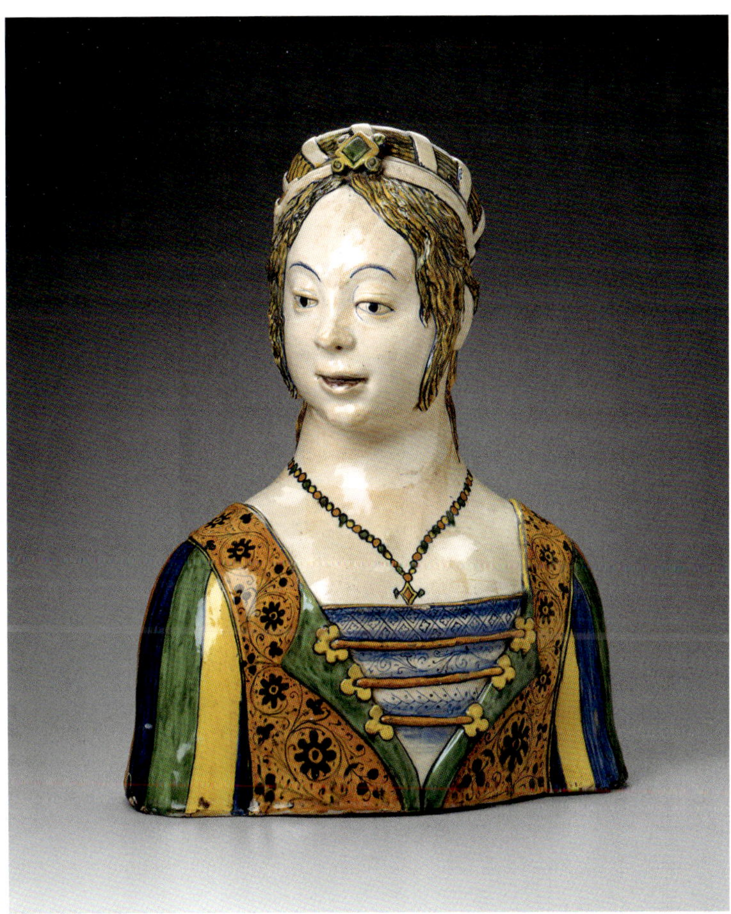

Portrait busts became popular in the fifteenth century, usually in materials such as unglazed terracotta and marble. This particular bust is one of few surviving in maiolica, or tin-glazed earthenware. Maiolica was traditionally used in making small vessels and plates. The young subject of this work, with her lively, quizzical expression and sumptuous clothing and jewelry, was likely just betrothed or recently married. The shiny glazed surface, which accentuates the realistic flesh tones and the saturated yellows, greens, and blues, makes this sculpture particularly engaging and lifelike.

The skill required to glaze and fire such a large piece was considerable. It is possible that the work was a collaboration between a sculptor who molded the figure and a ceramist who glazed and fired it. The first glazing was with a tin-based glaze, giving the sculpture an overall white color after firing. This would then be painted with colored glazes before it was fired a second time. The strong, bright colors were fixed by this second firing and remain to this day as bright as when they were created.

This sculpture and others that share stylistic similarities were long associated with the city of Faenza in northeastern Italy. However, recent scientific analysis and archaeological evidence now point to the Tuscan town of Montelupo.

Tin-glazed earthenware (maiolica)
53.3 x 43.2 x 21.6 cm (21 x 17 x 8½ in.)
William Francis Warden Fund 54.146

Giovanni Francesco Rustici

Italian (Florentine), 1474–1554

Saint John the Baptist, about 1505–15

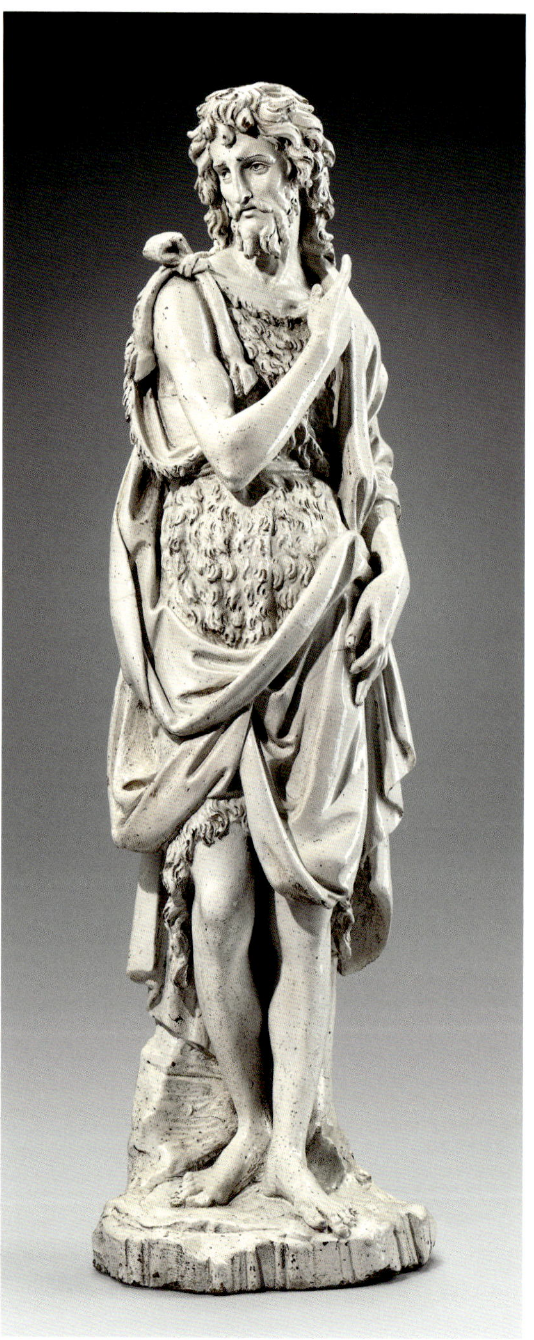

Saint John the Baptist, slender and elongated almost to the point of distortion, stands barefoot on rough terrain. He wears the animal-skin tunic that identifies him, hooves tied over his right shoulder, emphasizing the forward twist of his upper body. Right arm crossed over his chest, he points with his right index finger. This is his characteristic gesture, embodying the Gospel verse often written on scrolls in scenes of his life: "Behold, the Lamb of God." The statue calls to mind John's time in the wilderness, when he withdrew from family and society for a period of reflection, repentance, and preparation for his mission as the precursor of Jesus Christ.

The sculpture presents Saint John, patron saint of the city of Florence, as a role model for penitence. It would have embodied the need for spiritual if not physical asceticism for its Renaissance viewers, many of whom would have heard sermons in the decades around 1500 exhorting them to repent. Florentines would have been very familiar with the story of the saint's life, and this statue recalls earlier representations, including the mosaics in the vault of the town's famous baptistery. Its original location is unknown, but its humble material of local clay, elevated by a transcendent white glaze, and its emphasis on the ascetic body of John point to a setting that would have encouraged contemplation, prayer, and penitential devotion.

Glazed terracotta

H. 100.3 cm (39½ in.)

Gift of Mrs. Solomon R. Guggenheim 50.2624

Lorenzo Lotto

Italian (Venetian), about 1480–1556

Virgin and Child with Saints Jerome and Nicholas of Tolentino, about 1522

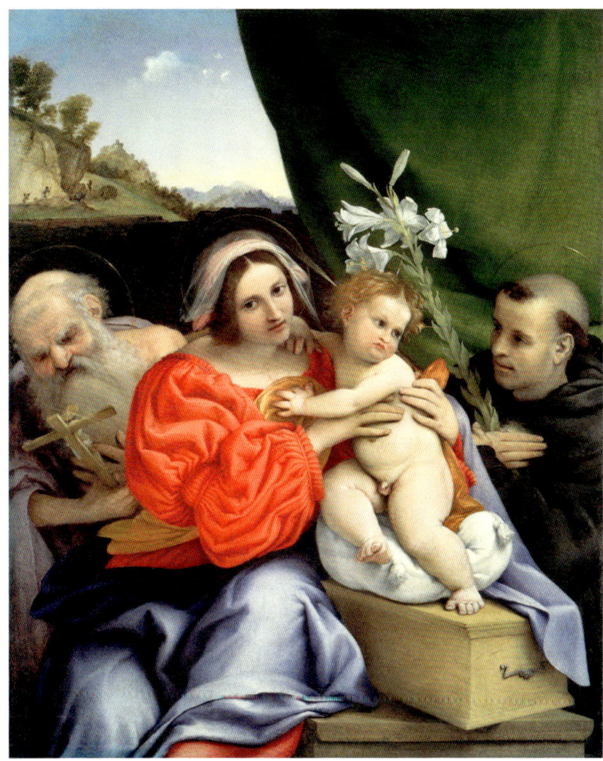

Born in Venice and a member of Titian's generation, Lorenzo Lotto worked in a number of centers throughout Italy. He produced this *Virgin and Child with Saints* toward the end of his residency in Bergamo, part of the Venetian mainland empire, where he lived from 1513 to 1525. The picture displays Lotto's characteristic vibrant palette, skillfully conveyed textures, and intense piety.

This scene condenses the beginning and end of the life of Jesus Christ into a single composition. As Mary gazes out with concern, the infant Jesus writhes uncomfortably; both seem aware of his eventual sacrifice by crucifixion. The baby sits on a cushion atop a child-size coffin, underscoring his fate. On the right is Nicholas of Tolentino, identifiable by his black monk's robe, the radiance on his chest, and the lily, a reference to the Annunciation. At left, the hermit Jerome prays fervently to a figure of Christ on the cross, whose golden halo gleams. A single tear falls from Jerome's eye. In the background, a partially drawn curtain reveals distant mountains similar to the landscape surrounding Bergamo. The deep recession at the upper left and the projecting coffin at the lower right create a powerful push-pull effect, enhancing the sense of drama captured in the expressions on the four faces.

Another version of this composition, signed by the artist and dated 1522, is in the National Gallery, London, although its condition is compromised. It is believed that the two paintings were executed simultaneously in the artist's studio. Bold changes to the underdrawing on the Boston canvas, visible using infrared light, confirm that Lotto worked out the composition on the present work before copying it onto a second canvas placed alongside the first. The Boston painting also features abundant ultramarine pigment used in creating the rich blues of the Virgin Mary's drapery and the subtle lilac of Jerome's garment. The London version employs azurite, comparatively economical.

Oil on canvas

94.3 x 77.8 cm (37⅛ x 30⅝ in.)

Charles Potter Kling Fund 60.154

Giovanni Angelo del Maino

Italian, about 1475–about 1525

Massacre of the Innocents, with Herod in His Court, and the Flight into Egypt, about 1520

Giovanni Angelo del Maino is one of the greatest sculptors of the Italian Renaissance, though his work is not well known. A virtuoso wood carver who worked in northern Italy in the area around Milan, he produced small-scale sculptures for private use, individual statues, and monumental altarpieces for churches. This relief sculpture demonstrates his extraordinary technical skill: the three separate scenes, each with numerous carefully carved figures, are all sculpted from a single panel of wood, with the exception of one small piece at the lower left that was attached separately. Once carved, the relief was painted and ornamented using *sgraffitto* (Italian for "scratched"). In this process, brilliant gilding was laid down, a layer of paint was applied above the gold, and patterns and details were scratched through the paint to reveal the gold underneath. All was contained inside a four-sided box with a backboard painted to help set the scenes.

Two of the three scenes have been associated with famous prints; the third likely derives from an as yet unidentified print as well. The Massacre of the Innocents, occupying the bottom half of the relief, is based on an image designed by Raphael and engraved by Marc Antonio Raimondi. It is one of the most famous prints of the Italian Renaissance, admired for its pathos and expressive power. It represents a biblical episode from the infancy of Jesus in which King Herod (shown in the scene at upper left) ordered the killing of all infant boys after being warned that a newborn child would usurp his power. In the scene at upper right, the Flight into Egypt—based on a print by the German artist Martin Schongauer—Mary, Joseph, and the infant Jesus escape the massacre, guided by angels.

Del Maino was inspired by prints from Northern Europe and central Italy, brilliantly weaving these sources into a complex narrative. His creativity is displayed as he transforms flat, monochrome designs into a three-dimensional, colorful, and highly ornamented sculptural relief. This work would have pleased an enlightened owner who might have marveled at the transformative power of the artist's imagination and skill.

Wood with paint and gilding

63.5 x 64.45 x 20.32 cm (25 x 25 3/8 x 8 in.)

H. E. Bolles Fund 42.563

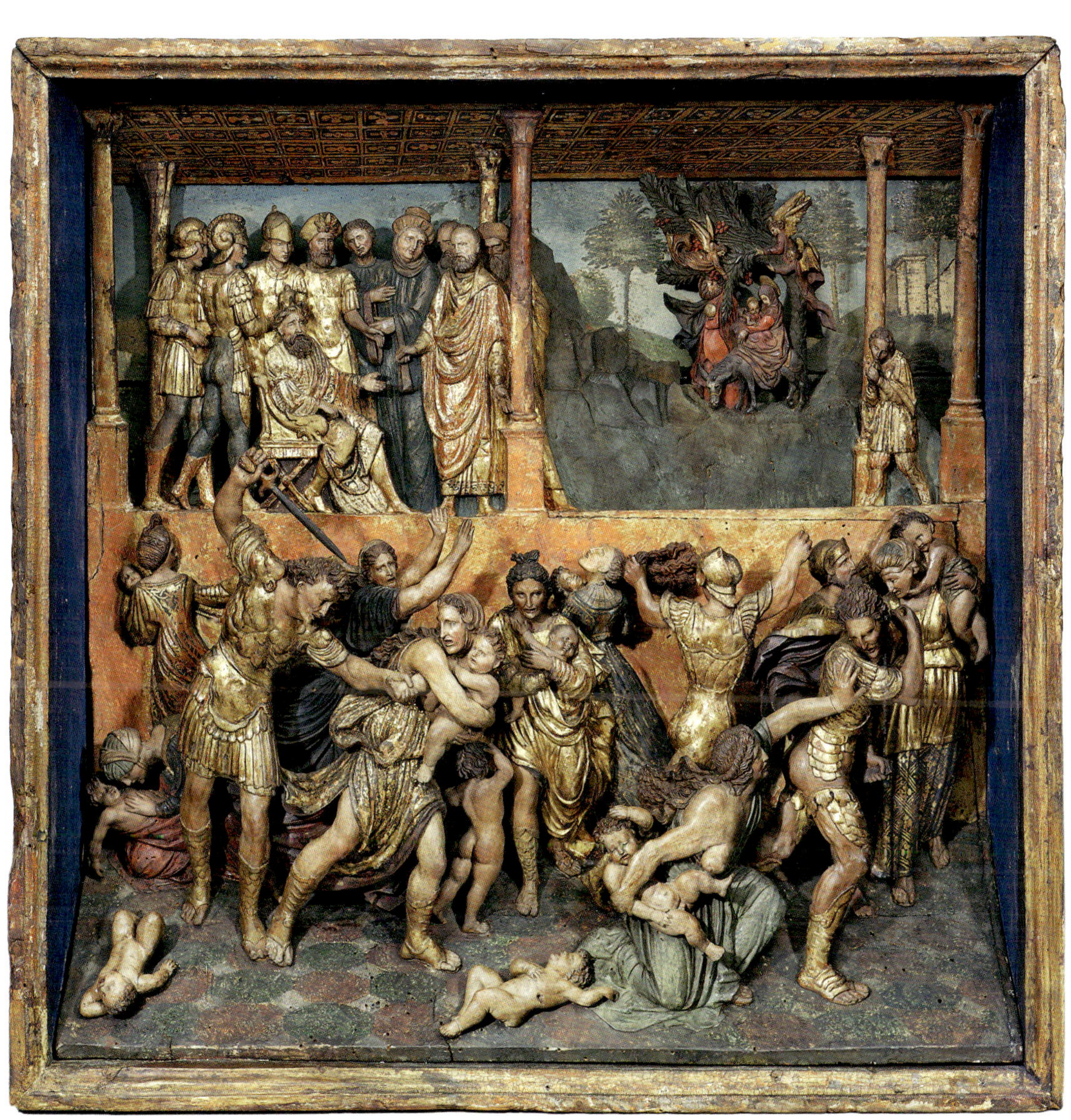

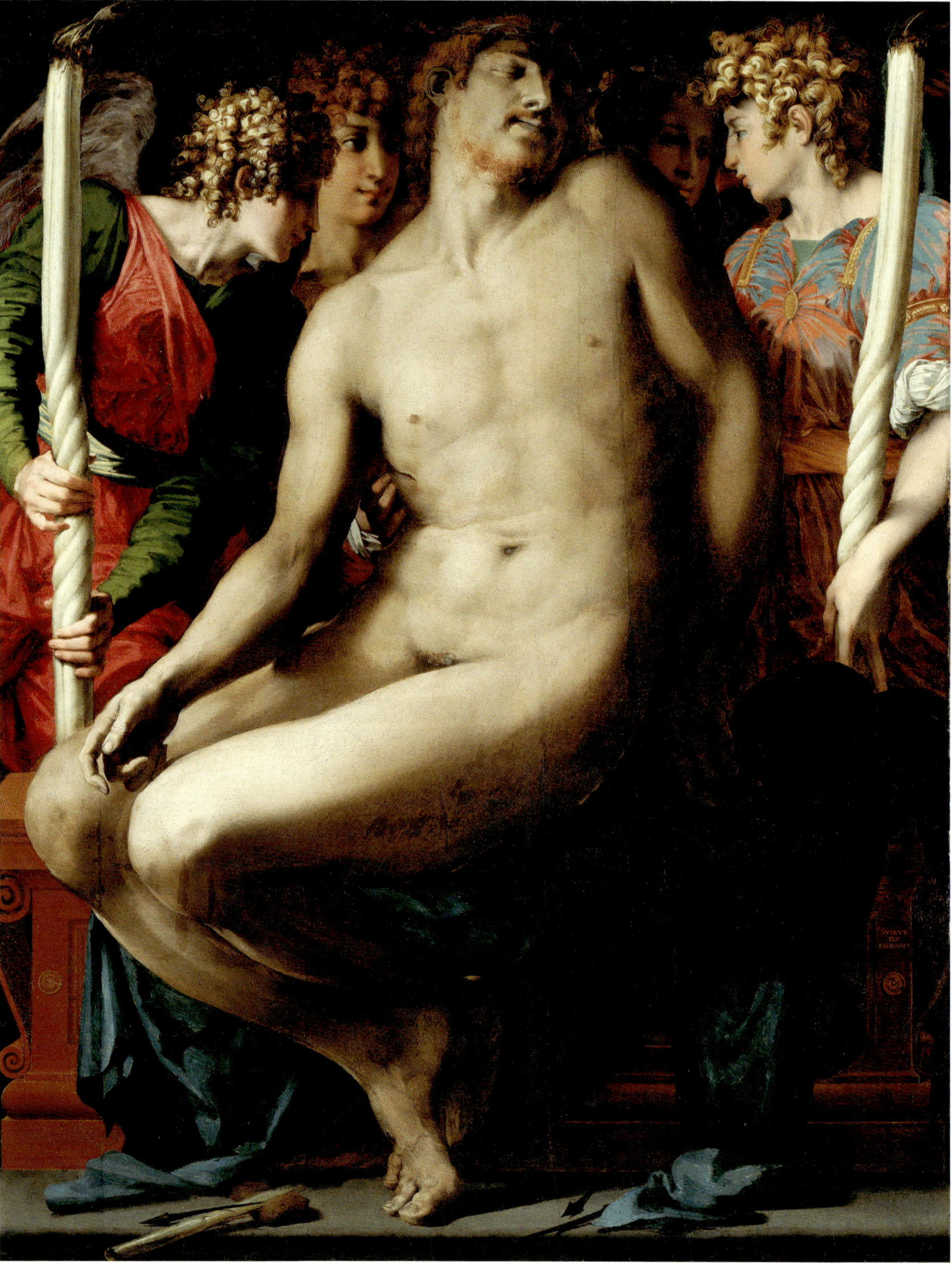

Rosso Fiorentino (Giovanni Battista di Jacopo)
Italian (Florentine), 1494–1540
The Dead Christ with Angels, about 1524–27

Inside a dark, hushed space, a slight movement interrupts a vigil kept by a group of angels. Sensing something special is happening, they lean in closer to the body of Jesus. This is the moment of Christ's resurrection on Easter morning: the stone blocking the tomb has been rolled away, and wind has extinguished the angels' candles. Christ's massive form stirs to life. His left arm hangs limply in shadow, and in contrast his muscular right arm, brightly illuminated, tenses as his body awakens. Most depictions of Jesus during or after the Crucifixion show a body racked with pain, demanding that viewers reflect on his suffering. Here, his figure is nearly pristine, its perfection anticipating Christ's reign in heaven. Such an extraordinary conception must have been the artist's own invention.

Giovanni Battista di Jacopo—known as Rosso Fiorentino, or "redheaded Florentine"—made the unusual choice to depict Christ with red hair and beard, surely an autobiographical touch. The artist deeply admired Michelangelo's statues and frescoes, and the sculptural presence of this Christ resembles the nudes on the Sistine Chapel ceiling painted some fifteen years earlier. This work is one of the foremost examples of the style often called Mannerism, defined by strong, unconventional colors (note the turquoise and salmon-colored garment on the angel at right), claustrophobic pictorial space, and elongated figures in twisted poses. Mannerism's refined approach also favored sophisticated details, such as the corkscrew curls of the hair and the crisply rendered fingers of the angel at left.

Probably intended as an altarpiece, this panel was certainly painted in Rome, perhaps for a chapel there. Most scholars believe the client was Leonardo Tornabuoni, bishop of Borgo San Sepolcro. This cleric would have appreciated a painting depicting the miracle inside the holy sepulchre.

Oil on panel
133.4 x 104.1 cm (52½ x 41 in.)
Charles Potter Kling Fund 58.527

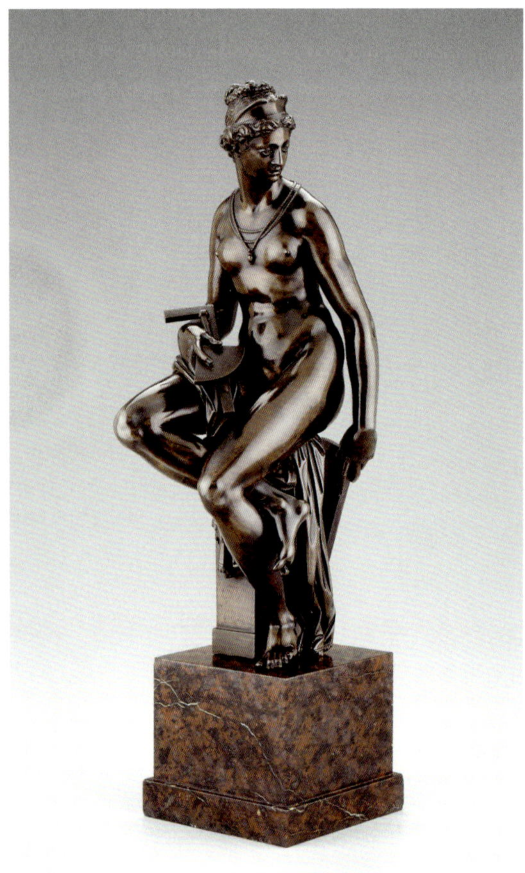

Giambologna (Jean Boulogne)
Flemish (worked in Italy), 1529–1608
Architecture, about 1600

This small, exquisitely made bronze figure, an allegory of Architecture, embodies the elegance typical of Giambolonga's bronzes. Born in Flanders, Giambologna traveled to Rome in 1550 to study ancient sculpture and architecture and ultimately remained in Italy. He worked extensively for the Medici dukes and the Florentine court, creating both monumental sculpture and smaller works, such as this piece, that might have been used as diplomatic gifts. Giambologna was also an architect but is perhaps better known today as a sculptor. The head of a large workshop active in bronze and marble, his small bronzes are a highlight of his production.

Here, the female figure is seated in graceful repose on a thin block, her body comfortably relaxed and weighty. The items she holds—a framing square, a protractor, a compass, and a drawing tablet—all speak to her identification as Architecture. Her delicate necklace supports not a jewel but a plummet, an architect's tool that further confirms her identity. This cast was taken from the model at an early stage, as later versions of the subject indicate that the model had deteriorated and the detail of the plummet is indistinguishable. The detail, the fine casting, and the finish of the Boston sculpture, which still retains traces of its reddish patina, make this one of the best surviving examples of Giambologna's small sculptures. Like many of the artist's most refined works in bronze, this one is dated after 1580, when the Italian bronze caster Antonio Susini joined his workshop.

The sculpture is signed on the lower edge of the tablet behind the figure, a hidden spot where perhaps only an initiated viewer would know to look. Its small scale would have made it well suited to private enjoyment, while the lithe posture of Architecture encourages viewing in the round. Giambologna's finest work, in both small and large scale, often features serpentine, twisting bodies.

Bronze with later marble base
45.1 x 12.1 x 15.2 cm (17¾ x 4¾ x 6 in.)
Maria Antoinette Evans Fund and 1931 Purchase Fund 40.23

Pier Jacopo Alari Bonacolsi, known as **Antico**
Italian, about 1460–1528
Bust of Cleopatra, about 1519–22

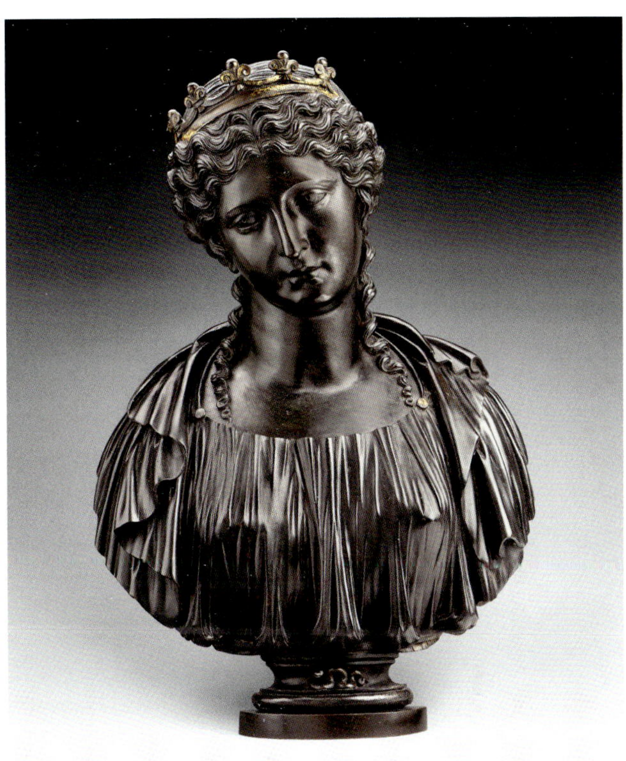

Pier Jacopo Alari Bonacolsi's sculptural style so strongly evoked ancient art that he was nicknamed "Antico," or "the Antique One." His *Bust of Cleopatra* exemplifies this quality, as it recalls ancient portraits, including Roman marble busts, carved gems, and coins. This image of the ancient Egyptian queen was likely made for Isabella d'Este, Marchesa of Mantua.

The subject is identifiable by the small snake that decorates the segment of a socle upon which the bust seems to rest. According to legend, Cleopatra committed suicide through the bite of a poisonous asp. In Antico's time, it was often the snake that helped identify images of the queen. For example, a famous ancient Roman marble sculpture of a reclining female figure wearing an armlet in the form of a serpent was believed to be Cleopatra, but today is recognized as the sleeping nymph Ariadne.

Antico's representation is a radical rethinking of the figure of Cleopatra, aligned with a new appreciation for her as a heroic, thoughtful woman. Though the fourteenth-century poet Giovanni Boccaccio described her in his book *On Famous Women* as one known for "greed, cruelty, and lustfulness," Renaissance writers saw her as more complex. They lauded her decision to kill herself as a choice of death before dishonor, which saved her from becoming part of the booty displayed in Augustus Caesar's triumphal procession through the streets of Rome. Antico presents Cleopatra looking downward, lost in thought, as if contemplating her fate. Her clothing and headdress exude elegance and refinement, the shiny bronze highlighted by areas of gilding. Originally, she even wore real earrings. Yet, it is her sense of introspection and melancholy that intrigues the viewer, while the snake below hints at the promise of release from her earthly troubles.

Bronze, with traces of gilding
H. 64.45 cm (25⅜ in.)
William Francis Warden Fund 64.2174

Sofonisba Anguissola

Italian (Cremonese), about 1532–1625

Self-Portrait, about 1556

Sofonisba Anguissola was one of the most successful female artists in Renaissance Italy. She was the eldest of six sisters, all of whom painted. Anguissola attained fame in her own day, reaching a pinnacle of professional success working at the court of King Philip II of Spain. Best known as a portraitist, she painted herself a number of times over the course of her long life. Twelve self-portraits are known today, the most of any Italian Renaissance artist, male or female.

Sofonisba made this oval miniature self-portrait while she was in her twenties. She is dressed in what might be considered her work clothes: a simple black doublet over a deep-purple sleeved garment and white shirt with lace-trimmed collar. (In another self-portrait now in Łańcut, Poland, she wears similar clothes and depicts herself painting.) She holds up a large medallion like a shield in front of her body. A descriptive signature in Latin around the medallion's edge reads: SOPHONISBA ANGUSSOLA VIR[GO] IPSIUS MANU EX [S]PECULO DEPICTAM CREMONAE (Sofonisba Anguissola the maiden, painted this with her own hand from a mirror, in Cremona). This inscription surrounds a mysterious emblem, still to be convincingly deciphered, set against a blue background. It contains all the letters of her father's name, Amilcare, but there are additional letters as well. Sofonisba's self-image connects her to antique traditions associated with female artists, including the Roman Marcia, who is described by Giovanni Boccaccio as using a mirror while painting a self-portrait.

The artist included a sly yet witty acknowledgment of her gender. As she holds the oversize medallion in her hands, she masks with her left thumb the last two letters of the word *virgo*, or virgin. This might attest to her chastity but, with the letters blocked, reads as *vir* (man) and encourages the viewer to think of another characteristic not usually ascribed to women: *virtù*, or manly virtue, the root of the word virtuoso, an apt description of this talented artist.

Varnished watercolor on parchment

8.3 x 6.4 cm (3¼ x 2½ in.)

Emma F. Munroe Fund 60.155

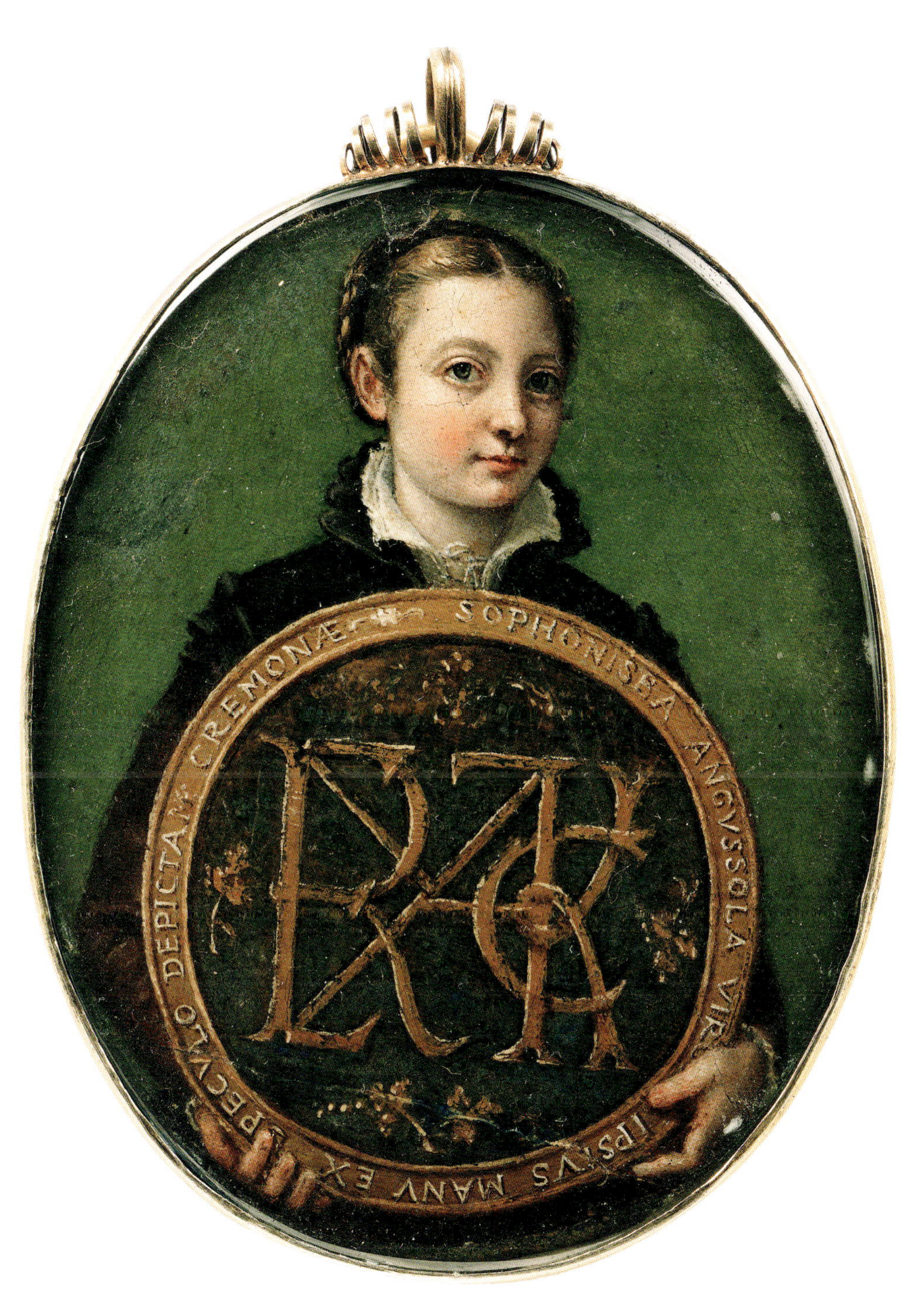
SOPHONISBA ANGVSSOLA VIR IPSIVS MANV EX SPECVLO DEPICTAM CREMONÆ

Titian (Tiziano Vecellio)

Italian (Venetian), about 1488–1576

Portrait of a Man Holding a Book, about 1540

The star artist of sixteenth-century Venice, Titian profoundly influenced painters of his generation as well as those much younger. Exploiting the new expressive possibilities of oil paint on a canvas support, Titian used his deft brushwork to convey, better than any predecessor, myriad details and textures, including cloth, fur, and flesh. He transformed the conventions of all the genres he undertook, from religious and mythological narratives to portraits.

In this portrait, the palpable sense of presence and meticulously rendered costume exemplify why Titian's portraits were prized across Europe. The man's flashy dress—note the pearls on the collar and at the cuffs, and the aglets (gilded tips originally used on the ends of laces to fasten clothing but employed for decorative purposes here)—is not Venetian. Such accessories allow the painting to be dated to around 1540, based on comparisons with portraits of fashionable men on the Venetian mainland, such as Moretto da Brescia's *Count Fortunato Martinengo* of 1540–45 (now in the National Gallery, London), whose subject wears a hat nearly identical to the one here.

The Boston sitter's red hair and beard, carefully executed without being precious, may indicate he is of Northern European origin. Various names have been proposed for the sitter over the years, including most recently Gianfrancesco Gonzaga (1502–1539), a soldier and an aristocrat, but evidence is lacking. Whoever he was, he commands the viewer's attention. His sword emphasizes his nobility; the book, closed with a silver clasp, his erudition or piety. Titian's authorship is manifest in his subject's self-assurance, itself paralleled by the assuredness of the paint handling. This confidence is summed up in one tiny detail: the impasto stroke between the subject's nose and left eye. Such a bold, surprising touch indicates not the hand of a workshop assistant but rather that of the master.

Oil on canvas

97.8 x 77.2 cm (38½ x 30⅜ in.)

Charles Potter Kling Fund 43.83

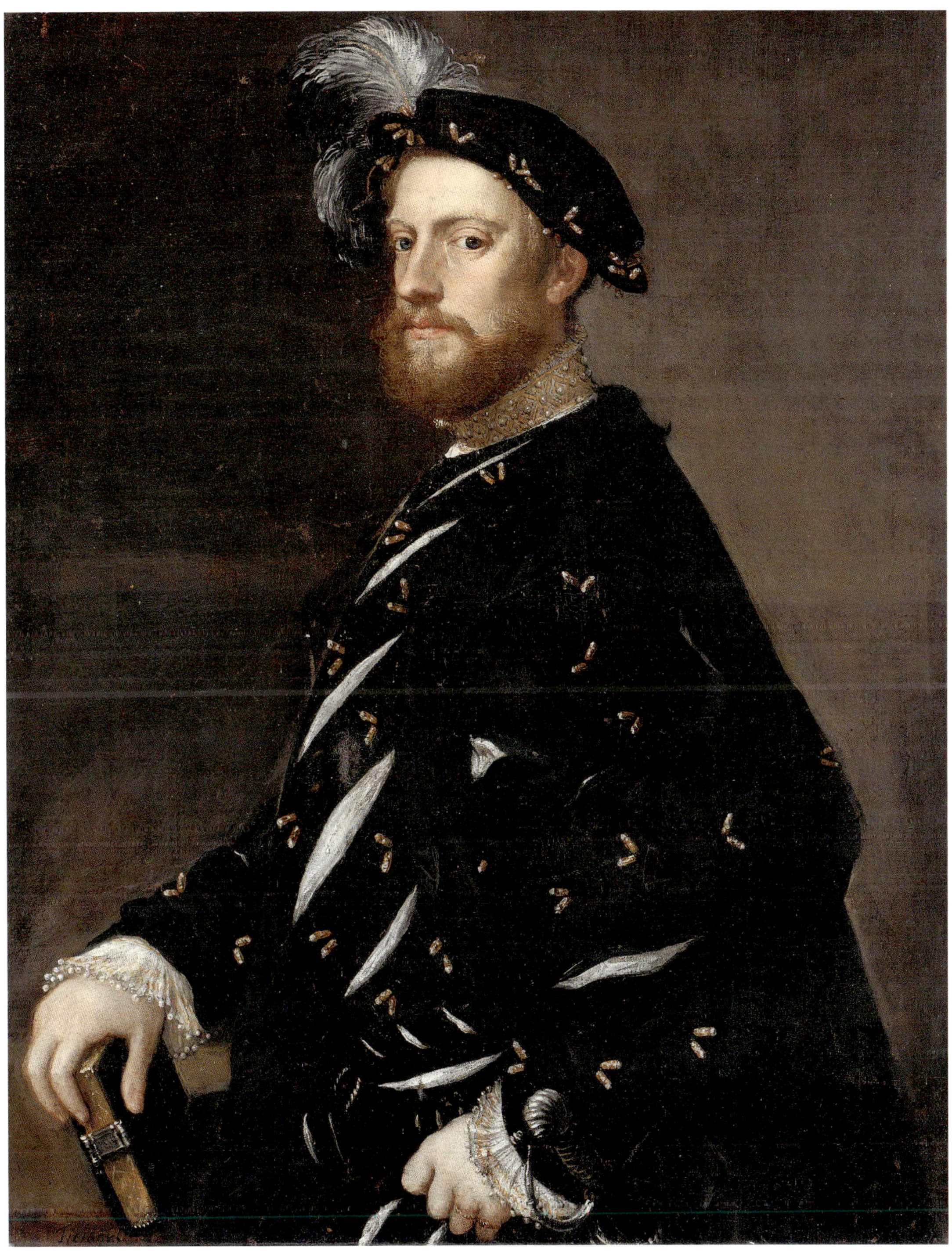

Jacopo Tintoretto (Jacopo Robusti)

Italian (Venetian), about 1518–1594

The Nativity, late 1550s, reworked 1570s

Markedly uneven in quality, this painting has long confounded experts. Some passages, particularly the Virgin Mary at left and Saint Anne at right, are beautifully executed while others, such as Saint Joseph and the Christ Child at center, lack convincing definition. The vignettes in the upper corners have an insubstantial aspect and may have been carried out by another hand entirely. Moreover, this scene does not appear as a Nativity should. Saint Anne is not typically present in this episode, yet here she flings out her arms vehemently, a gesture more of alarm than of joy. The old shepherd at far right stares up and out of the picture, ignoring the infant, who should be the center of attention.

Scientific investigations have offered an explanation. X-radiography, used to penetrate the surface of a painting, reveals that the picture underwent extensive changes in Jacopo Tintoretto's workshop. What is now a horizontal Nativity was initially a vertical Crucifixion set in the heavens. The original painting either stayed with Tintoretto or was returned to him, perhaps because it was damaged or the client was dissatisfied with it. More than a decade later, Tintoretto, ever frugal, repurposed sections as the building blocks for a Nativity. The two female figures, typical of the artist's style in the 1550s, were recycled from the Crucifixion scene. Although superfluous elements of that earlier scene would have been painted over, pigments have altered with time; today the legs of Jesus on the cross are faintly visible just above Joseph's shoulders.

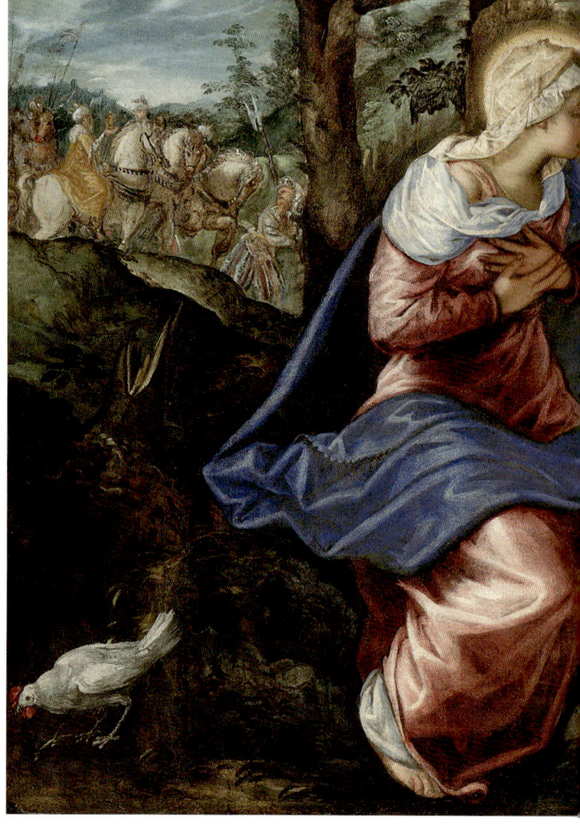

The sketchier background scenes, depicting the Journey of the Magi and the Annunciation to the Shepherds, were added by an assistant after the canvas was enlarged by attaching vertical strips of canvas at the center and at the left and right edges. Tintoretto himself reworked the shepherd's head.

Oil on canvas

155.6 x 358.1 cm (61¼ x 141 in.)

Gift of Quincy A. Shaw, Jr. 46.1430

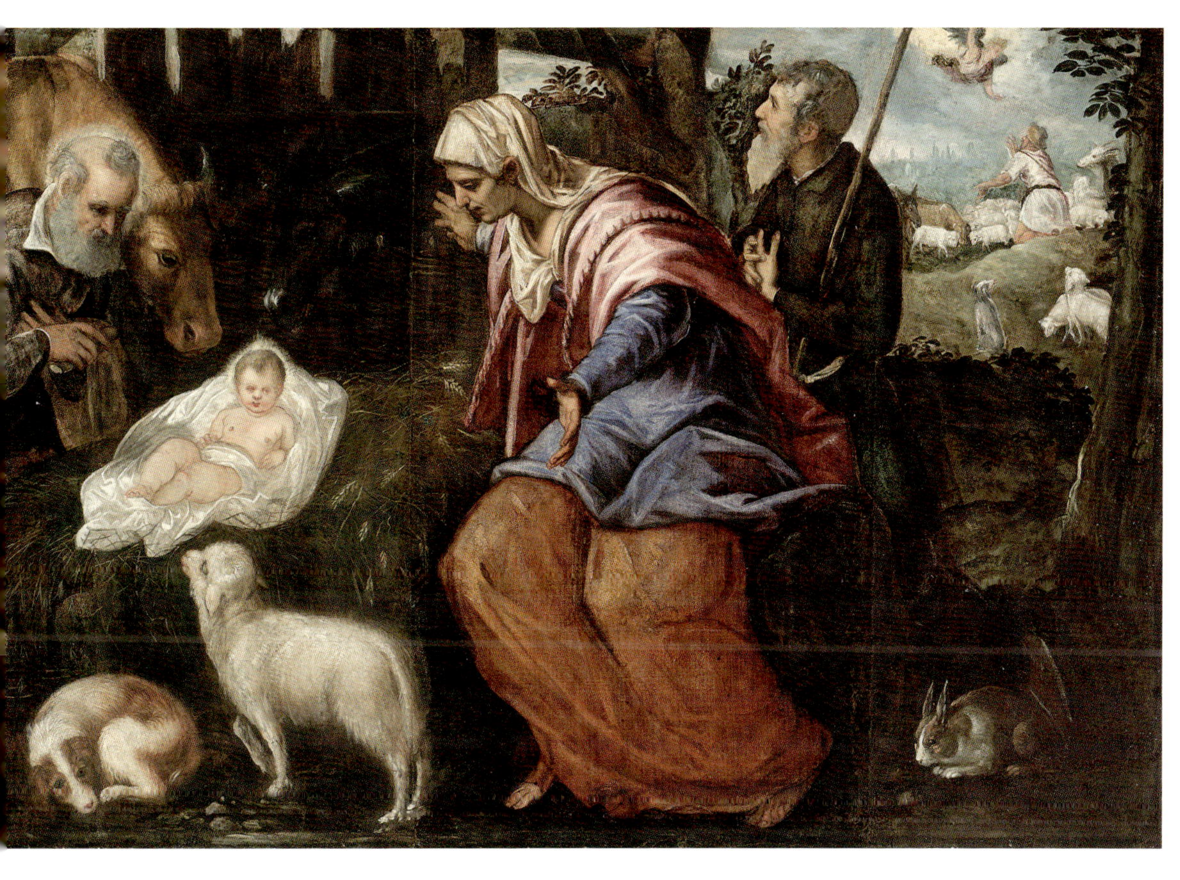

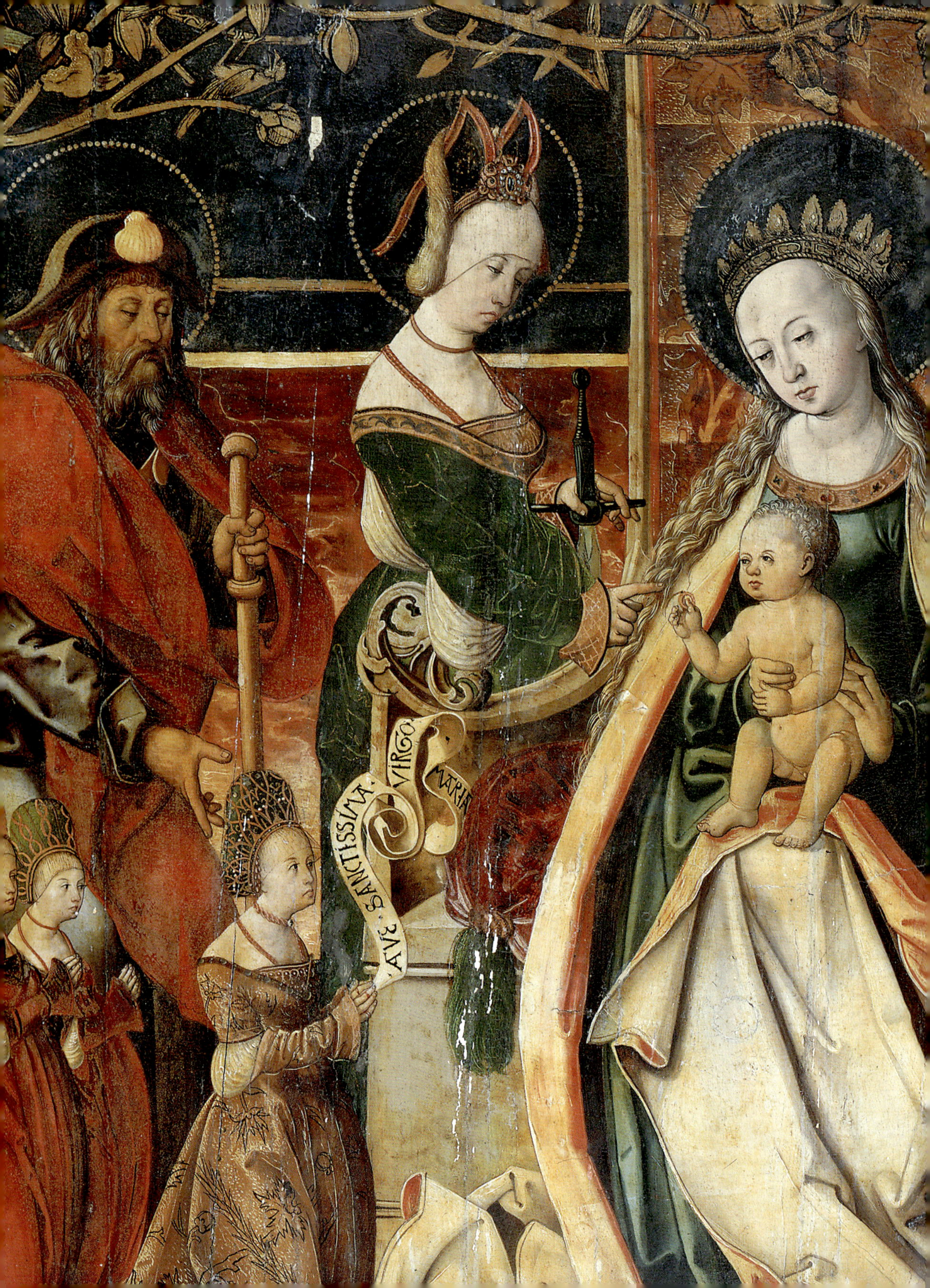
AVE SANCTISSIMA VIRGO MARIA

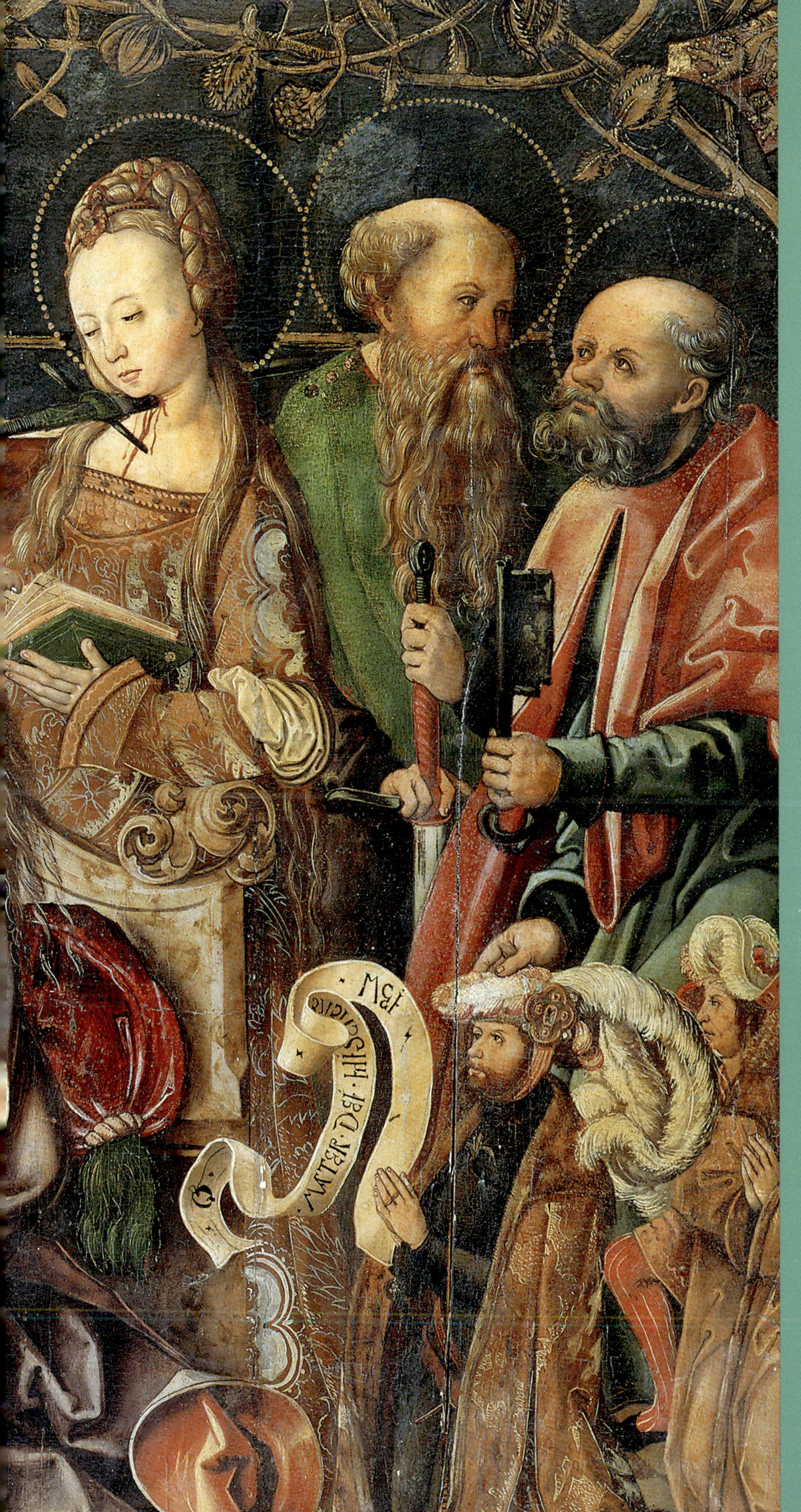

3 THE RENAISSANCE IN NORTHERN EUROPE

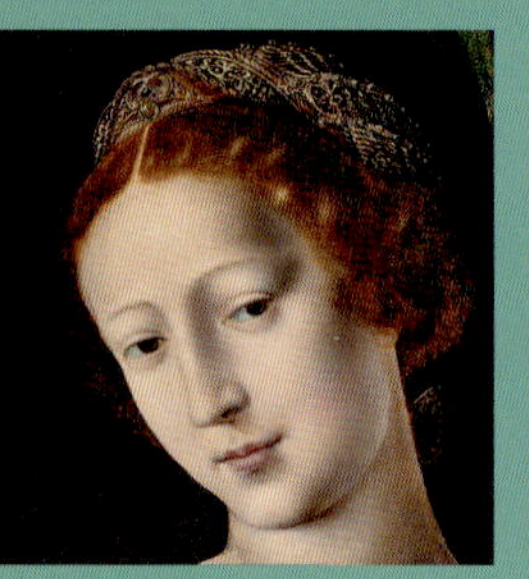
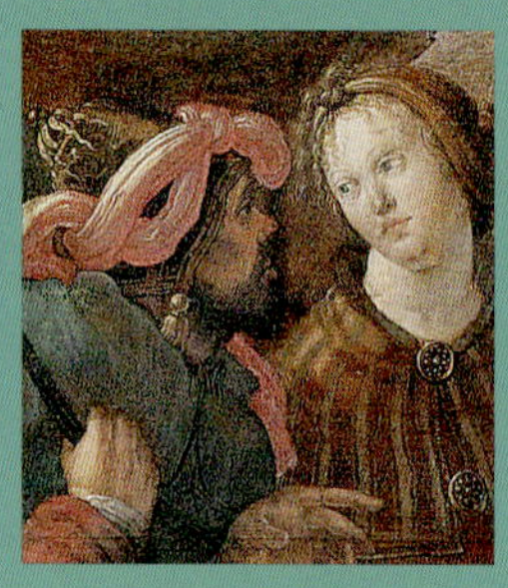
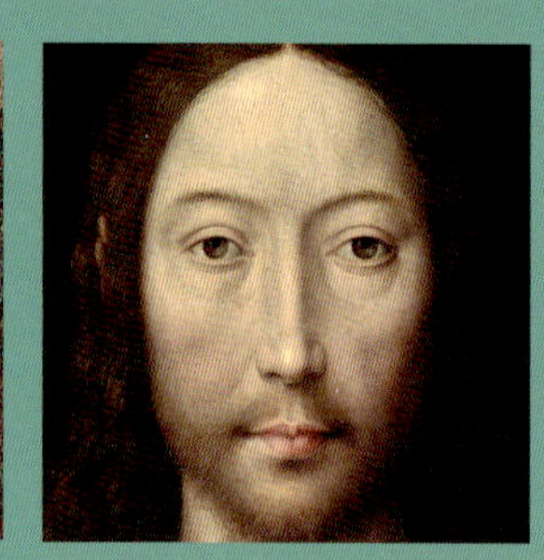
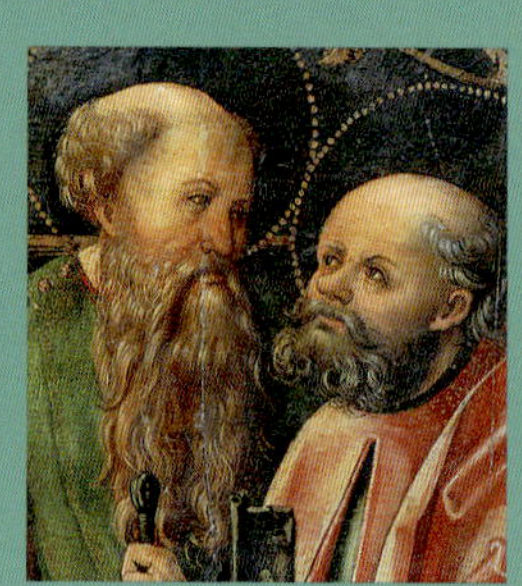
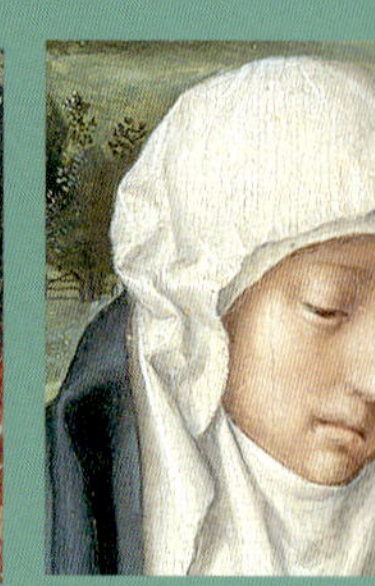

The Renaissance in Northern Europe

The Low Countries, acquired by the dukes of Burgundy through canny marriages, became a source of great wealth and culture in the fifteenth century and boasted some of the most important centers of finance and trade in Europe. Artists enjoyed the patronage of the court and its officials as well as newly rich merchants. The latter commissioned altarpieces for their family chapels and portraits that not only recorded their features for posterity but also showcased their power and wealth.

Early Netherlandish painting was primarily religious in nature. Easel painting emerged as a new medium during this period; its production had much in common with manuscript illumination, which was used in the devotional practice of both religious orders and wealthy individuals. Like manuscripts, much of the painting of this period is small in scale, requiring close looking. Naturalism made biblical stories feel immediate, transporting the viewer into a detailed personal realm that was deeply engaging.

Indeed, one of the most remarkable characteristics of Northern Renaissance art is a striking interest in the natural world. Artists turned their attention to plants and animals, people and objects, materials and textures, and lovingly described them all in paint. Reflection and sheen could be masterfully rendered in the new technique of oil painting. Unlike the tempera used by Italian artists, oil paint takes longer to dry, allowing changes to be made more easily during the painting process. By varying the proportion of pigment to oil, artists could achieve a range of optical effects—from opaque to translucent. Transparent layers of glazes, applied over the vibrant colors painted on an oak panel prepared with a white ground, contributed great depth and luminosity to the painted surface.

Northern artists for the most part did not share the Italian interest in the accurate depiction of antique forms, nor were they concerned with classical ideas of decorum or compositional harmony. The approach of early Netherlandish painters to the visible world was more empirical than scientific. Rather than using one-point perspective for their depictions, they sought to capture the way the eye sees: figures overlap or their scale diminishes as they recede into space; the color and definition of forms vary from foreground to background in landscapes (some of which feature fantastical outcroppings and buildings); and aerial perspective changes from green to a hazy blue as forms become less distinct in the distance.

Some of the naturalistic details in these paintings carried symbolic meaning, like the frequently appearing white lilies that allude to the Virgin Mary's purity. Despite the apparent realism of these flowers, their presence would have signaled something deeper to those who knew how to read the paintings. In addition, figures and narratives from the Old Testament were depicted not only for their educative value—as a way for a largely illiterate population to know their Bible stories—but also typologically, as prefigurations of New Testament subjects. The Virgin Mary was the new Eve; the Sacrifice of Isaac referred to the Crucifixion of Christ.

In Germany, then part of the Holy Roman Empire, trade flourished under the auspices of the Hanseatic League, an association of cities and trading outposts. German merchants and their bankers became wealthy, and commissioned portraits of themselves and fine furnishings for their homes. Wood carvers fashioned poignant devotional sculptures of all sizes as well as major polychrome altarpieces, sometimes with ensembles of panel paintings as wings.

Northern Europe was transformed both politically and religiously in the sixteenth century. The Reformation, the Protestants' break with Catholic Rome, began in Germany and spread throughout Northern Europe. Through marriage, the House of Burgundy united with the Hapsburgian Holy Roman Empire, which came to control not only Germany and the Netherlands but also Spain. Under the reign of the Spanish King Philip II, the Netherlands revolted, in part motivated by religious conflict. The successful Spanish siege of Antwerp in 1585 was a defining moment in the separation of the Netherlands into north (independent and Protestant) and south (Spanish and Catholic).

Artists in the southern Netherlands now created images that encouraged meditation, spiritual alliance, and empathy on the part of the viewer. Instead of the seamless integration of the real and symbolic, the sacred and secular realms began to compete for attention. Decorative elements, including lavish costumes, dramatic gestures, unlikely anatomy, and acid colors engaged the eye.

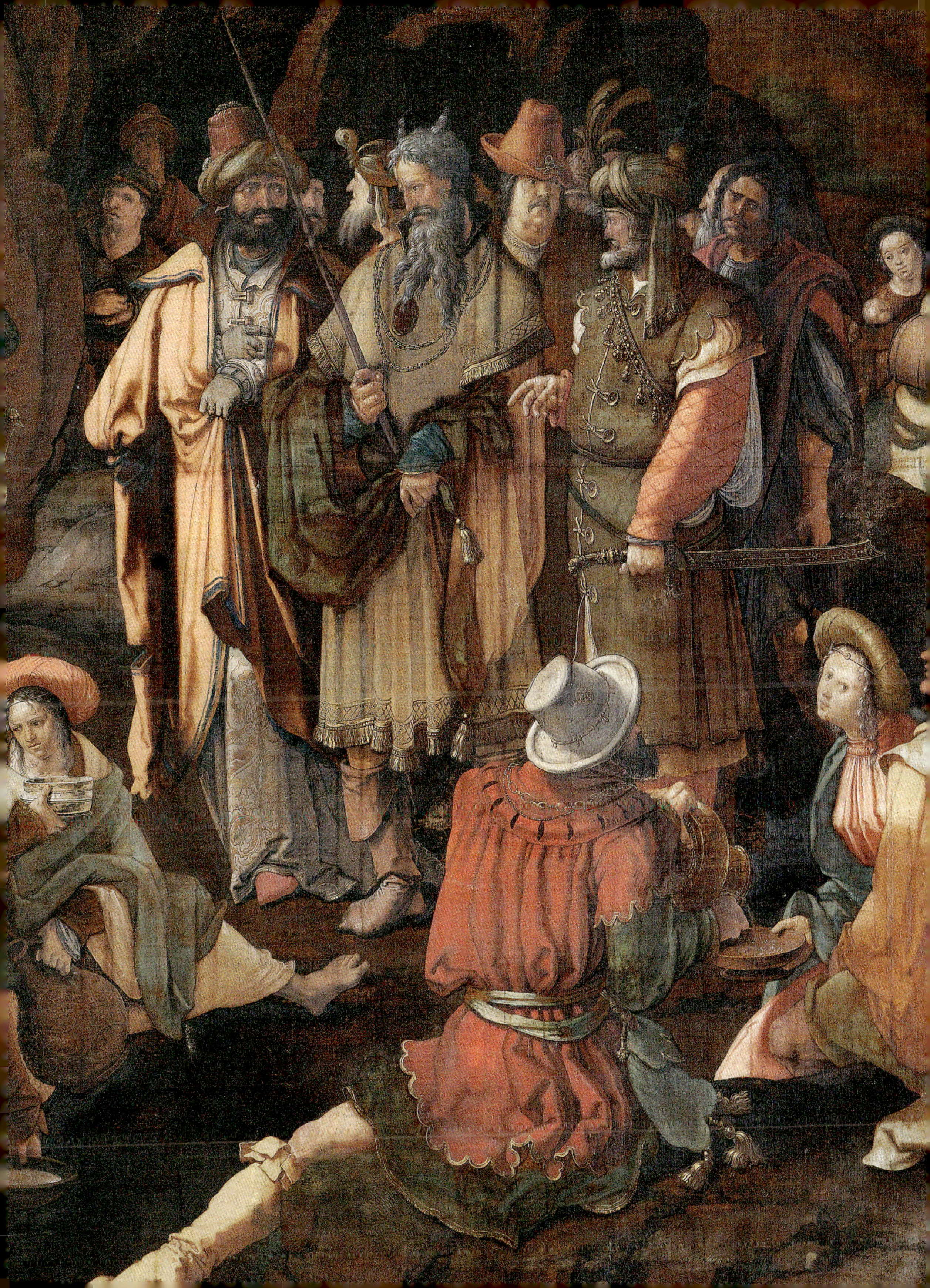

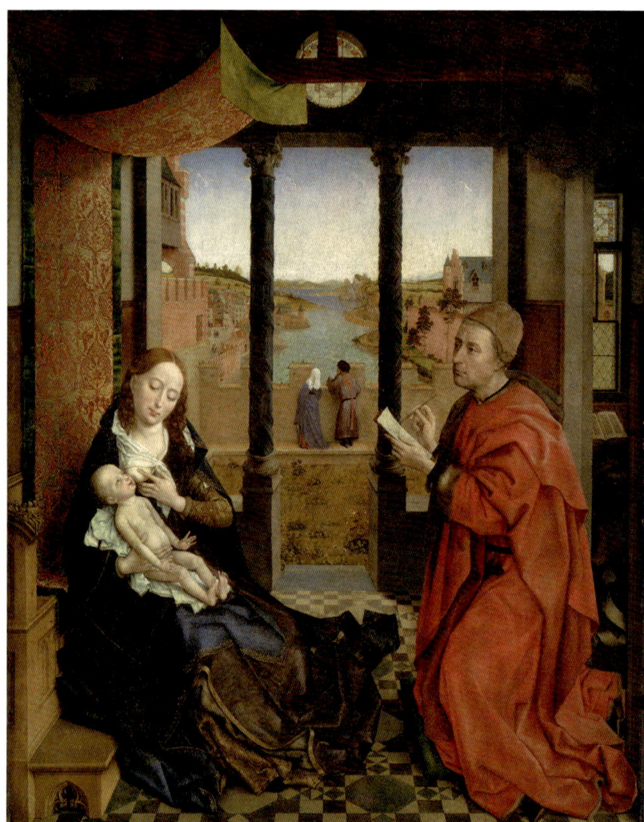

Rogier van der Weyden
Netherlandish, about 1400–1464
Saint Luke Drawing the Virgin, about 1435–40

Rogier van der Weyden likely painted this work at the time of his appointment as official city painter of Brussels. It probably hung in the artists' guild chapel in the Church of Saint Gudule. The panel displays the angular drapery folds, sense of patterning, and crisp delineation typical of Rogier's style. Today, at least three full-size copies of this composition are known, now in Munich, Bruges, and Saint Petersburg. Numerous motifs depicted here, such as the Virgin nursing the infant Christ, appear in many smaller devotional paintings of the fifteenth and sixteenth centuries.

The subject is among the earliest portrayals of an artist at work. According to tradition, Saint Luke, the patron saint of artists, was a contemporary of Mary. Rather than showing him crafting an image that appeared to him in a vision, as in earlier conceptions of the scene, Rogier depicts the saint engaging with Mary directly, portraying her in silverpoint, an exacting medium used in preparatory drawings. Rogier takes great pains to describe minutely a contemporary Flemish town in the distance. Most remarkably, the specificity of Luke's features suggests that he is a portrait of the artist.

The composition is based on one by Jan van Eyck, an earlier pioneer of Netherlandish painting, but omits the angels and halos often found in that artist's work. Despite the apparent naturalism of the image, the panel is replete with traditional symbolic elements, some more apparent than others. The Virgin Mary is placed under and in front of a brocaded cloth of honor, alluding to her future role as Queen of Heaven. In addition, a *hortus conclusus*, or enclosed garden, representing her purity and including flowers with Marian associations, appears just beyond the columns. Saint Luke's attribute, an ox, kneels discreetly on the floor of his study at right. Adam and Eve, the Old Testament corollaries to Mary and Christ, are carved into the armrest of Mary's throne.

Oil and tempera on panel
137.5 x 110.8 cm (54 1/8 x 43 5/8 in.)
Gift of Mr. and Mrs. Henry Lee Higginson 93.153

Tilman Riemenschneider
German, 1460–1531
Virgin and Child, about 1490–95

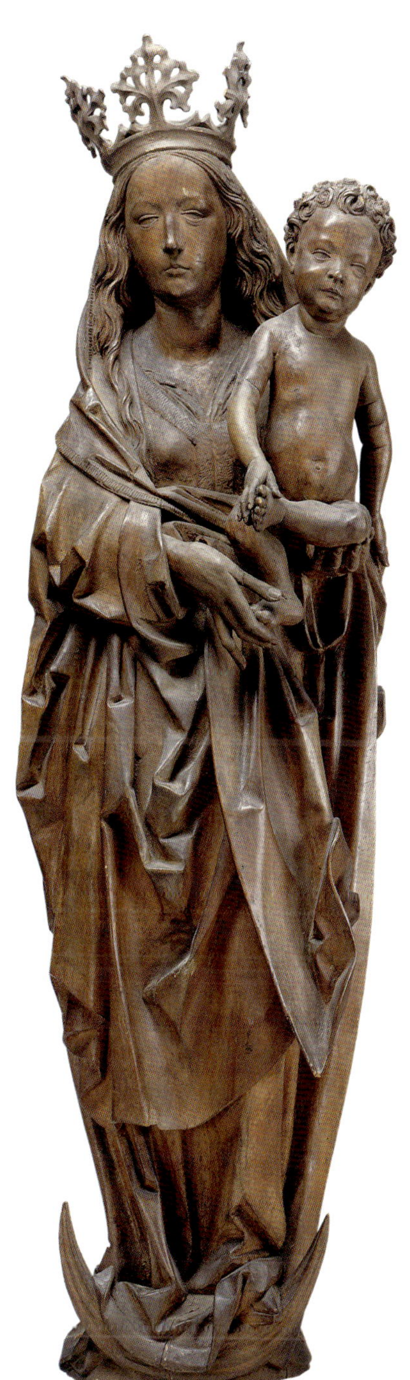

Among the notable sculptors active in the fifteenth century in the region that is today Germany, Tilman Riemenschneider was particularly influential in the Upper Rhineland area. He worked in both wood and stone to create ecclesiastical decoration as well as objects for private devotion. His fellow sculptor Nikolaus Gerhaert von Leyden, who trained in Leiden, may have in turn served as an important influence on Riemenschneider. In this work, the tender manner in which the Christ Child plays with his foot may be a nod to this Northern influence. The sculpture's scale suggests it was originally intended for a religious setting, perhaps over an altar in a church.

While much German wood sculpture was polychromed and gilded, it is not known if this sculpture was painted. Riemenschneider is known for working in both painted and unpainted wood. As it exists today, without color, this sculpture's fine handiwork can be especially appreciated. Carved from a single piece of lime or linden wood, it is hollowed out in the back. Both the Virgin and the toddler-age Christ Child face the viewer, yet their open poses and the dynamic quality of the drapery lead the eye around the sides of the sculpture. The lozenge shape is emphasized by its culmination in the Virgin's crown and by the narrowing of the garment at her feet. Mary's crown and her stance on a crescent moon identify her as the Virgin of the Apocalypse, a reference to the book of Revelation in which she is described as "a woman clothed with the sun, and the moon under her feet, and upon her head a crown of twelve stars."

Limewood
120.7 x 38.1 x 20.2 cm (47 ½ x 15 x 8 in.)
Gift in memory of Felix M. Warburg by his wife Frieda Schiff Warburg 41.653

Hans Memling

German (worked in Flanders), about 1430–40 to 1494

Christ Blessing, 1481

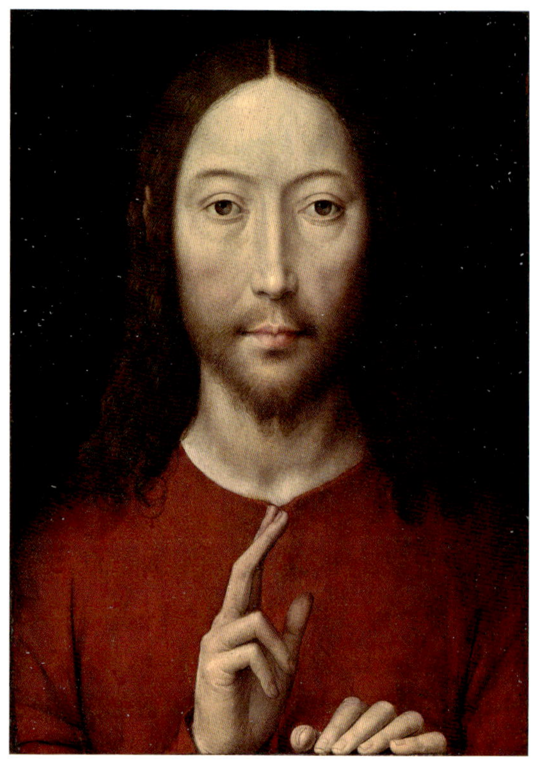

Christ Blessing retains its original engaged frame bearing the date of the painting at the top. Part of the panel on which the artist painted, intact frames such as this are rare. Hans Memling used the frame to help create the illusion of three-dimensional space. Jesus's hands appear to press against the lower edge, almost extending into the viewer's space.

When Memling painted this panel, he had already established himself as a highly sought-after portraitist. His naturalistic depiction of Jesus, with hazelnut, shoulder-length hair parted down the middle and a beard forked slightly at the chin, is based on a purportedly first-person account of Christ's appearance recorded in an apocryphal medieval document known as the Letter of Lentulus. This text was published twice in the late fifteenth century, so both Memling and his patrons were likely familiar with the description.

The iconographic motif of Christ Blessing is found in earlier Byzantine and Christian art. Unencumbered by symbolic attributes, Memling's image updates earlier Netherlandish depictions by endowing Jesus with an extraordinary sense of immediacy. Filling most of the picture plane, he levels his calm gaze at the viewer, providing a mesmerizing simulation of a direct personal encounter with the son of God.

Oil on panel

35.1 x 25.1 cm (13⅞ x 9⅞ in.)

Bequest of William A. Coolidge 1993.40

Saint Sebastian
German (Upper Rhine), about 1470

This painted wood sculpture represents the early Christian saint, Sebastian. Sebastian was condemned to death by the Roman emperor Diocletian, who ordered him to be taken out into the country and killed by archers. Here, Sebastian is bound to a tree trunk, his right wrist tied with a strap to a high branch and his left arm caught on a lower one. His slender torso is stretched out and his feet rest on the ground, one crossed in front of the other but barely seeming to support his weight. Long curls frame his face, and his eyes have a slightly unfocused quality that lends sadness to his expression. Holes in Sebastian's flesh originally would have held arrows, probably made of metal. The sculptor presents the figure in the midst of the assault, so that those viewing it—probably as part of an altarpiece in a church—would empathize with the saint's distress. The painted wood would have seemed akin to real flesh, heightening the sense of suffering.

However, devotees would know that though Sebastian was left for dead by his executioners, he survived the attack (only to be later clubbed to death by Diocletian's soldiers). Sebastian came to be viewed as a saint who endured pain and persecution, offering hope to those suffering physical and mental afflictions and anxieties. He was one of the most venerated saints because he was considered a protector against illness. In the mid-fourteenth century, the Black Death raged through Europe, and in the centuries that followed, numerous smaller outbreaks of bubonic plague created fear and killed many. Not surprisingly, Sebastian was one of the most frequently represented saints in works of art.

Wood with paint and gilding
99.69 x 41.9 x 29.8 cm (39¼ x 16½ x 11¾ in.)
Bequest of Dr. Siegfried J. Thannhauser in memory of his wife Franziska Peiner Thannhauser 63.589

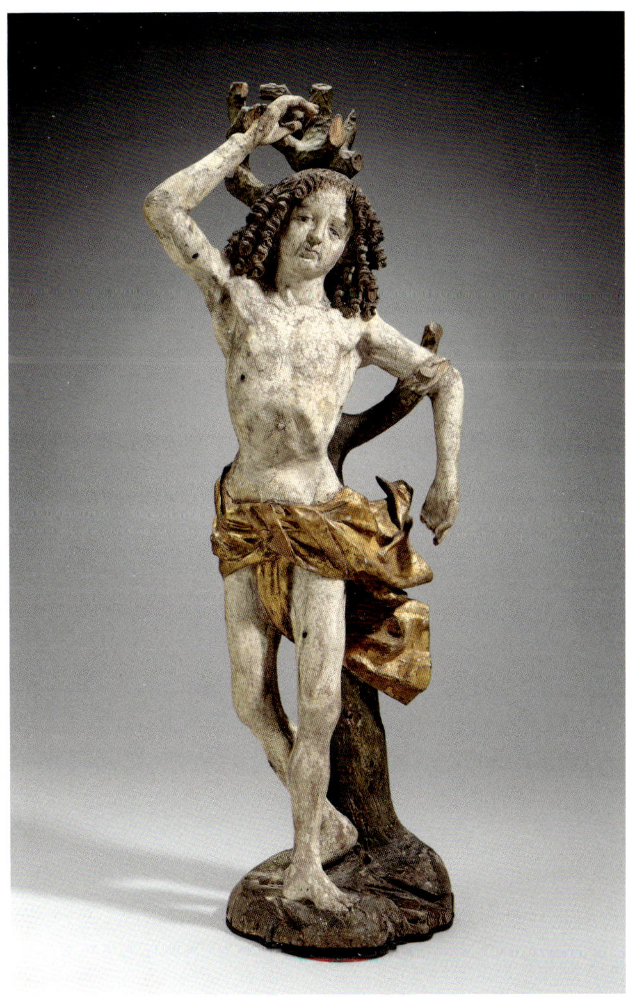

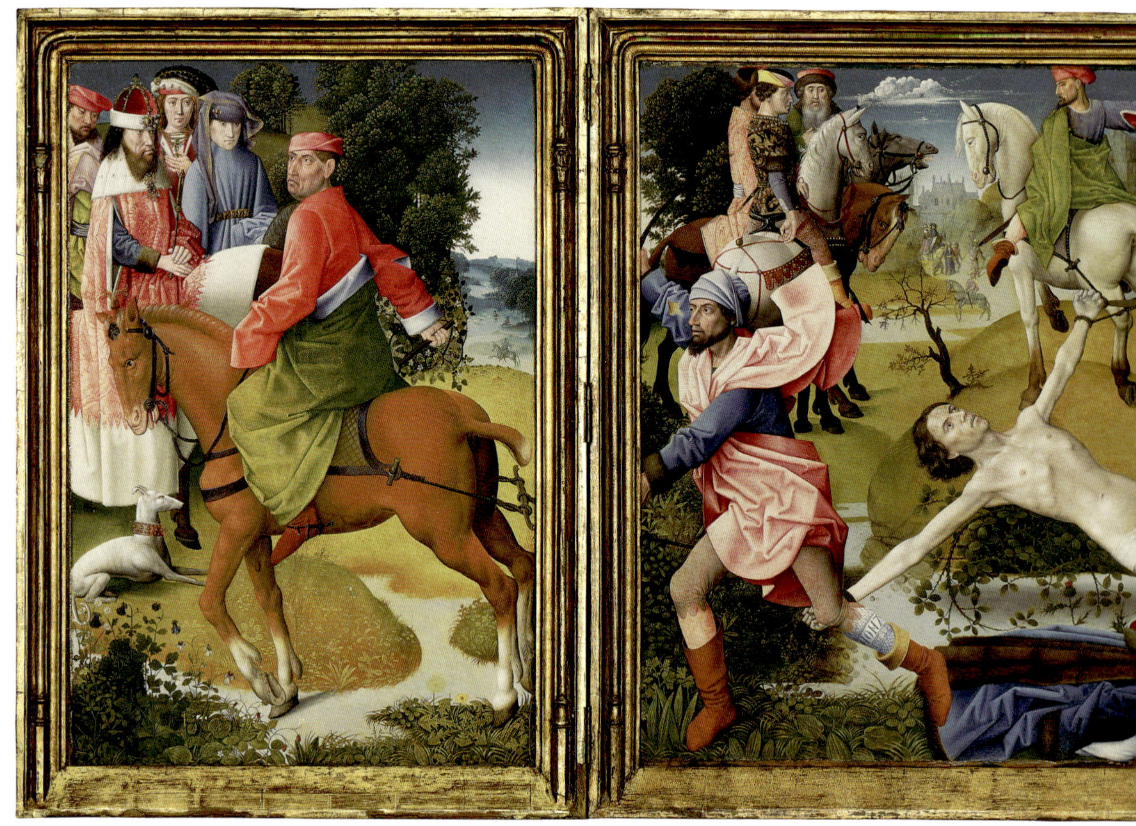

Martyrdom of Saint Hippolytus
Netherlandish, 1490s

During his lifetime, Hippolyte de Berthoz, a prominent financial adviser at the Burgundian court, commissioned two altarpieces depicting the martyrdom of his patron saint. Both altarpieces are triptychs consisting of two wings, painted on both front and reverse, that close over a central panel. On each triptych, the outside wings are grisaille paintings made to look like statues of Saints Hippolytus and Elizabeth, the name saint of Hippolyte's wife, Elisabeth Hugheins. The coats of arms of the Berthoz and Hugheins families accompany the saints. The first altarpiece, in Sint-Salvatorskathedraal in Bruges, was painted by Dirk Bouts and Hugo van der Goes in the 1470s; this second altarpiece, by an anonymous Brussels master, was likely painted in the 1490s.

Saint Hippolytus was a Roman soldier who converted to Christianity after witnessing the martyrdom of Saint Lawrence. When he refused to renounce his new faith, he was condemned to be drawn and quartered. In the earlier altarpiece, a continuous landscape extends across the three panels, with Hippolytus's martyrdom depicted in the central panel, donors on the left wing, and onlookers on the right. In this second triptych, the artist stretched the action across all three panels. Hippolytus's body—his arms

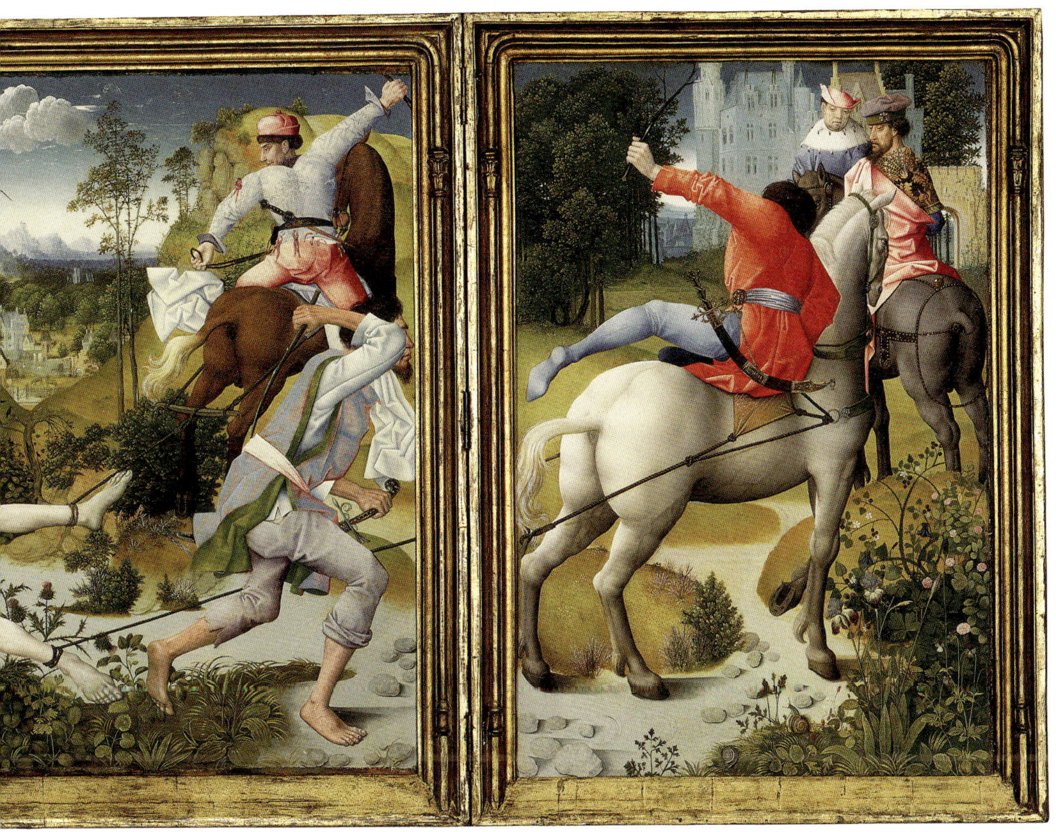

spread wide in a horizontal variant of the Crucifixion—and the frenzied horse-beaters fill the central panel. Each wing features a powerful steed and rider intent on the saint's dismemberment. This unique compositional arrangement, dependent on but wholly different from the earlier altarpiece, emphasizes the brutality of Hippolytus's martyrdom.

Tempera and oil on panel
87.6 x 253.1 cm (34½ x 99⅝ in.)
Walter M. Cabot Fund 63.660

Workshop of Jacquemart de Hesdin

Netherlandish, (worked in France) active 1384, died after 1413

Annunciation to the Shepherds (Opening of Terce, Hours of the Virgin), about 1400

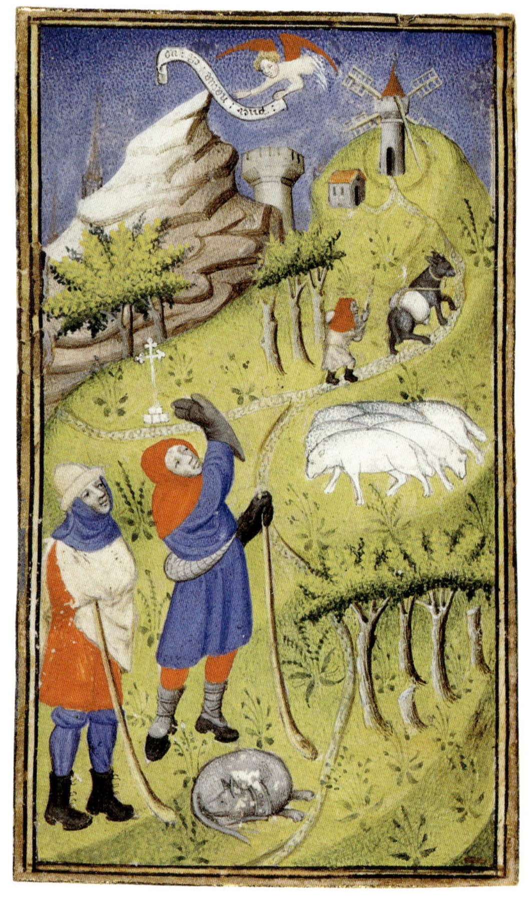

Tempera and gold on parchment

10.2 x 5.8 cm (4 x 2¼ in.)

Helen and Alice Colburn Fund 43.212

This miniature, cut from its manuscript long before it entered the MFA's collection, originally belonged to a book of hours, a luxury prayer book written in French and Latin, consisting of texts, psalms, and litanies to be recited at the canonical hours of the day. The Hours of the Virgin, from which this leaf came, was a prominent section of such books because of Mary's role as intercessor between man and God.

Illustrations for the Hours of the Virgin, meant to inspire delight, reflection, and meditation, included events in Mary's life surrounding the birth and infancy of Jesus. These scenes also helped the reader locate particular prayers in the text. Depictions of an angel announcing Jesus's birth to the shepherds traditionally introduced the fourth set of prayers and psalms, known as Terce, which was recited at nine o'clock in the morning.

The illuminations in these manuscripts were carried out collaboratively in workshops under the direction of a master artist. This painting features solid, stocky figures placed into a convincing spatial environment, elements that diverge stylistically from the willowy figures and decorative linearity of the earlier International style. The artist also included whimsical anecdotal details such as a windmill, a castle tower, rows of trees, and a sleeping dog. The style of this miniature is associated with the Parisian workshop of Jacquemart de Hesdin, a prominent painter active at the French court in the late fourteenth and early fifteenth centuries.

Joos van Cleve
Netherlandish, about 1485–1540/41
The Crucifixion, about 1525

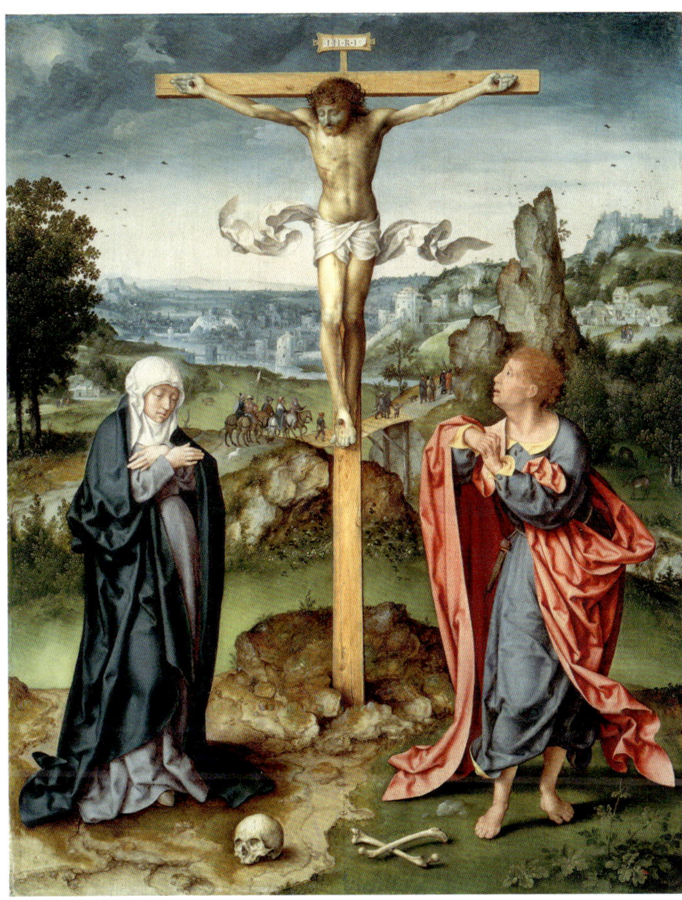

Based in the mercantile city of Antwerp, Joos van Cleve received commissions from patrons throughout Europe, painting portraits as well as a wide range of religious subjects in both large- and small-scale formats. Many of his compositions are known in more than one version, indicating an active workshop and eager clients. Because the bustling port city of Antwerp was home to the richest, most vibrant art market in Northern Europe, Joos was exposed to both established and new stylistic currents. This depiction of the Crucifixion, one of the most important and enduring subjects in Christian art, epitomizes his eclecticism, combining stylized, decorative elements indicative of emerging trends with naturalistic details typical of earlier Netherlandish painting.

The cross is placed in the exact center of the composition. The greenish color of Jesus's face, fingers, and toes heightens the impression of his lifelessness, while the fluttering, symmetrical ends of his loincloth lend a curious animation to the scene. At right, the intense emotion on Saint John's face is reflected in his agitated demeanor and rumpled cloak, which contrasts with the restrained grief of the Virgin, who is turned in on herself, enveloped by her voluminous robes. The artist suggests a depth of perspective using bands of color: brown for the foreground, green for the middle ground, and blue for the background. Joos was among the first painters to make use of the panoramic vistas and strange rock formations of the landscapes devised by his older contemporary, Joachim Patinir.

Oil on panel
80.4 x 63.2 cm (31⅝ x 24⅞ in.)
The Picture Fund 12.170

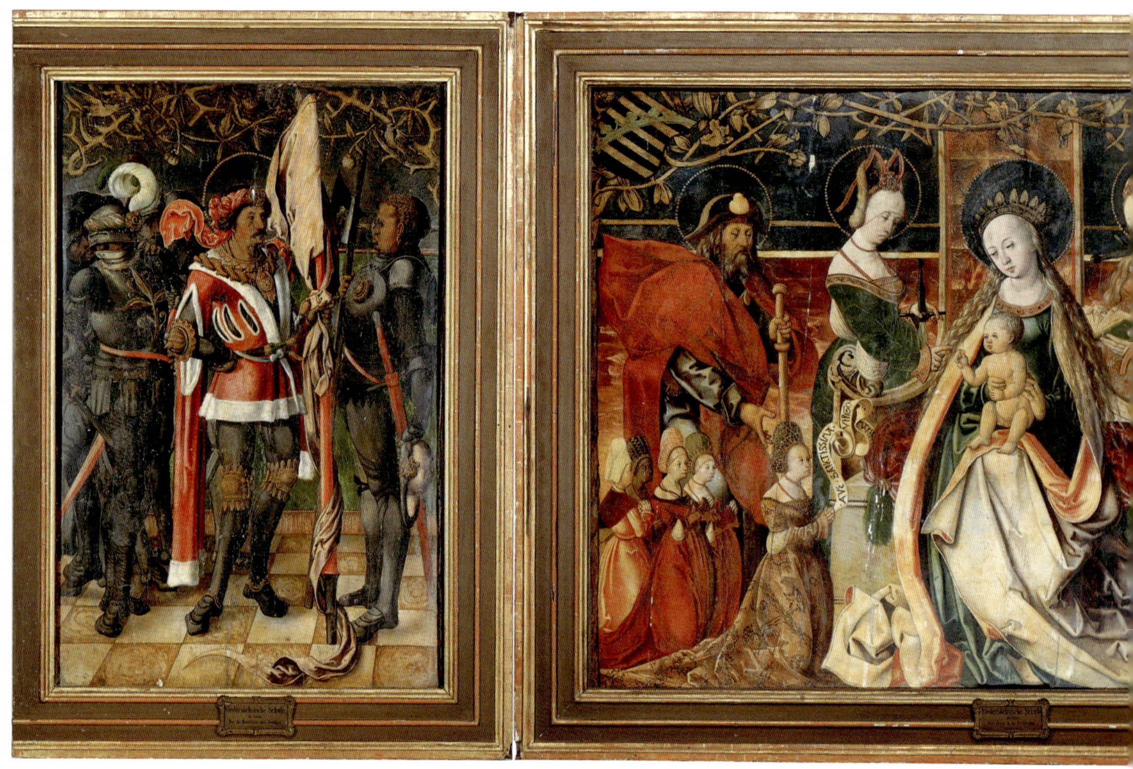

Master of the Goslar Sibyls
German
The Calenberg Altarpiece, first quarter of the 16th century

Intact examples of early German altarpieces are rare, as the central panel and wings were often separated and sold off individually. In the case of the Calenberg altarpiece, one of the wings was in fact split lengthwise, separating the front from the back. Considering this history, the panel's present, reassembled condition is quite remarkable.

Dating to the early sixteenth century, the Calenberg altarpiece was created for a castle chapel in Lower Saxony in northwestern Germany. The central panel features an assembly of saints and donors arranged symmetrically on either side of the Virgin Mary and the infant Jesus, who are seated on a throne. Jesus offers a ring to Saint Catherine, his spiritual bride.

The altarpiece's patrons were Erich I, Duke of Braunschweig-Calenberg (1470–1540) and his first wife, Katharina of Saxony (1468–1524). As was customary, they are depicted as small figures kneeling at either side of the base of Mary's throne, with Katharina in front of her patron saint. The banderoles issuing from their hands offer prayers to the Virgin. Their coats of arms are incorporated into the tracery along the tops of the panels, Saxony on the left and Calenberg on the right. As the couple were childless, the figures accompanying them may be attendants. The inclusion of an African woman in Katharina's entourage is particularly unusual for the period and has yet to be explained.

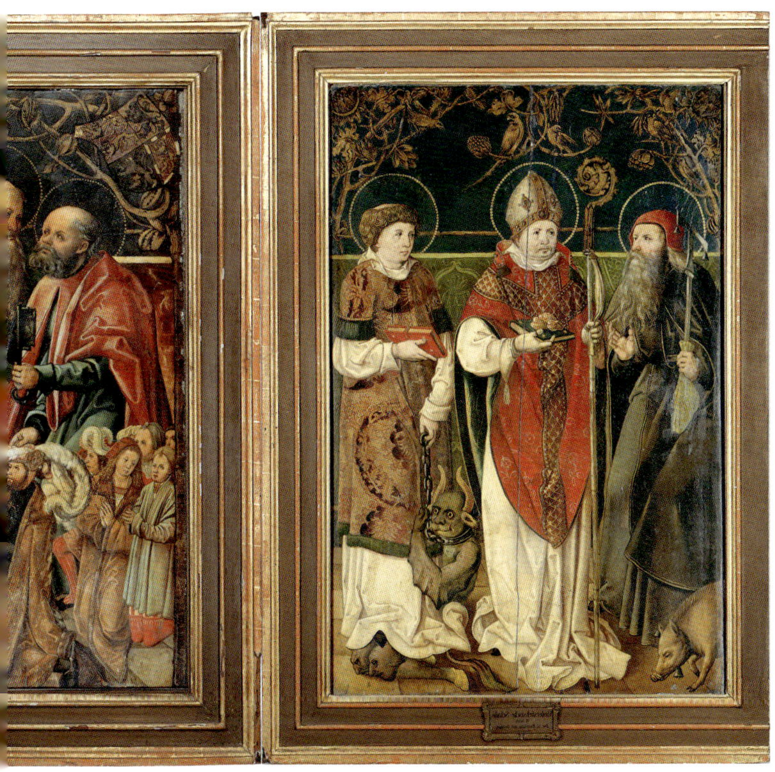

In areas where the paint has become transparent, extensive underdrawing—outlines, hatching, and cross-hatching—is visible to the naked eye. This, as well as qualitative differences in paint handling, indicates that more than one artist executed the work, a practice not unusual at the time. The unknown master who was head of the studio that produced this altarpiece is named for the elaborate decorations in the council chambers in the town hall of Goslar, located fifty miles southeast of Calenberg Castle. The Goslar wall panels feature an alternating motif of emperors and sibyls in the same distinctive style as that of the MFA's triptych.

Oil on panel
Central panel: 99 x 144.5 cm (39 x 56⅞ in.)
Museum purchase with funds donated anonymously and Charles H. Bayley Picture and Painting Fund 2005.195.1-4

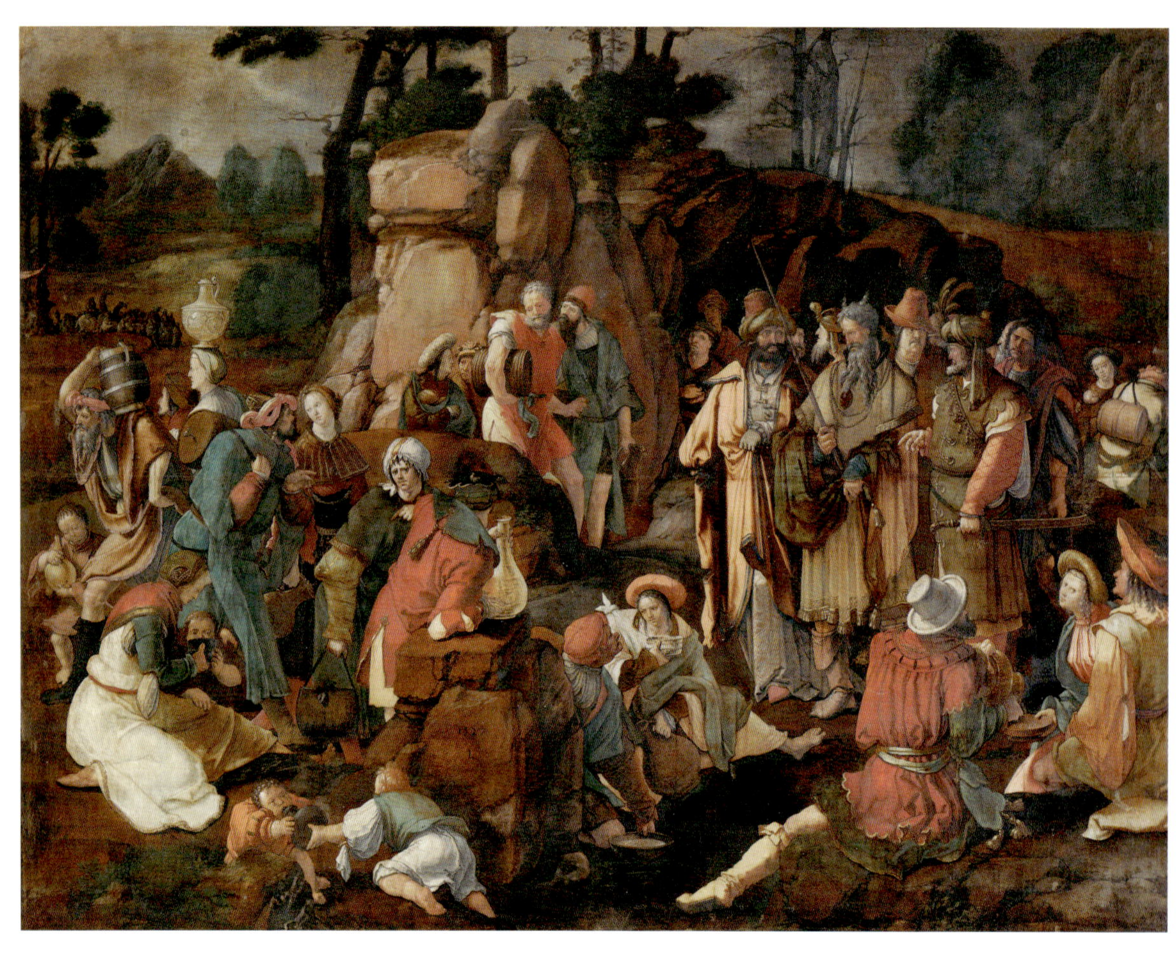

Lucas van Leyden
Netherlandish, about 1494–1533
***Moses and the Israelites after the Miracle of Water from the Rock*, 1527**

Glue tempera on linen
181.9 x 237.5 cm (71⅝ x 93½ in.)
William K. Richardson Fund 54.1432

Moses and the Israelites is the only work on canvas by Lucas van Leyden still extant. In the sixteenth century, most Northern artists worked on panel. According to contemporary sources, Lucas painted other large works on linen, but unfortunately the water-soluble tempera and delicate fabric did not fare well in the damp climate of Northern Europe. During the seventeenth century, this painting was among the masterpieces at the Villa Borghese in Rome, where the warmer, drier climate may have helped prevent the work from deteriorating.

Lucas was a master storyteller. Here, he portrays a miracle from the Old Testament. According to the Bible, the Israelites ran out of drinking water while crossing the desert to escape enslavement in Egypt. After turning to God for guidance, their leader, Moses, struck a rock with his rod and water began to spill out. Lucas depicts the moment after the miracle, as the jubilant if confused Israelites fill their vessels and begin to drink. Just right of center, Moses, identifiable by his horns, his brother, Aaron, and two elders are depicted with elongated bodies swathed in richly decorated garments, while the Israelites around them are shown in a variety of stylized poses. The painting's colors have darkened over time and originally were more vibrant, with their acid tones in bold juxtaposition.

Lucas van Leyden was a celebrated artist in his own day, and through the circulation of his distinctive engravings and woodcuts, his name became known throughout Europe. Roughly fifteen of his paintings survive, with this canvas and a panel in Munich being the only ones signed and dated by the artist.

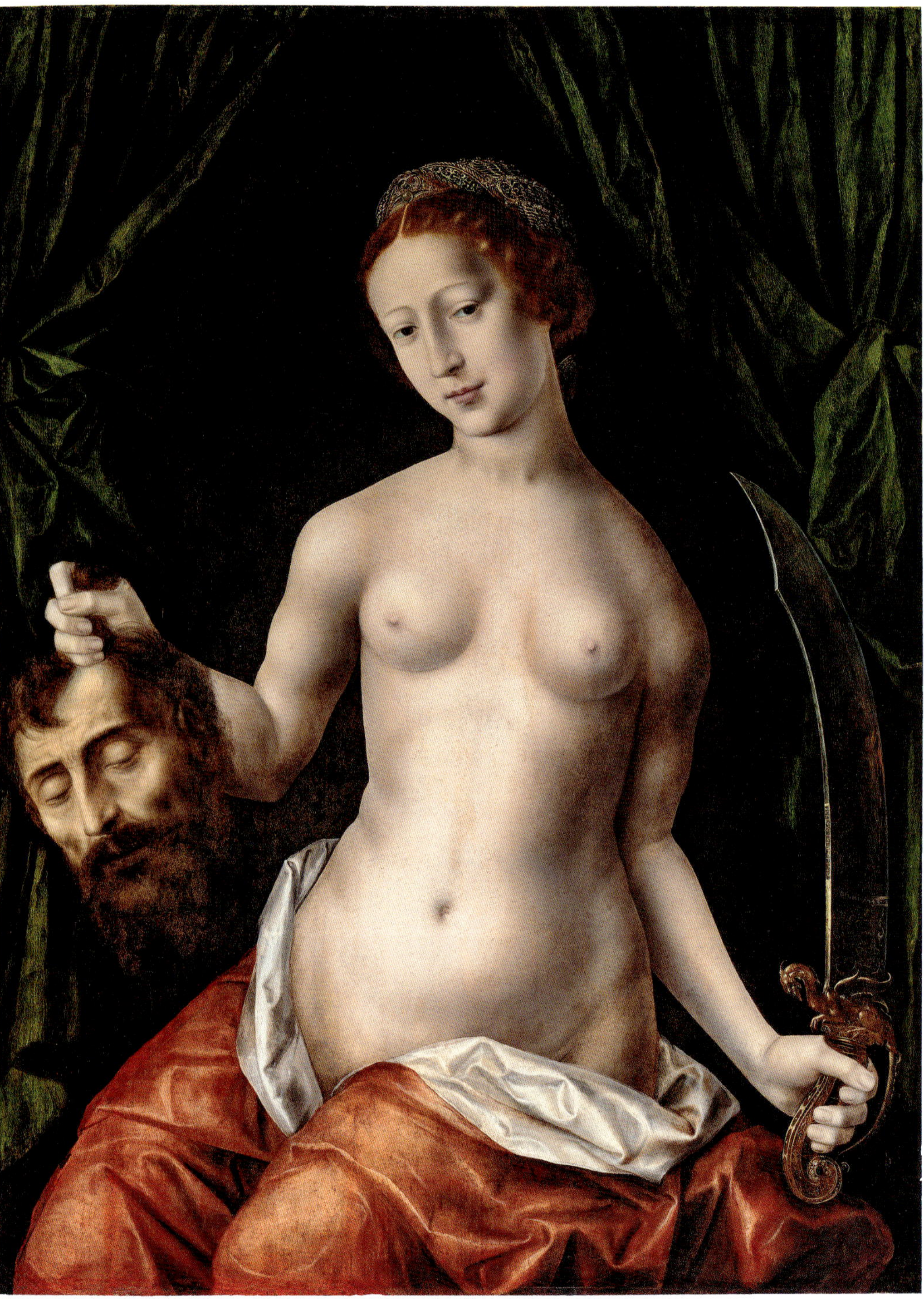

Jan Massys
Netherlandish, 1509–1575
Judith with the Head of Holofernes, 1543

This is the earliest signed and dated work by Jan Massys, son and pupil of the celebrated Netherlandish artist Quentin Massys. Jan's interpretation of Judith reveals his father's influence in the soft shading of her face, her static pose, and the refined elegance of her figure. Jan has cleverly integrated his name and the date of the painting into the ornamentation on Judith's sword such that they appear etched into the metal.

Best known for his female nudes, Jan Massys often took his subjects from the Old Testament. As recounted in the deuterocanonical book of Judith, the widow Judith saved her fellow Israelites from the forces of the Assyrian king Nebuchadnezzar by cunningly ingratiating herself with the king's general, Holofernes, who desired her. Judith waited for Holofernes to fall into a drunken sleep, then beheaded him.

In the Middle Ages, Judith was regarded as a model of humility and chastity. Beginning in the early sixteenth century, however, Northern artists began to play up the element of her nakedness. Here, her erotically charged body is on display. Unperturbed, she focuses her knowing gaze directly on the viewer, proudly presenting the severed head. Her pale, marble-like skin is accentuated by the dark green bed-curtains in the background and the scarlet satin drape in her lap. She, along with other Old Testament heroines, provided the perfect excuse for a male artist to depict a female nude.

Until relatively recently, this painting was largely obscured beneath a thick, yellowed varnish. Cleaning revealed a beautifully intact face and sword but much abrasion on Judith's body. It appears that at some point, clothing had been painted over Judith's body—a more substantial garment than the diaphanous dresses Massys painted on his other heroines—and was subsequently, and rather forcefully, removed, causing the damage.

Oil on panel
102.2 x 75.6 cm (40¼ x 29¾ in.)
Abbott Lawrence Fund and Picture Fund 12.1048

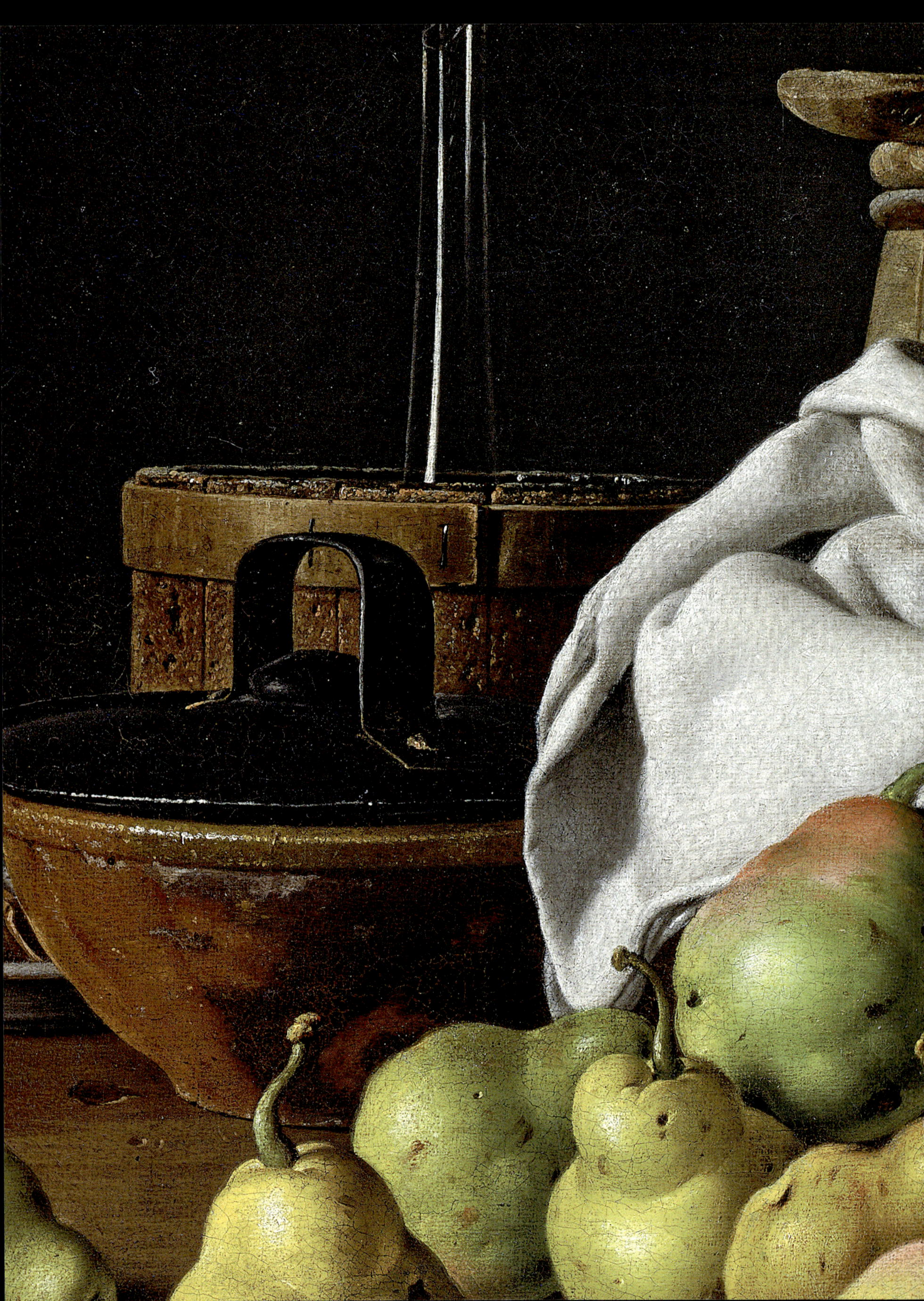

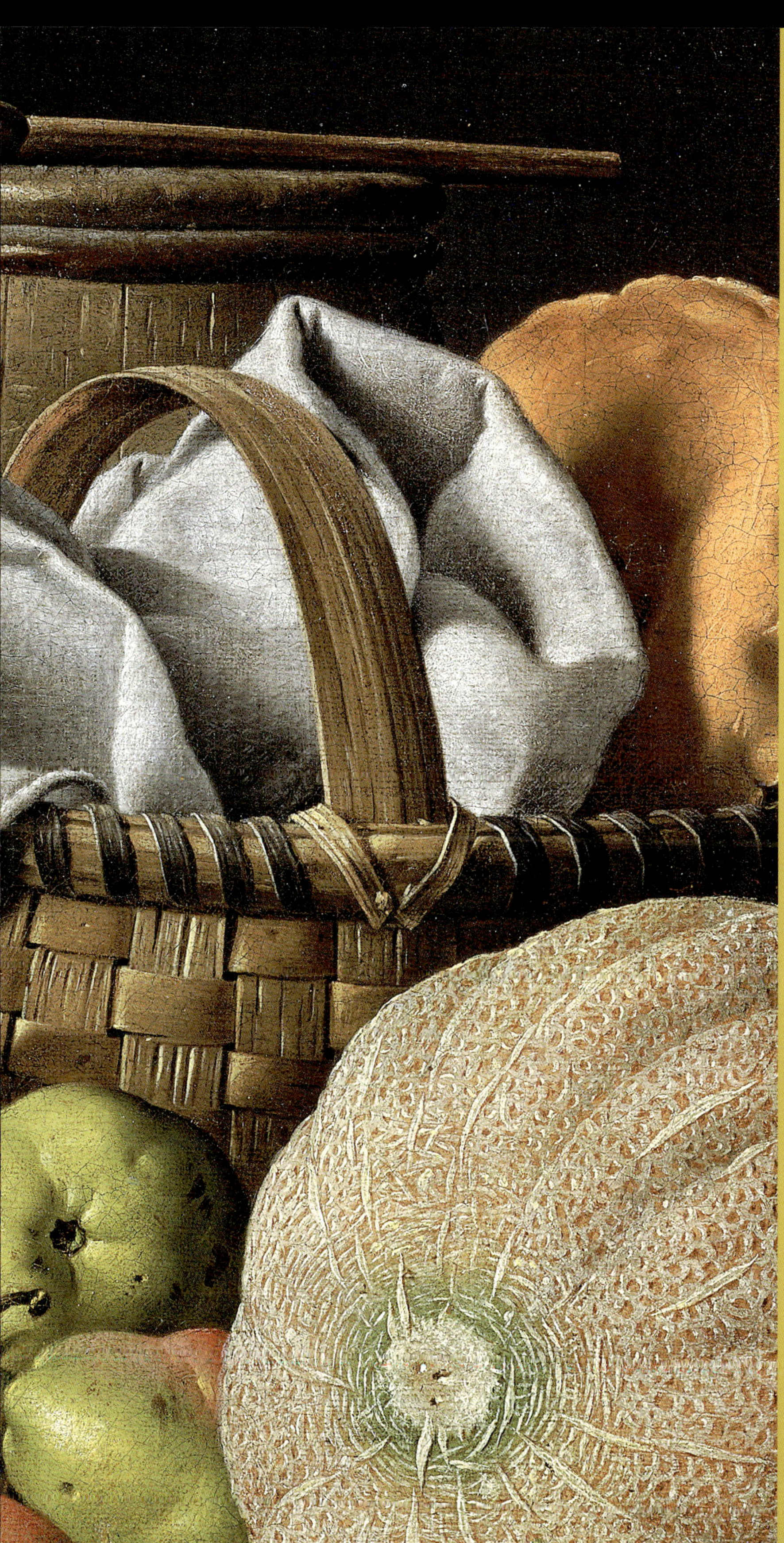

4 THE SEVENTEENTH CENTURY IN ITALY, SPAIN, AND FRANCE

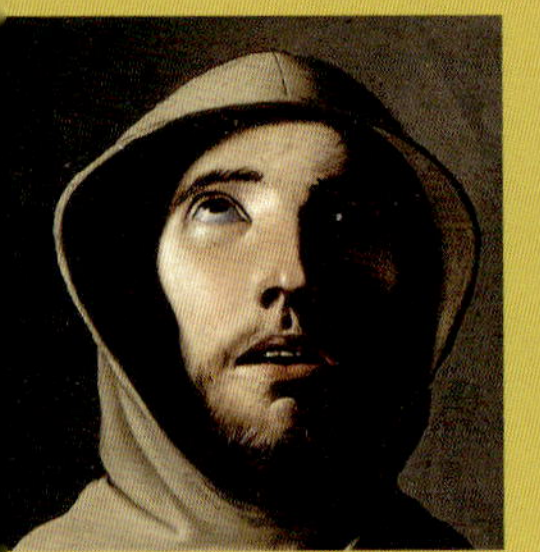
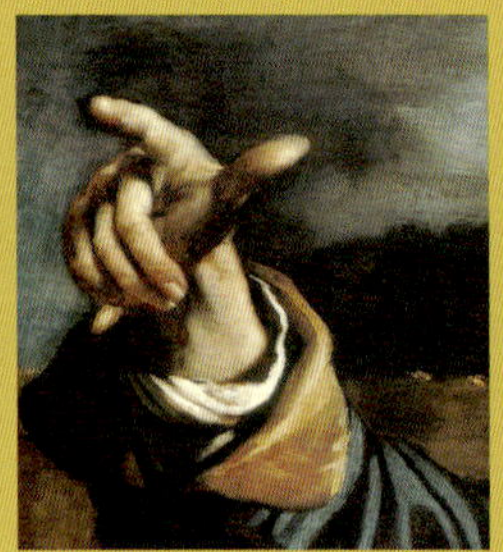

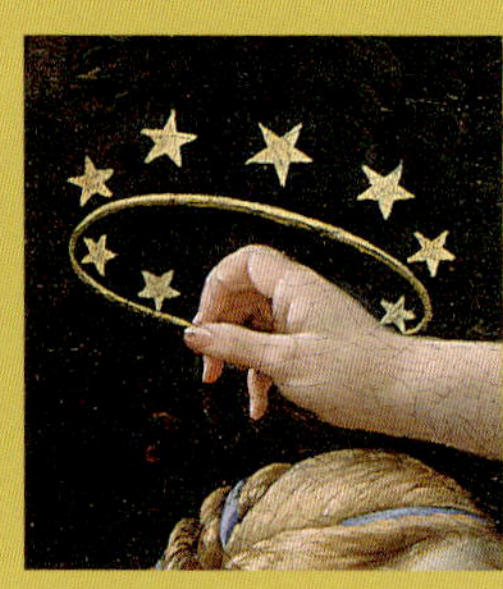
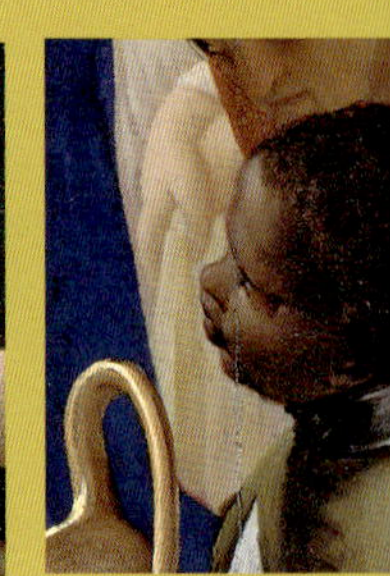

The Seventeenth Century in Italy, Spain, and France

From 1545 to 1563, the Catholic Church convened the Council of Trent in an effort to muster its strength against the growing influence of Protestantism as well as clarify its doctrines and teachings. From these sessions grew a demand for art that was more naturalistic and readily understandable; paintings that would appeal to the senses, inspire empathy and devotion in the viewer; and ultimately reinvigorate Christian practice and belief.

In southern Europe, where Catholicism maintained its primacy, artists were asked to embellish churches, satisfy the demands of powerful cardinals, and glorify mighty secular rulers. In seventeenth-century Italy, two dominant strains of painting developed. In the city of Bologna, the brothers Agostino and Annibale Carracci, together with their older cousin Ludovico, began painting in a style that tempered the ideal with a careful study of the real world. In their art academy, they encouraged others to join them in copying older works of art and drawing from life. The other, more revolutionary style was a dramatic, in-your-face naturalism exemplified by the work of Caravaggio, who began his career in Milan. Caravaggio daringly took the people he saw in the streets around him as models and organized his compositions for greatest impact and immediacy, employing strong contrasts of light and shade and pushing his large figures toward the front of the picture plane. Important commissions eventually brought both the Carracci and Caravaggio to Rome, the seat of power and patronage. While the Carracci had pupils, Caravaggio had followers, and the impact of his art would be felt throughout Europe. The interplay of these two artistic poles would inform Italian painting throughout the seventeenth century.

Spanish art and literature blossomed in the seventeenth century, despite political turmoil, constant warfare, and the financial crises of the preceding decades. Dramatic and readily accessible imagery gave form to a new, intense devotion based on the practices of contemporary Spanish mystics. Scenes from the life of Christ and images of the Infant Jesus, characterized by his compassion and vulnerability, carried great emotional impact. Art became a devotional aid, inspiring intense meditation and fervency in the believer.

Spanish painters and sculptors were also called upon to depict heroic themes or scenes from ancient history and mythology. Using bold gestures and strongly delineated forms, artists effectively animated these literary narratives. Portraiture was commissioned by royalty, leaders or founders of the religious orders, and celebrated men. Artists employed dazzling technical means and insightful characterization to capture the majesty, devotion, or intellectual acuity of their sitters.

Like Spain, France in the seventeenth century was ruled by powerful monarchs and their ministers but was less dogmatically Catholic. As elsewhere in Europe, artists traveled to and from the capital city, bringing with them ideas and approaches that effectively cross-fertilized local production. The Flemish artist Philippe de Champaigne trained in Brussels and settled in Paris in 1621, where he worked for magistrates, the clergy, and the court. His particularized physiognomies, simple compositions, and painstaking technique redolent of Flemish art found a sympathetic audience in the French capital. The development of French art in the period, however, was most closely linked to Italian painting. Early in the century, Simon Vouet was given a royal pension to study in Italy. After more than ten years abroad, he returned to Paris, bringing back lessons he had learned from the art of Caravaggio as well as the smoother, more idealizing manner of the Carracci.

Nicolas Poussin and Claude Lorrain, Frenchmen by birth, spent virtually their entire working careers in Rome. Poussin's rigorously ordered and highly idealized figures and compositions fueled the classicism that by mid-century was the official style promulgated by the newly founded Royal Academy of Painting and Sculpture. Claude's landscape paintings, based on a careful study of nature, emphasized atmosphere, masterfully created through subtle tonal values and subdued light and colors.

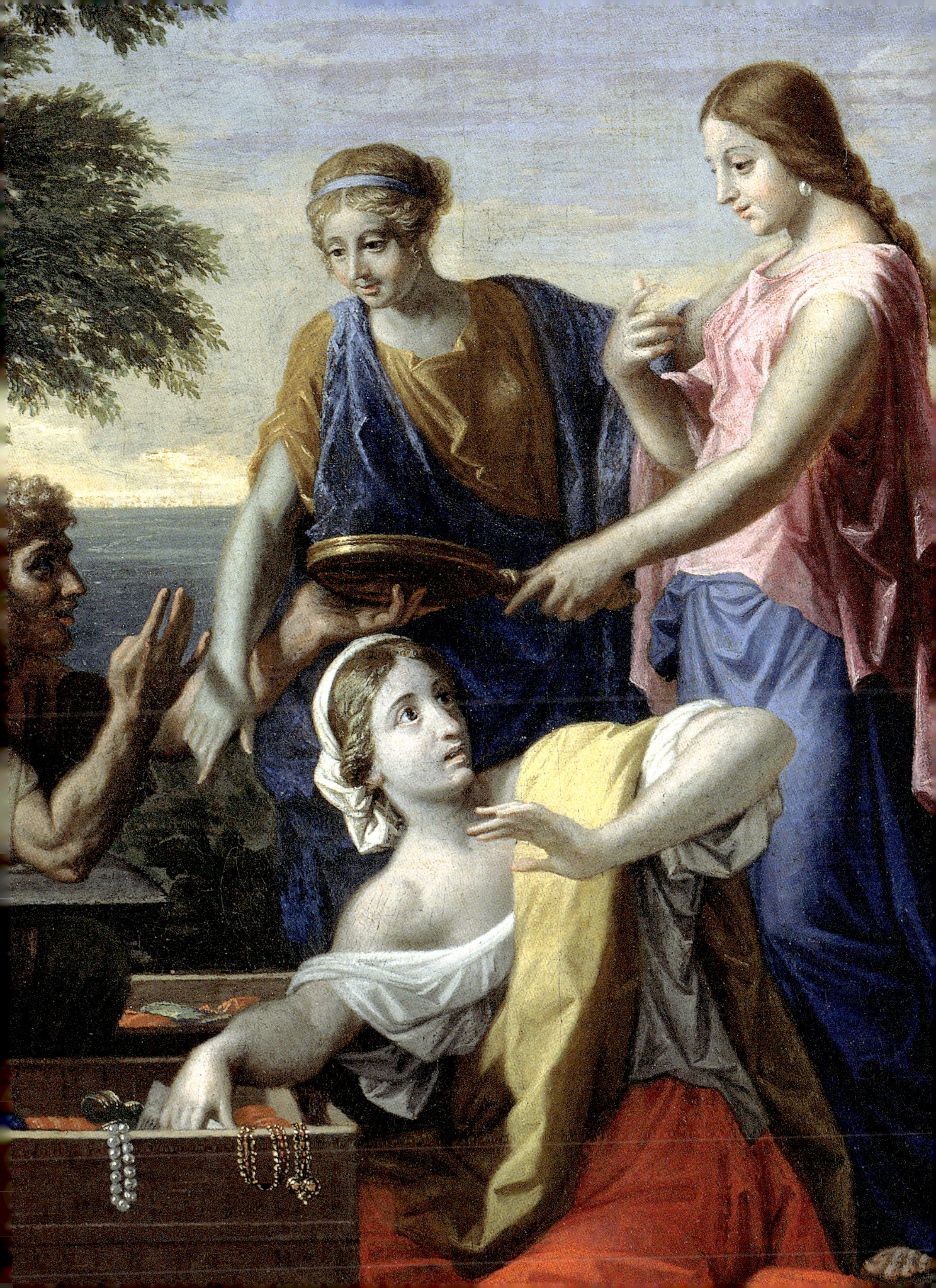

Orazio Gentileschi

Italian, 1563–1639

Saint Francis Supported by an Angel, about 1600

According to his biographers, in 1224 Saint Francis saw a divine vision while at prayer on Mount Alvernia. The experience left his body imprinted with the wounds of the crucified Christ. Emotionally charged depictions of Francis swooning in an angel's arms became popular during the Counter-Reformation, when the Catholic Church used such intense imagery to encourage the faithful to resist Protestantism. In this work, painted by Orazio Gentileschi in about 1600, the saint's pose echoes Mary's traditional posture at the foot of the cross, further underlining Francis's identification with Christ. The background of the painting references the strange rock formations on Mount Alvernia, and the two figures bathed in light might allude to the angelic vision that brought on the stigmata.

A few years earlier, Caravaggio had been the first to paint Saint Francis cradled by an angel, minimizing the physical signs of the stigmata and emphasizing instead the spiritual experience. The MFA's work is probably the earliest of the four known versions that Gentileschi painted of this subject in the early years of the seventeenth century. Stylistically, it is the least Caravaggesque of the four, but it shares elements with the others that suggest the artist made frequent use of studio paraphernalia. It appears that Caravaggio also relied on Gentileschi's props. As part of a libel suit, Gentileschi testified on September 14, 1603, that Caravaggio had asked to borrow from him a Capuchin's robe and a pair of wings, perhaps the ones seen in this painting.

Oil on canvas

139.4 x 101 cm (54⅞ x 39¾ in.)

Charles H. Bayley Picture and Painting Fund 2010.374

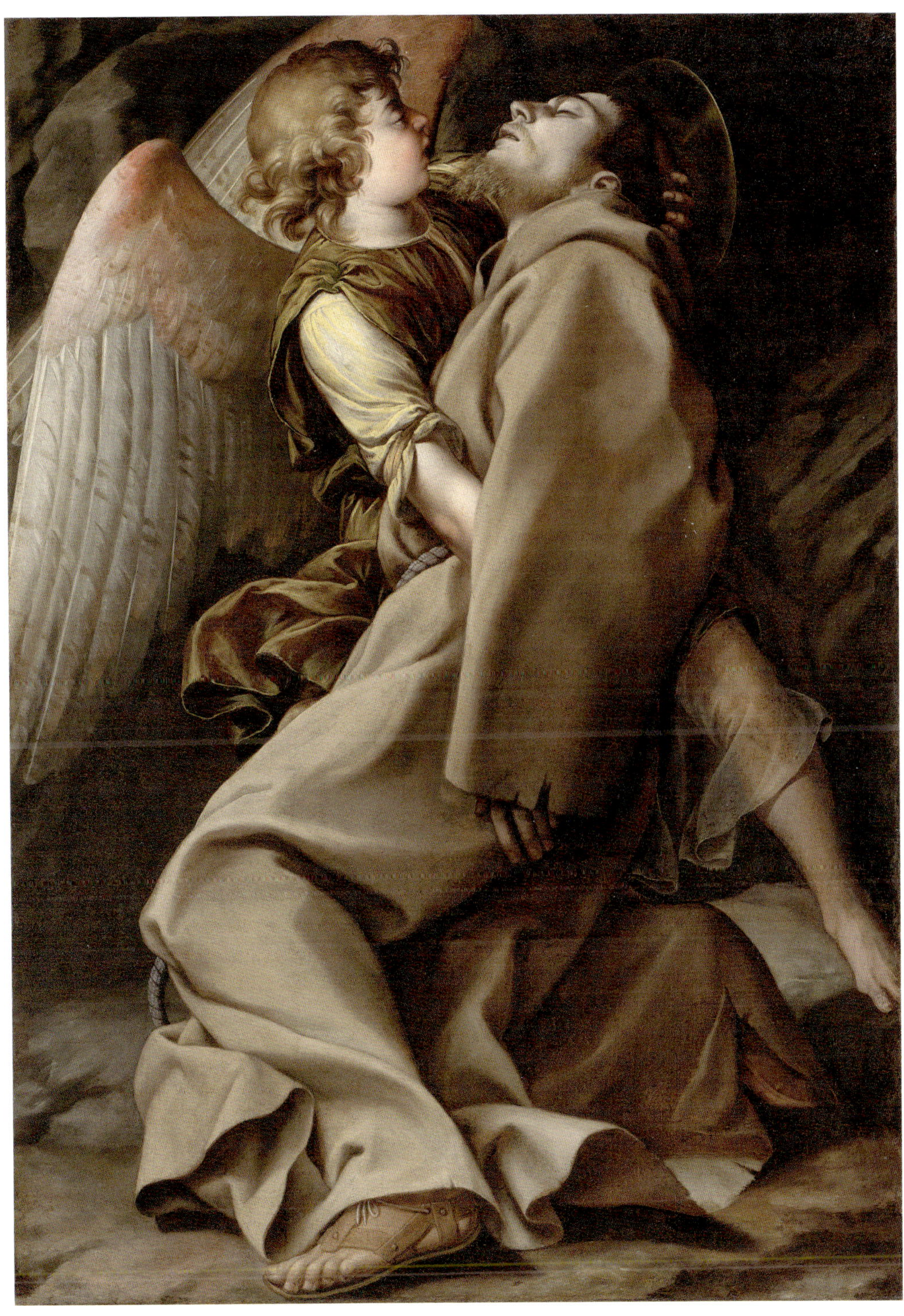

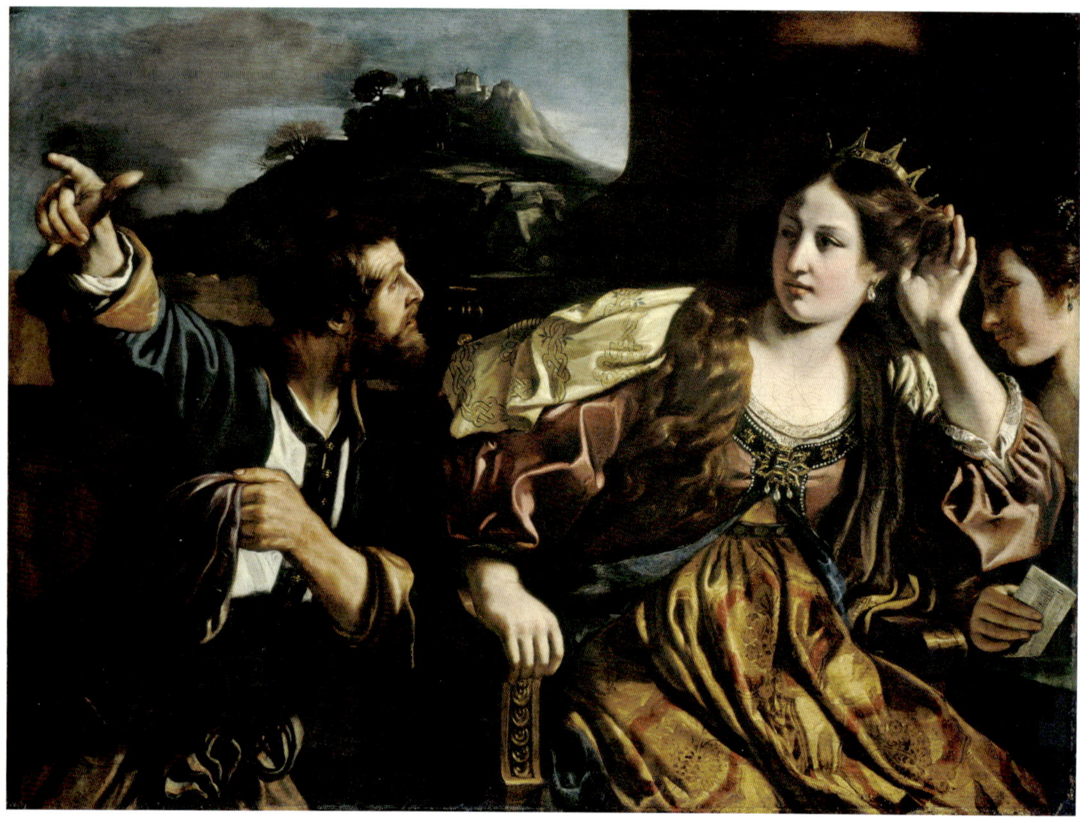

Guercino (Giovanni Francesco Barbieri)
Italian (Bolognese), about 1591–1666
Semiramis Receiving Word of the Revolt of Babylon, 1624

The subject of this painting derives from a historical anecdote recounted by the first-century CE Roman writer Valerius Maximus. In his account, the historian describes how the Assyrian queen Semiramis, a woman of unrivaled beauty, received news of the revolt of Babylon while at her toilette. As a testament to her strength, she refused to finish having her hair dressed until she had personally led an army to crush the rebellion and execute its leaders.

This is the earliest of three known versions of the composition by Guercino, made only a year after the artist returned to his native Cento from Rome. It exhibits the painter's robust use of light and shade that was the hallmark of his style in the first half of the 1620s. The composition is marked by a heightened sense of drama and theatricality in which the figures appear like actors on a shallow stage. Semiramis listens to a messenger gesturing emphatically in the direction of the revolt, while her maid, comb in hand, appears at right. The queen's left hand fingers her half-coiffed hair, and her right hand grips the arm of the chair, as if she is preparing to propel herself into action.

Unusual for a work from the seventeenth century, the early ownership of this painting is well documented. It was commissioned by Daniele Ricci in Bologna in 1624 before passing into the important collection of Italian paintings formed by the Amsterdam merchant Gerrit Reynst (1599–1658), where it was recorded in an engraving by Jeremias Falck (1610–1677). Shortly thereafter, the States-General of the Netherlands acquired it and made it part of the "Dutch Gift" presented to Charles II of England (1630–1685) in 1660 upon his restoration to the throne.

Oil on canvas
112.4 x 154.6 cm (44 ¼ x 60 ⅞ in.)
Francis Welch Fund 48.1028

Attributed to Ferdinando Tacca
Italian, 1619–1686
Hercules and the Erymanthian Boar,
mid-17th century

Hercules strides forward with his prey, the fierce Erymanthian boar, slung over his shoulder. The scene represents the fourth of the twelve Labors of Hercules, in which the ancient hero was ordered by King Eurystheus to capture the wild beast that had been ravaging the countryside and bring it to him alive. Thus the viewer must imagine the large animal still breathing and fighting, making Hercules's legendary strength even more astonishing. He holds the boar firmly by one leg and moves quickly and lightly, his cloak billowing in the breeze.

This bronze statue was made in Florence in the seventeenth century, probably by Ferdinando Tacca, who inherited his sculptural workshop from his father, Pietro. The figure of Hercules was a popular subject in Florentine art during the Renaissance and came to symbolize civic fortitude and resilience. In its expert casting and finishing, the sculpture is evidence of the long tradition of excellence in the making of bronze statuary in Florence. Hercules's open stance, with all of his weight balanced on his front foot and only the toes of his right foot touching the ground behind him, is made possible by Tacca's expert comprehension of the tensile strength of bronze.

Bronze
H. 74.2 cm (29 ¼ in.)
Bequest of William A. Coolidge 1993.48

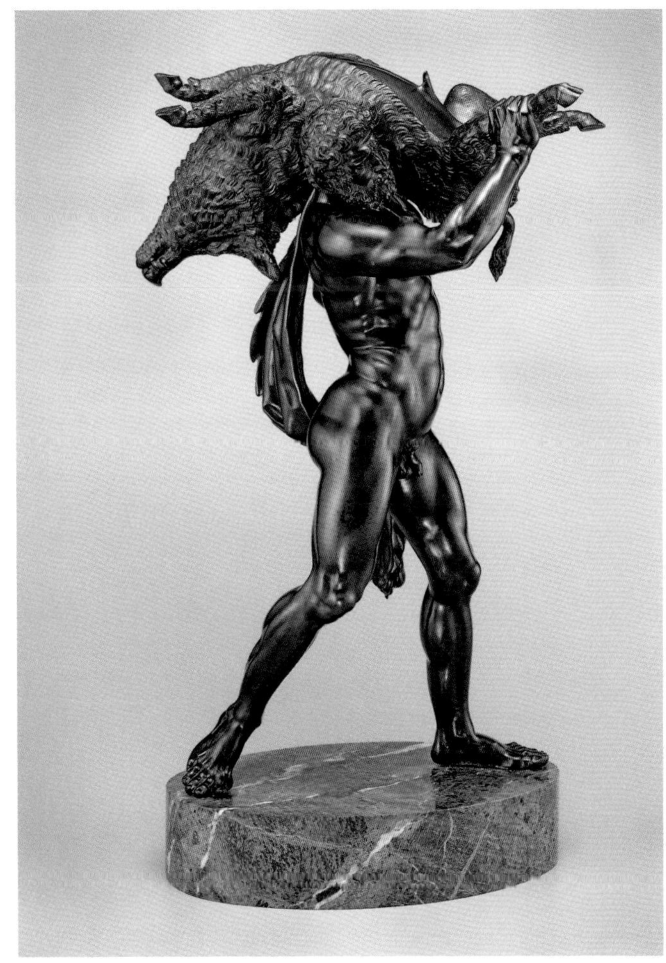

El Greco (Doménikos Theotokópoulos)
Greek (active in Spain), about 1541–1614
Fray Hortensio Félix Paravicino, 1609

Born on the island of Crete and trained in Italy, El Greco moved to Spain in his mid-thirties. Best known for his intense, spiritual religious paintings, he was also a perceptive and powerful portraitist. The subject of this work is the well-known Trinitarian monk, poet, theologian, and court orator Fray Hortensio Félix Paravicino (1580–1633). Paravicino was a friend of the artist, though it is not known when and under what circumstances painter and patron met.

In this late masterpiece, El Greco adopts the sixteenth-century portrait format of the full-length seated ecclesiastical figure made famous by Raphael and Titian. He positions the chair so that the sitter's body faces the viewer directly, facilitating Paravicino's concentrated gaze. The monk holds two books on his lap, most likely a Bible and a book of poetry to signify his dual calling, and wears the habit of his order—a black cape over a white hooded robe bearing a red and blue cross. Apart from these color notes, the artist painted in a restricted palette of whites, browns, and blacks over a red-brown ground that shows through in places and gives warmth to the whole painting. Long, animated strokes that describe the drapery seem to cascade out and into the viewer's space. This lively technique and the long, slender fingers, one of which marks the sitter's place in the book, imply movement, notwithstanding the figure's stillness. The subtle, compelling image emphasizes the cleric's psychological as well as physical presence.

Paravicino displayed this painting in his cell, praising it and the artist effusively in one of four sonnets he addressed to El Greco. The work later made an equally favorable impression on the American painter John Singer Sargent (1856–1925), on whose recommendation the MFA acquired the portrait in 1904.

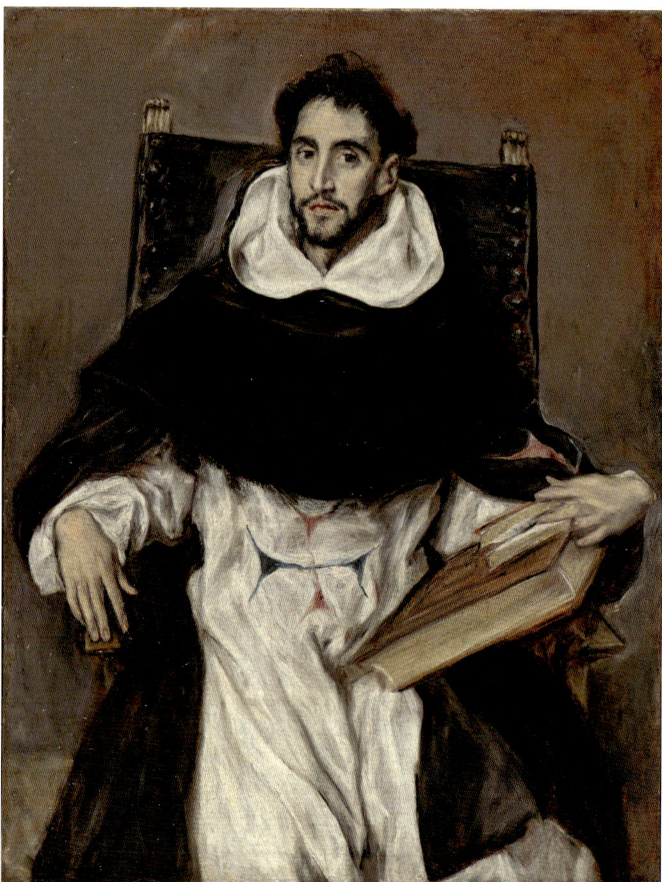

Oil on canvas
112.1 x 86.1 cm (44⅛ x 33⅞ in.)
Isaac Sweetser Fund 04.234

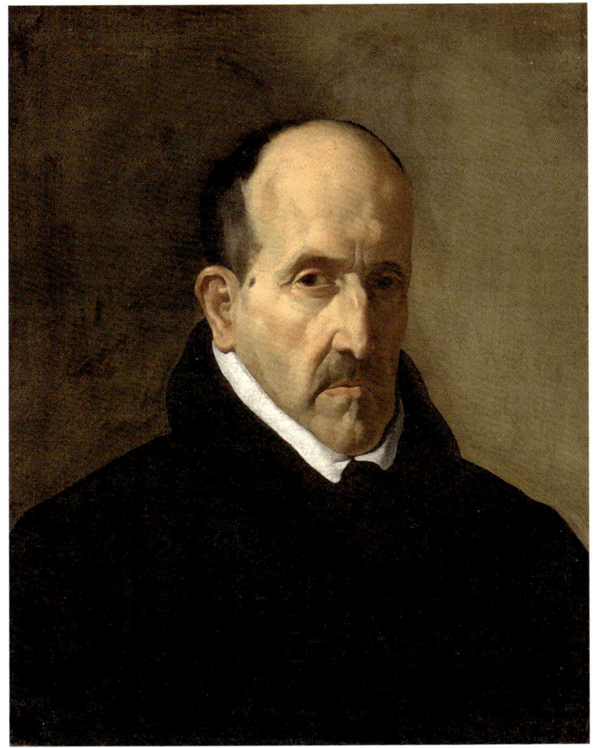

Diego Velázquez
Spanish, 1599–1660
Luis de Góngora y Argote, 1622

In 1622, Diego Velázquez embarked on his first trip from his native Seville to Madrid. His teacher and father-in-law, Francisco Pacheco, the most important Spanish theorist of the seventeenth century, introduced him to friends there who were well connected at court. While these contacts did not immediately result in a royal commission, Velázquez did succeed in painting the poet Luis de Góngora y Argote (1561–1627), one of the most celebrated literary figures in Madrid. Góngora had instituted a new style of writing characterized by complex imagery and interpretative difficulty. He was not, however, universally admired and suffered many personal and professional setbacks.

Pacheco had likely wanted Velázquez to paint Góngora as a model for Pacheco's own *Libro de retratos*, a book of bust-length portrait drawings of famous Andalusians, which included ecclesiastics, poets, and other eminent figures. X-rays of the MFA's painting reveal that Velázquez originally encircled the sitter's head with a laurel wreath, the traditional attribute of the poet, which featured in other contemporary portraits of illustrious men. In this depiction, the subject turns a stern—or perhaps sorrowful—gaze outward, his mouth downturned and his brow furrowed. His face, half in shadow, is described in flat, broad planes of flesh-colored tones enlivened by pink and is set off from the black bulk of his body by a thin white cleric's collar. The artist's economy of means, in palette and application of paint, is extraordinary.

Velázquez's portrait of Góngora had its desired effect, and the young painter's abilities became known in the capital. The following year, Velázquez would be summoned back to Madrid to paint the king.

Oil on canvas
19¾ x 16 in. (50.2 x 40.6 cm)
Maria Antoinette Evans Fund 32.79

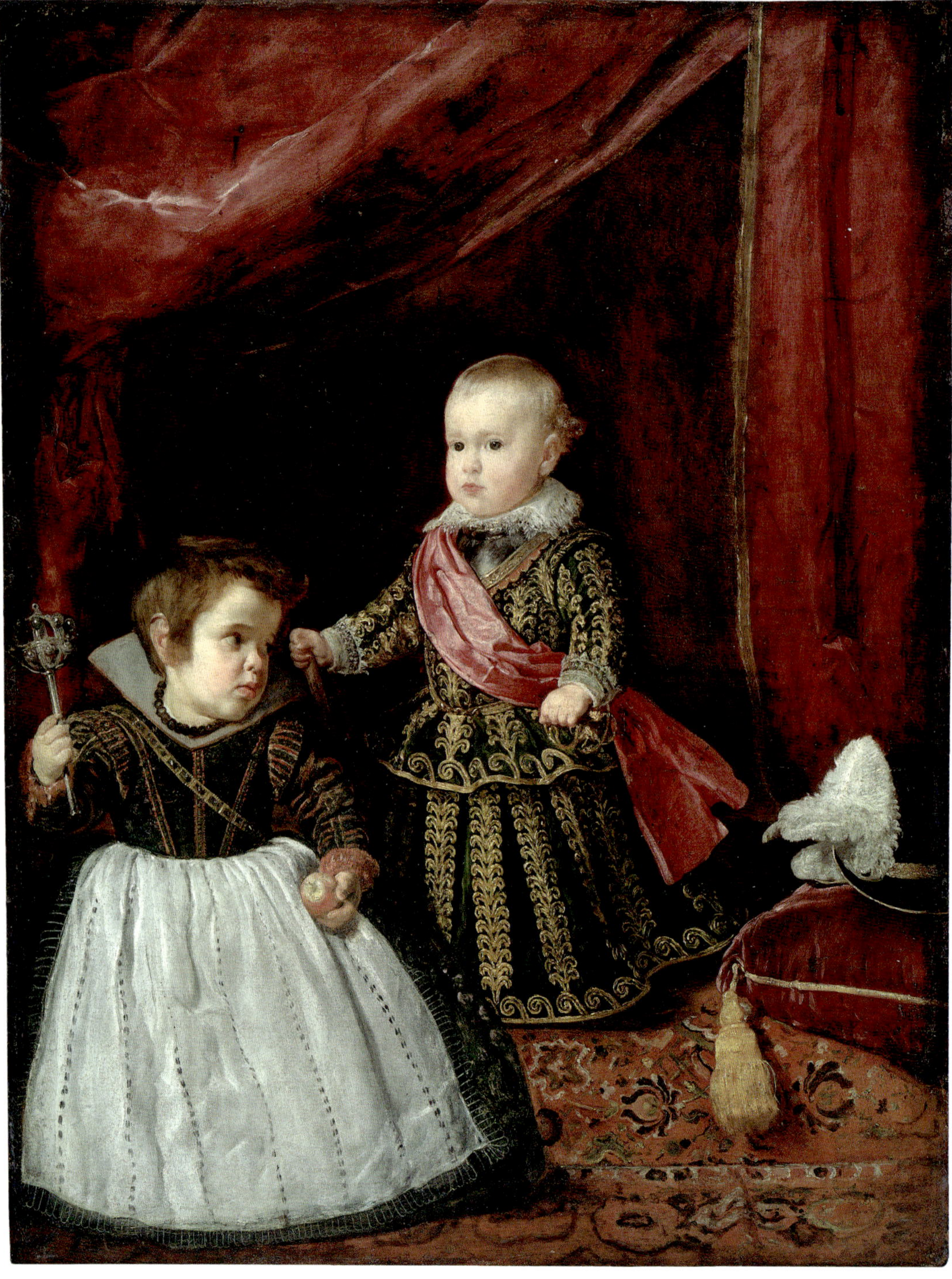

Diego Velázquez

Spanish, 1599–1660

Don Baltasar Carlos with a Dwarf, 1632

From the moment of his appointment as *Pintor del Rey* to Philip IV on October 6, 1623, Diego Velázquez worked exclusively for the King of Spain. Though Prince Baltasar Carlos (1629–1646), the king's son with Isabel de Bourbon, was born during the artist's first sojourn in Italy, Philip waited for Velázquez's return to Madrid to have the child painted. The work likely commemorates the occasion of the swearing of allegiance by the nobles of Castile to the young prince, the moment when he was recognized as heir to the powerful Spanish throne. Velázquez portrays the two-year-old with the attributes of a military commander. He wears the sash of office and a metal breastplate, holds the captain general's baton in his right hand, and grasps the hilt of a sword with his left. A plumed helmet rests on a velvet cushion at his side. Tragically, the boy would never be king, as he died just shy of his seventeenth birthday.

In the painting, Baltasar Carlos is accompanied by a dwarf. Dwarves traditionally served as royal jesters and companions at court and figured in depictions of Spanish royal sitters as foils to their princely perfection. This dwarf, placed a step below Baltasar Carlos as befits his status, holds symbols of the monarchy in the form of a rattle as scepter and an apple as orb. His twisting posture is in marked contrast to the rigid verticality of the young prince.

Velázquez created an effect of splendor through colors and textures. Baltasar Carlos sparkles against a ground of deep reds and crimsons. The artist varied his painting technique, employing, for example, a relatively painstaking touch for the embroidery on the prince's garment compared to the more loosely handled carpet. The result is a work that, even at this early date, exhibits the artist's dazzling ability to manipulate paint.

Oil on canvas

128 x 101.9 cm (50 3/8 x 40 1/8 in.)

Henry Lillie Pierce Fund 01.104

Juan de Montejo

Spanish, died 1601

Tomb effigy of Alonso de Mera (died May 22, 1553),
1592–94

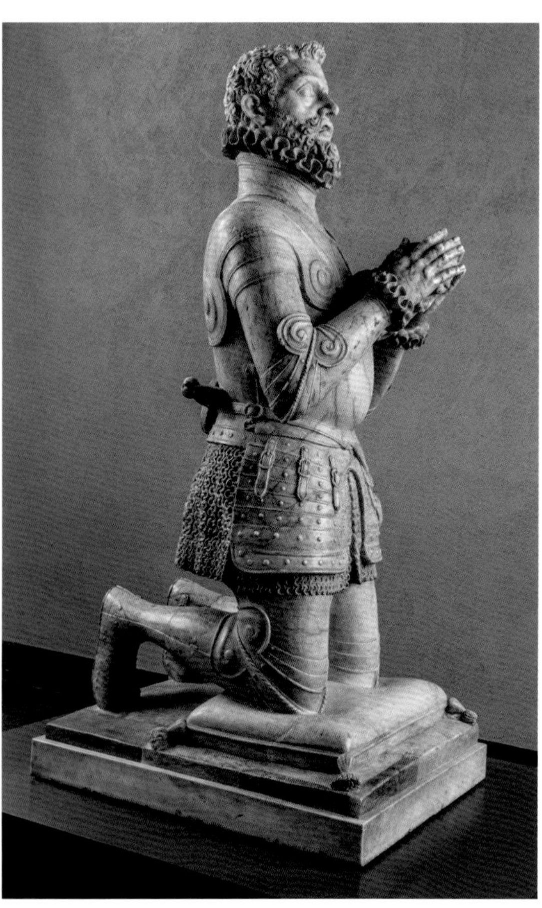

Alabaster
152.4 x 63.5 x 77.5 cm (60 x 25 x 30½ in.)
1939 Purchase Fund 44.813

In 2016, research revealed the proper identification of the sculptor, subject, and original location for this life-size alabaster sculpture. Incorrectly identified as Italian when the sculpture was acquired by the MFA in 1944, it was known simply as the Kneeling Knight. The knight can now be identified as Alonso de Mera, who spent much of his life abroad in the Spanish colony of Peru, returning to his home country late in life having amassed a large fortune. He used the money to found a monastery church in Zamora dedicated to Saint Pablo and Saint Ildefonso (now destroyed) but did not live to see it completed.

This large and exquisitely detailed sculpture, made of two pieces of carved alabaster, decorated the knight's tomb in that church, though it was not completed until nearly four decades after his death. Mera's will had called for a simple slab to cover his resting place, but his executors decided to commission Antonio Falcote to create a sculpture of Mera instead. However, Falcote died before the sculpture could be made. Juan de Montejo, best known as a figural sculptor and the most important artist active in Zamora and Salamanca, took over the commission, purchasing the alabaster from Falcote's widow. Alabaster as a medium was particularly popular in Spain, the Low Countries, and England, where marble was not as readily available as it was in Italy. The level of detail in the meticulous carving of his hair, beard, neck ruff, and chain mail is extraordinary and lends this portrait a particular vitality and immediacy.

José de Arce

Flemish (active in Spain), about 1600–1666

Infant Jesus, about 1640–50

A rosy-cheeked infant Christ strides forward, his right arm extended in benediction. The decoration on his cloak imitates rich, multicolored brocade and was created using *estofado* (from the Spanish word *estofa*, meaning a type of quilted silk). In this technique, gesso is applied to a wood surface and then covered in gold or silver leaf. The artist paints over the leaf with oil paint, which is scratched away to create a pattern.

José de Arce was born in Flanders. After starting his career there, he relocated to Spain in about 1637. Active in Seville, he engaged with the local tradition of nearly life-size polychrome sculptures of the Christ Child and saints. His works of religious figures display a sophisticated sense of movement—a nod to his knowledge of Baroque traditions—and the naturalism and emotion favored by local Spanish artists.

The sculpture, already full of vitality when stationary, would have been further animated by its use in ceremonial processions, which would have given the drapery of his cloak a sense of movement. The delicate modeling of Christ's face and legs highlights his innocence and vulnerability, while his firm stance foreshadows his future role as the Savior.

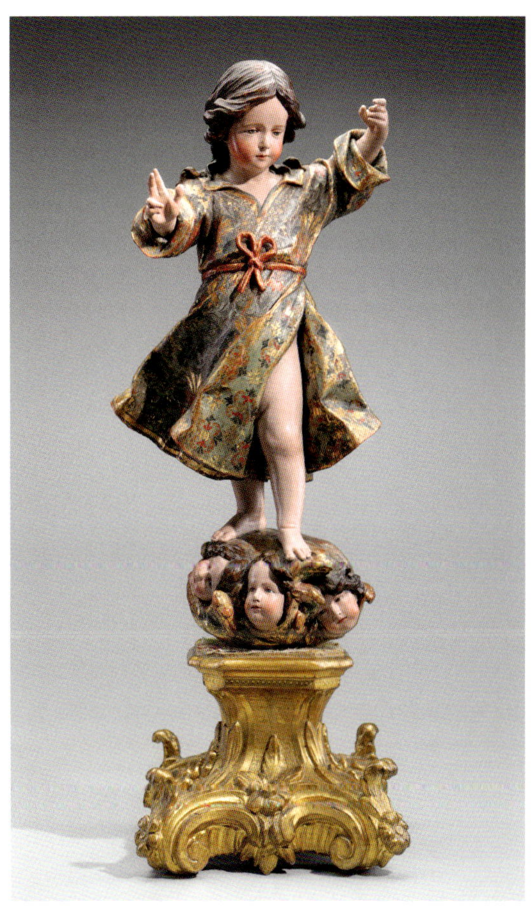

Painted wood

58 x 28 x 25 cm (22⅞ x 11 x 9⅞ in.)

John Lowell Gardner Fund, Marshall H. Gould Fund, Russell B. and Andrée Beauchamp Stearns Fund, and Tamara Petrosian Davis Sculpture Fund 2011.1637

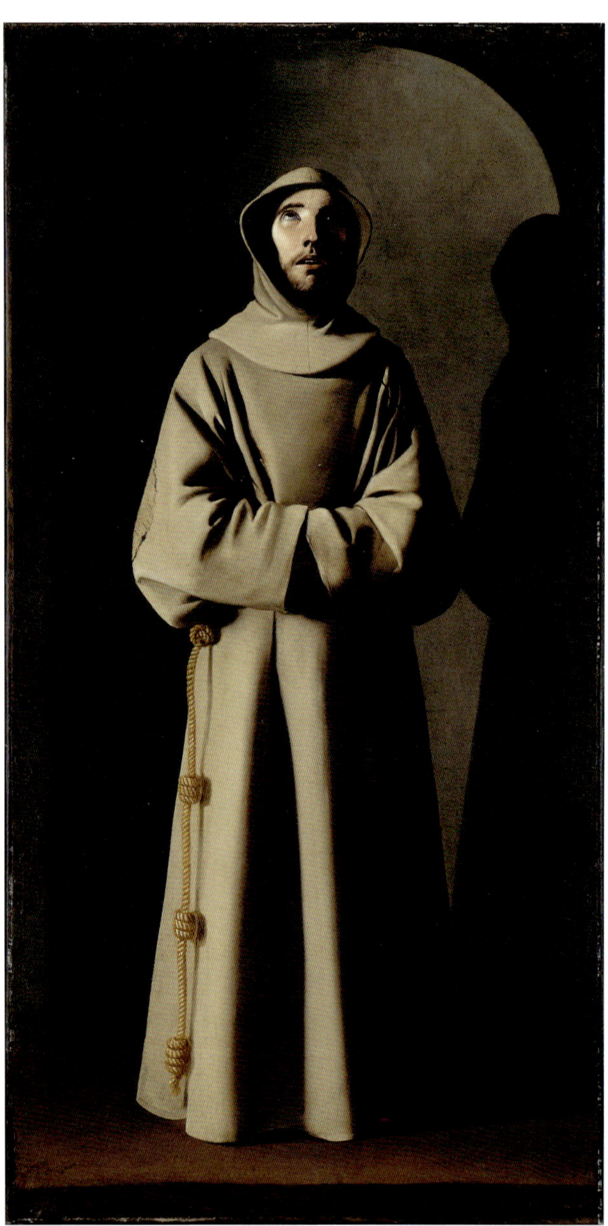

Oil on canvas
207 x 106.7 cm (81½ x 42 in.)
Herbert James Pratt Fund 38.1617

Francisco de Zurbarán
Spanish, 1598–1664
Saint Francis, about 1640–45

A contemporary of Diego Velázquez, Francisco de Zurbarán lived and worked mostly in the southern Spanish city of Seville, where he was highly regarded for his depictions of devotional subjects. This dramatically lit image of Saint Francis (1181/82–1226), identifiable by his brown habit with a large patch on the right sleeve (indicating his vow of poverty), depicts him in a moment of ecstasy. Some scholars believe the saint's specific facial features suggest he was painted from a live model; others emphasize the solidity of the drapery and its association with contemporary three-dimensional polychrome sculpture. The simple vaulted niche before which the saint stands would have been a common setting for such sculpture of the period.

Zurbarán's representation has much in common with a popular seventeenth-century account of a mystical legend involving the saint. While visiting the monastery of Assisi in 1449, Pope Nicholas V allegedly descended into the crypt by torchlight early one morning. Saint Francis was said to have appeared to the pope, standing, eyes open and cast toward heaven. Upon seeing this vision, the pope fell to his knees. Reaching out, he carefully lifted a corner of Francis's robe to reveal a bloody foot—one of the five wounds of the stigmata. Intriguingly, Zurbarán offers only the tips of a few toes on Francis's left foot, as if encouraging the viewer to play an active role in the moment of revelation.

Luis Meléndez
Spanish, 1716–1780
Still Life with Melon and Pears, about 1772

In 1771, the Prince of Asturias (later King Charles IV) commissioned Luis Meléndez to depict "every species of food produced by the Spanish climate." Meléndez subsequently delivered forty-four still lifes to the Royal Palace. The encyclopedic character and taxonomic approach the artist took to this endeavor was in keeping with the study of natural history, a new field of inquiry that especially interested the prince.

After fulfilling his commission, Meléndez expanded on his rather simple, contained compositions for the prince to create more ambitious, complicated works for private patrons. The MFA painting is one such composition. The large melon, for example, is painted from the same angle, with the same pattern of white reticulation on the rind, and the same configuration of ridges and dents as the melon in the artist's *Still Life with Melon, Jug, and Bread* from the royal series (now at the Museo Nacional Colegio de San Gregorio in Valladolid). Yet, the melons vary in color, size, and handling. The melon from the royal series is painted carefully, the rind built up with numerous small touches. In contrast, the melon in the MFA work is rendered more quickly and in a kind of shorthand, which implies it was painted from the prior work rather than from nature.

This painting provides insight into Meléndez's working method. It combines many of the artist's studio props: the wine cooler, the olive barrel with large wooden spoon on top, the woven basket with white kitchen cloth, and the ceramic bowl with iron lid are all familiar from other Meléndez paintings. He was a master of describing texture with paint, juxtaposing these various materials with foodstuffs, all placed on a ledge before a dark background. X-rays of the painting have revealed a partial figure holding a scrolled sheet of paper beneath the surface. This underlying work was probably not painted by Meléndez. He was a scavenger of canvas, likely seeing its reuse as a way to economize.

Oil on canvas
63.8 x 85.1 cm (25⅛ x 33½ in.)
Margaret Curry Wyman Fund 39.41

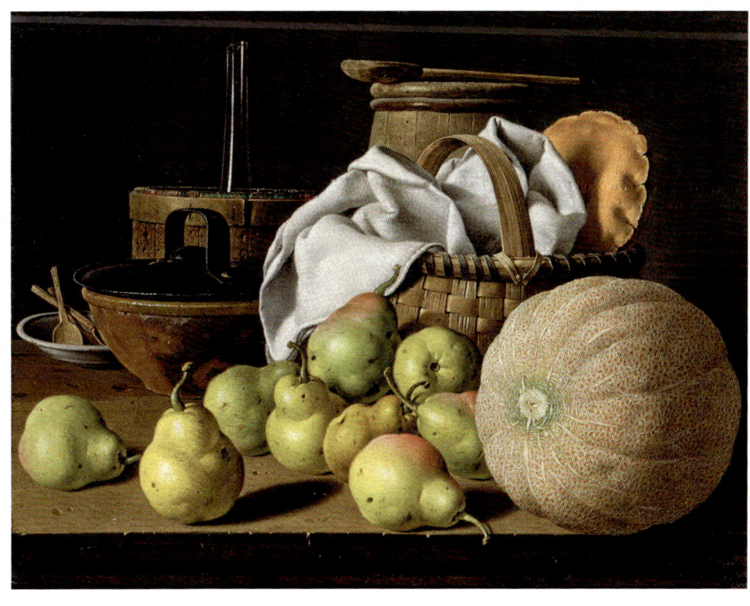

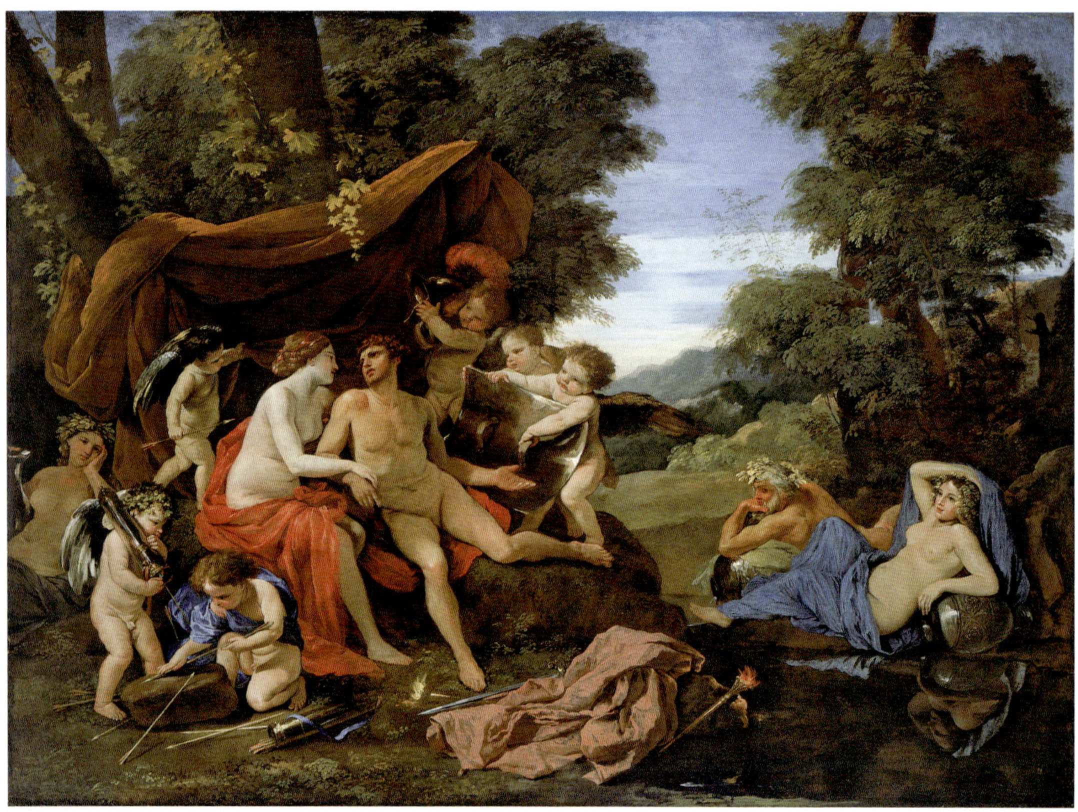

Nicolas Poussin
French (active in Rome), 1594–1665
Mars and Venus, about 1630

This early work by Nicolas Poussin depicts an allegory of the triumph of love over war that comes from the poem *De rerum natura* (*On the Nature of Things*) by the ancient Roman philosopher Lucretius. In the painting, Venus, goddess of love, is shown seducing Mars, god of war. Six cupids encircle the couple and aid the goddess in disarming Mars by removing his helmet, turning his arrows into playthings, and holding up his shield as a mirror to reflect Venus's beauty. On either side, two nymphs and a river god look on, framing the composition.

Though born in France, Poussin spent nearly his entire career in Rome. His admiration for Italian Renaissance painters, particularly those of the Venetian school, is evident in his use of warm colors and harmonious integration of figures and landscape. Two copses of trees serve as backdrops for each of the figural groups, while a vista of green hills appears between them. The figures' elegant poses derive in large part from those found in antique sculpture and sarcophagi. Such explicit allusions to classical antiquity likely intrigued the presumed patron of this painting, the Italian antiquarian Cassiano dal Pozzo (1588–1657). In addition to a number of important paintings, Cassiano amassed a sizable collection of illustrations after Roman sculpture and antiquities.

Oil on canvas
154.9 x 213.7 cm (61 x 84⅛ in.)
Augustus Hemenway Fund and Arthur William Wheelwright Fund 40.89

Nicolas Poussin
French (active in Rome), 1594–1665
Discovery of Achilles on Skyros, about 1649–50

By the mid-1640s, Nicolas Poussin had developed a new grand style in which his figures and forms have a solid monumentality, his use of primary colors is marked, and his compositions are severely ordered. This style was perfectly suited to the depiction of scenes from classical history. Poussin twice painted the subject of Achilles among the Daughters of Lycomedes. In order to thwart the prophecy that the great military leader Achilles would die young, his mother, Thetis, sent him to the island of Skyros disguised as a girl. Understanding that the Greek forces could not triumph over Troy without him, Ulysses, masquerading as a beturbaned merchant from the East, devised a plan to find him.

This painting shows the moment that Achilles's true identity is discovered. Faced with the choice of jewels or a weapon, Achilles delights in selecting and unsheathing a sword. Poussin has taken great care in describing the reactions of the onlookers: the eager Ulysses; the horrified Deidamia, Achilles's lover; and the excited warrior in disguise. The action is circumscribed within a broad pyramid anchored by architectural elements on either side and set within a verdant landscape. Poussin carefully planned the composition through a number of preparatory drawings in which he tried out various arrangements. It is possible he even used a three-dimensional model, which would have allowed him to study the fall of light.

Oil on canvas
97.5 x 131.1 cm (38⅜ x 51⅝ in.)
Juliana Cheney Edwards Collection 46.463

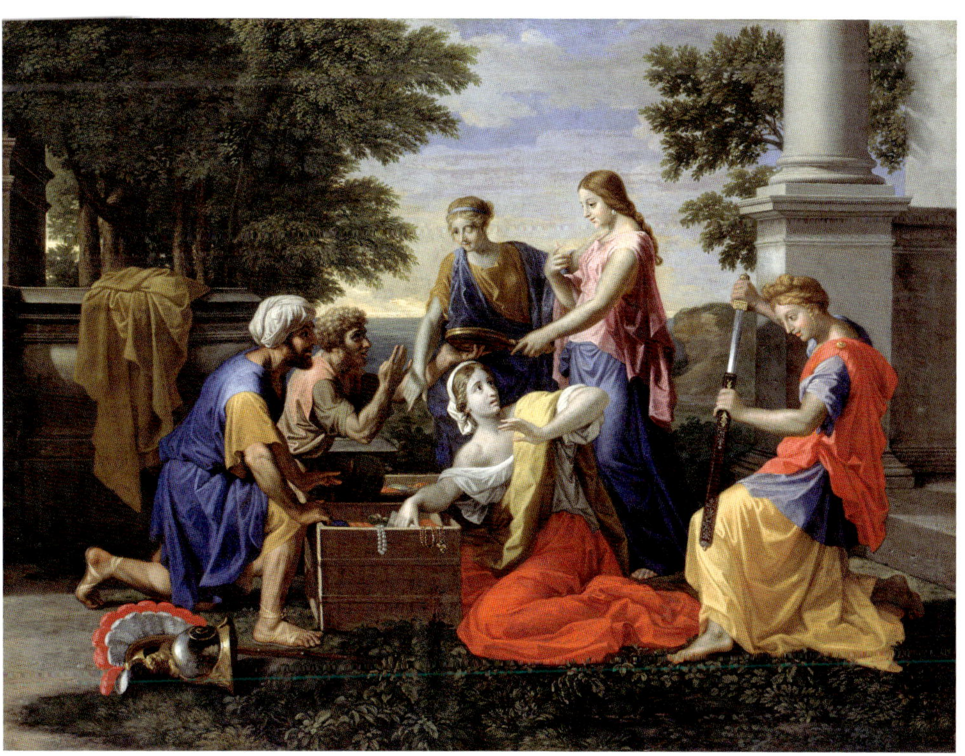

Eustache Le Sueur

French, 1616–1655

Bacchus and Ariadne, about 1640

This painting was acquired by the MFA in 1968 as a work by Simon Vouet, one of the most influential seventeenth-century French painters. It was only several years later that its maker was determined to be Eustache Le Sueur, who was among Vouet's most important pupils and collaborators. Vouet's style was formed in Rome, where he was inspired by the boldly modeled and dramatic life-size figures of Caravaggio and the elegant, highly polished forms of Giovanni Lanfranco, as well as sixteenth-century Venetian artists' use of light and color. Vouet brought this Italian idiom back to France, where it would revitalize painting, not least through the works produced by the talented artists in his workshop, including Le Sueur.

In Le Sueur's hands, the story of Bacchus and Ariadne has been distilled to its essence. Ariadne, daughter of King Minos of Crete, was deserted by Theseus on the island of Naxos. Bacchus, the god of wine, shown here with grape leaves in his crown and staff, came to her rescue and, as a sign of his love, hurled her crown into the sky, where it became the constellation Corona Borealis (Northern crown). The color harmonies, Bacchus's swirling draperies, and the robust, substantial figures reveal Vouet's influence. Le Sueur also relied on prints or drawings of ancient statuary. Bacchus, for example, was derived from the sculpture of Apollo Belvedere in the Vatican, and Ariadne from the lower portion of any number of Roman mythological sarcophagi of the second and third centuries CE.

Oil on canvas

175.3 x 125.7 cm (69 x 49 ½ in.)

Ernest Wadsworth Longfellow Fund and Grant Walker Fund 68.764

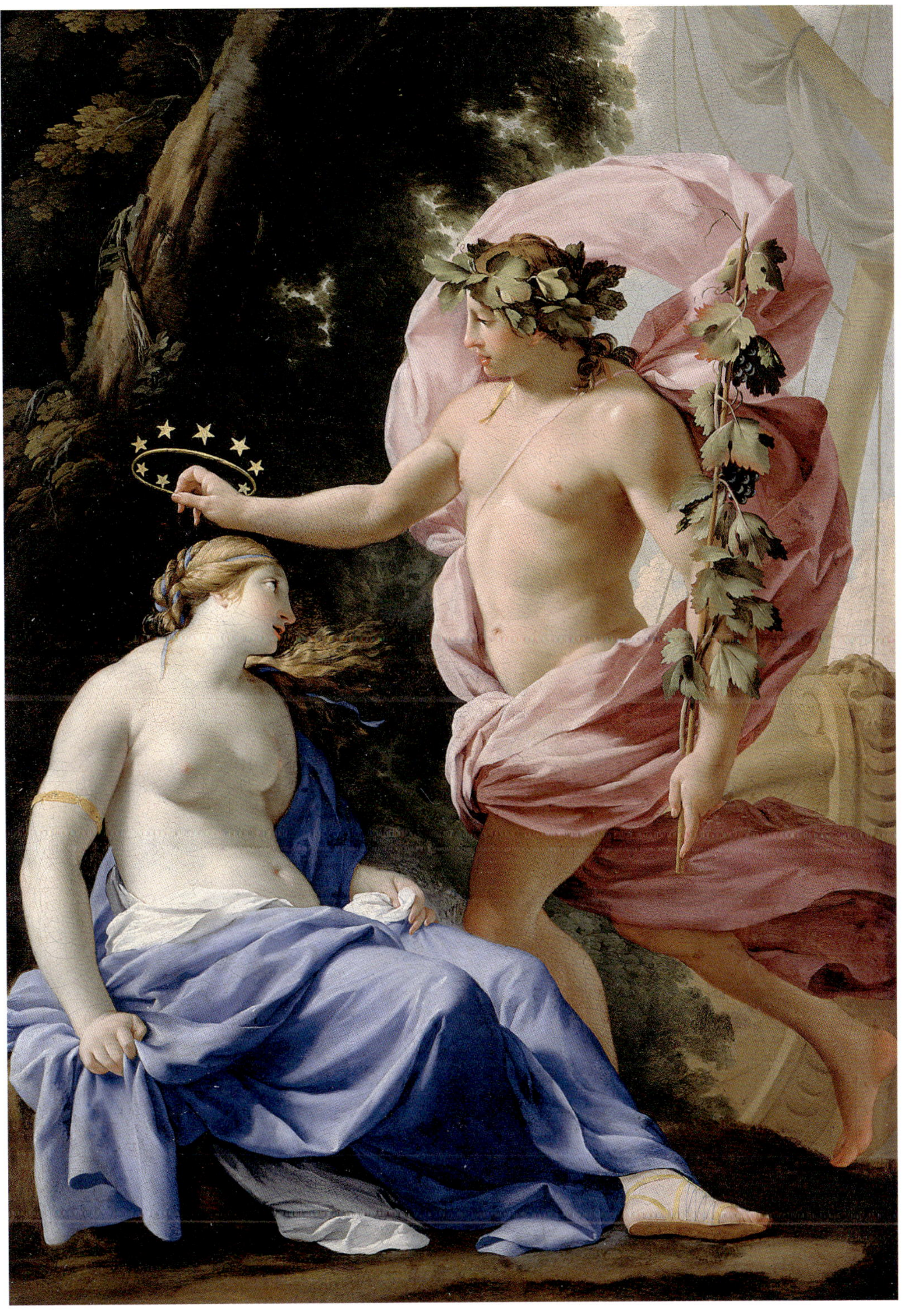

Eustache Le Sueur

French, 1616–1655

Camma Offers the Poisoned Wedding Cup to Synorix in the Temple of Diana, about 1644

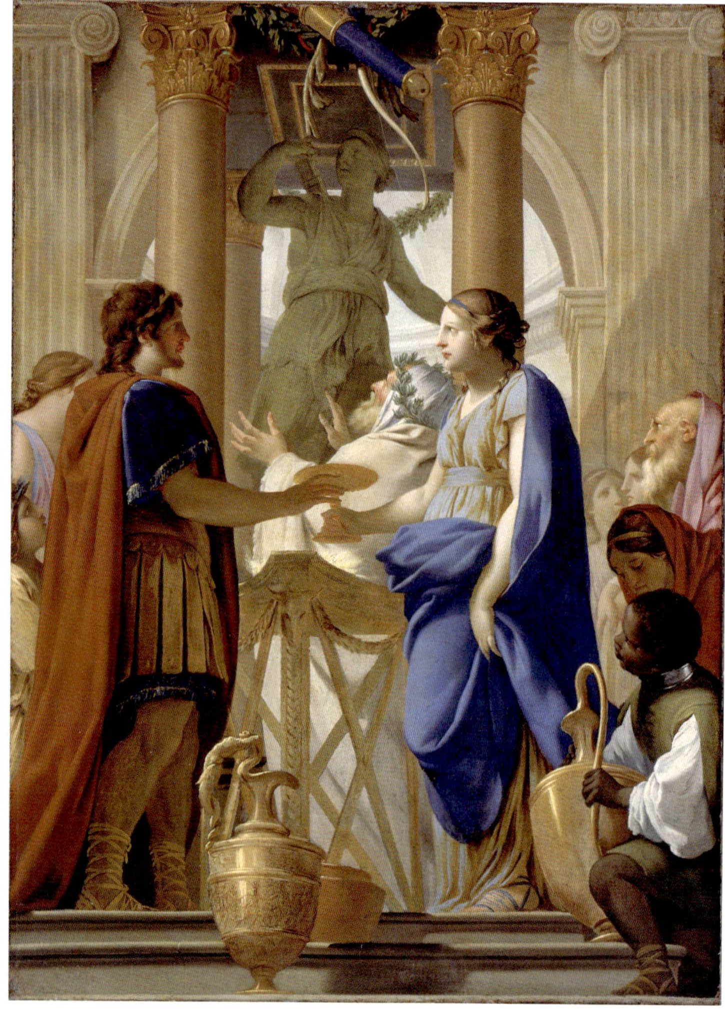

There is an obvious stylistic difference between this painting and the artist's earlier *Bacchus and Ariadne*. The shift illustrates Eustache Le Sueur's move away from Simon Vouet's voluptuous manner and toward the more severe style of Nicolas Poussin, which Le Sueur tempered with a nod to the classical art of Raphael. The monumental scale of the sculptural figures, relative symmetry of the composition, and coolly balanced palette of blues and golds that imbue the scene with a calm tranquility are all typical of Le Sueur's mature work.

Here, the story depicted comes from Plutarch's "On the Bravery of Women" in the Greek biographer's collection of essays and speeches known as the *Moralia* (about 100 CE), which was translated into French in the late sixteenth century. The priestess Camma, of the cult of Diana, plots to avenge her husband's death by agreeing to marry her husband's murderer, Synorix. Le Sueur shows the moment when Camma, having taken a sip from the poisoned wedding cup, extends it to Synorix, ensuring both his death and hers. A statue of the goddess Diana, based on an ancient marble sculpture brought to the Louvre from the royal palace at Fontainebleau in 1602, presides over the drama. Such narratives of moral exempla from ancient history and the Bible were popular among Le Sueur's private clientele of royal officials and wealthy financiers.

Oil on canvas

171.8 x 125.7 cm (67⅝ x 49½ in.)

M. Theresa B. Hopkins Fund 48.16

Philippe de Champaigne

French, 1602–1674

Reverend Father Giovanni Antonio Philippini, 1651

After moving to Paris from his native Brussels early in his career, Philippe de Champaigne enjoyed prestigious appointments and commissions from the French court, most notably from Louis XIII, Cardinal Richelieu, and Marie de' Medici, the Queen Mother. Though an important painter of religious histories, Champaigne was in high demand as a portraitist because of his adeptness at capturing a sitter's likeness and, at the same time, suggesting a certain spiritual inner life.

Champaigne made two versions of *Reverend Father Giovanni Antonio Philippini*, one for himself and one for the sitter. This painting was in Champaigne's personal collection at the time of his death, while the other was bequeathed by Philippini to the Roman church at San Martino ai Monti, which he had helped restore during his tenure there as prior.

Depicting Philippini at bust length, the painter's favored format in the mid-1640s, Champaigne turned the sitter's body slightly to one side but directed his gaze outward. He often included a stone parapet, as he did here, to create a sense of depth and exhibit his virtuosic ability to render different materials. The inscription on the marble slab states that Philippini belonged to the Carmelite order.

Champaigne's role as court painter to Marie de' Medici, an ardent Catholic instrumental in bringing the Carmelites to Paris, helped him secure commissions from prominent religious figures such as Philippini. Champaigne himself was also devout, especially later in life, and his relatively austere style and restrained palette might reflect his strong religious convictions.

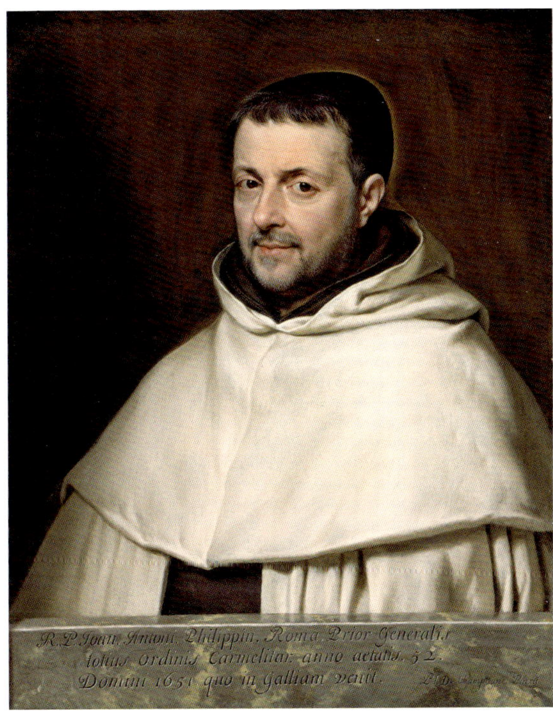

Oil on canvas

73.3 x 59.7 cm (28⅞ x 23½ in.)

Bequest of William A. Coolidge 1993.35

Claude Lorrain (Claude Gellée)
French (active in Rome), 1600–1682
Apollo and the Muses on Mount Helicon, 1680

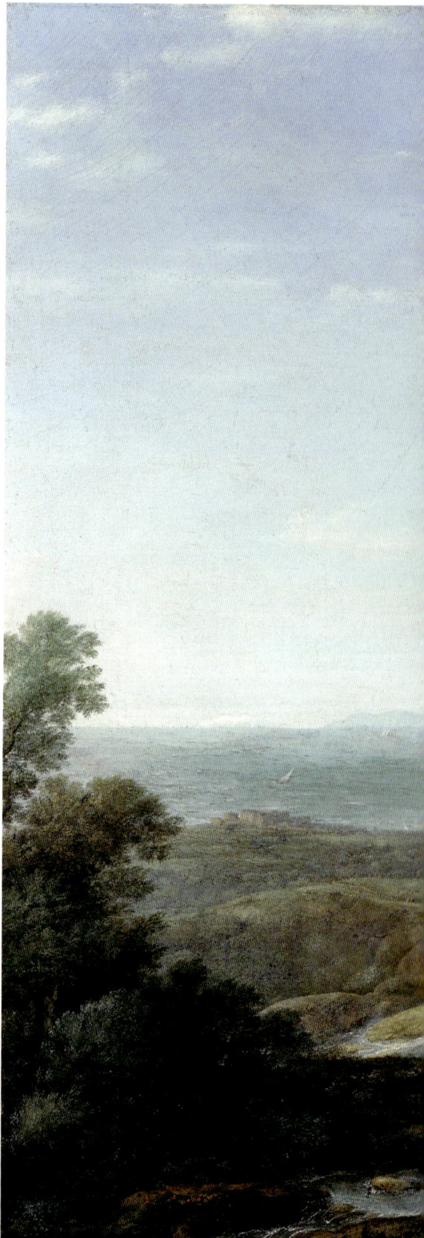

The Frenchman Claude Lorrain spent his entire career in Rome, painting idyllic landscapes bathed in atmospheric light. This particular scene depicts the god Apollo and the nine muses of Greek mythology. Claude's visits to the environs of Rome inspired the painting's carefully balanced fusion of countryside and coast. The mountain at right refers at once to Parnassus, site of the Temple of Apollo, and to Helicon, home to the muses and the Hippocrene fountain—the source of artistic creativity unearthed by a kick from Pegasus, the mythical winged horse seen at upper right. Apollo and the muses gather near a temple that resembles one of Claude's favorite motifs, the Temple of the Sibyl in the ancient town of Tivoli, about twenty miles from Rome. The figures of Clio, the muse of history, and Calliope, the muse of epic poetry, were adapted from a fresco by Raphael in the Vatican Stanze. Claude's drawing in the *Liber Veritatis*, where he recorded all his new paintings, indicates the composition originally included birds in the sky, a counterbalance to Apollo's sacred swans in the river below.

This painting was commissioned by Lorenzo Onofrio Colonna, Duke of Paliano and Grand Constable of Naples, an important patron of the artist. Colonna wanted to pair it with a painting already in his collection, *The Judgment of Paris*, by Claude's contemporaries in Rome, Gaspard Dughet and Carlo Maratti. Although Claude began his preparations for the composition in 1674, the painting was not finished until six years later. In a letter from 1679, the artist confirmed he had completed his patron's request to include the temple, Pegasus, and the wooded area in the foreground.

Oil on canvas
99.7 x 136.5 cm (39¼ x 53¾ in.)
Picture Fund 12.1050

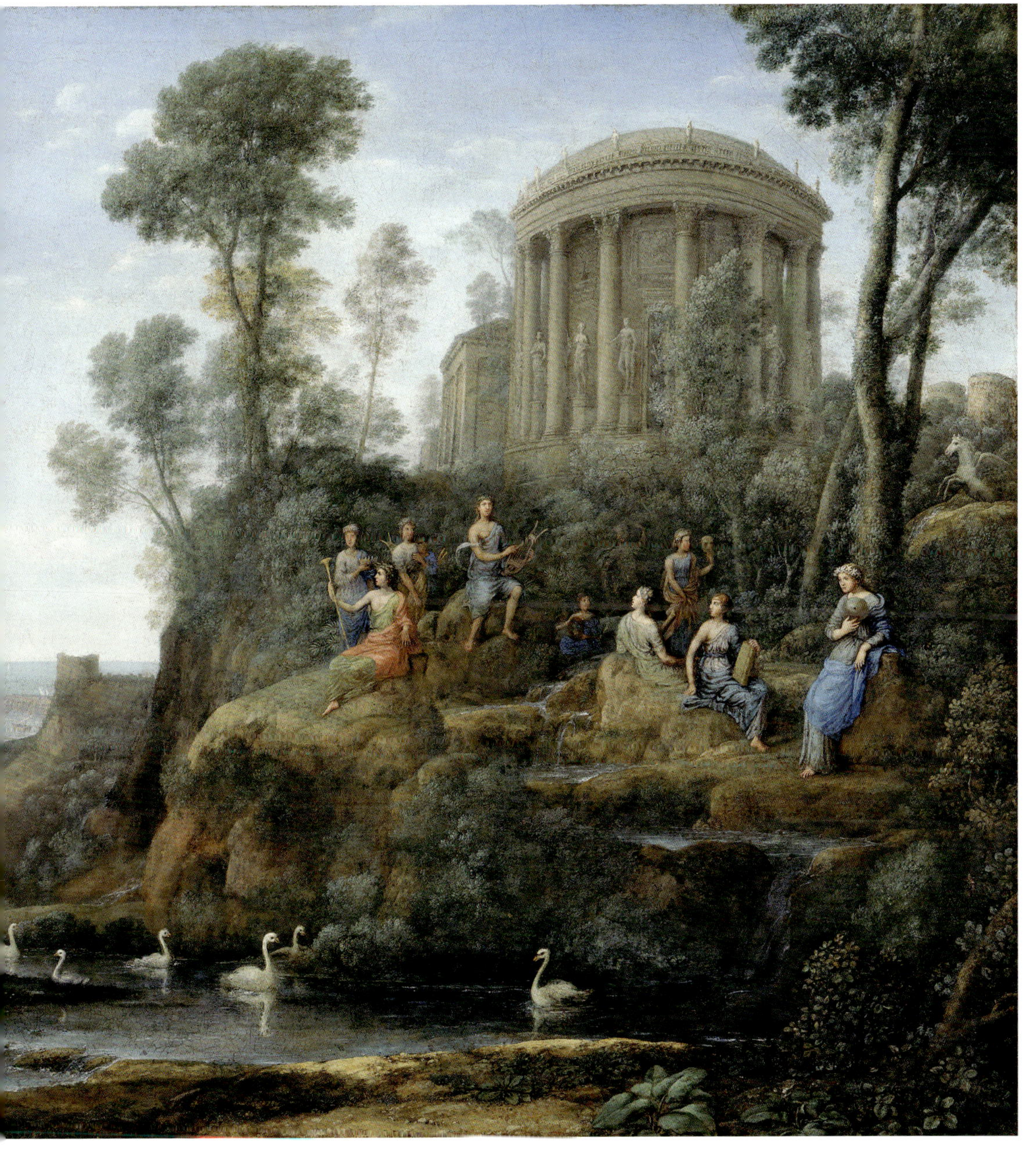

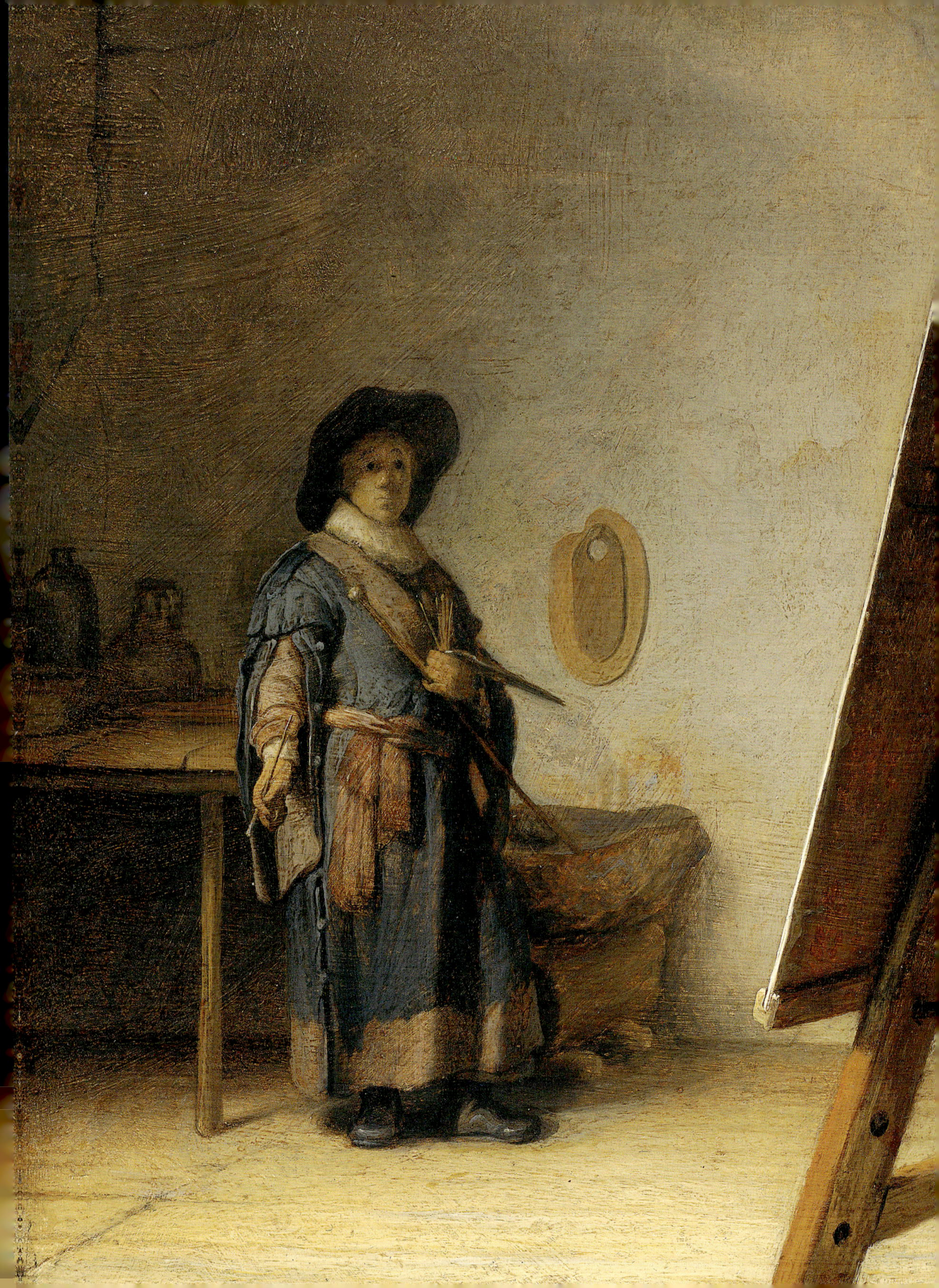

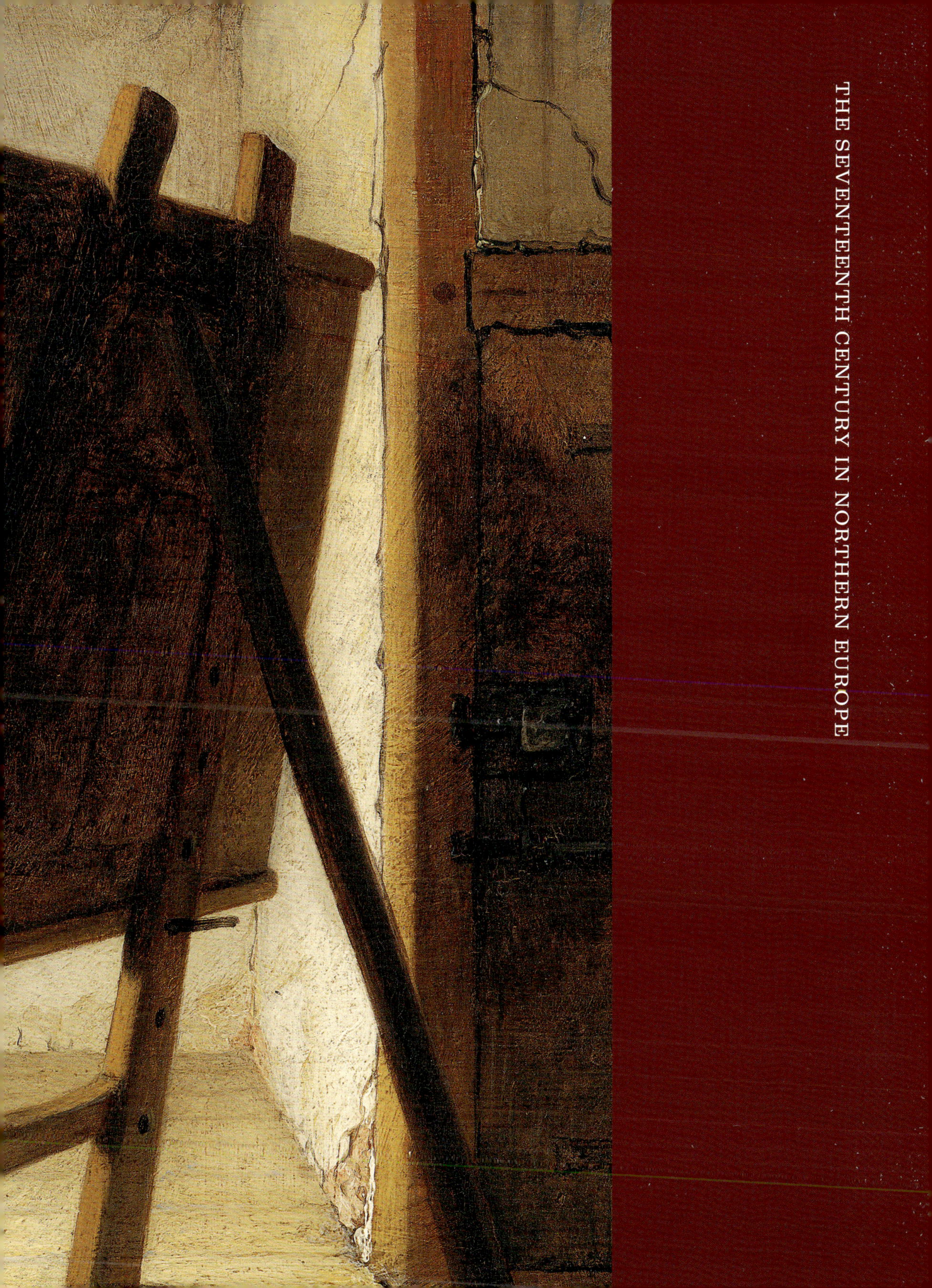
THE SEVENTEENTH CENTURY IN NORTHERN EUROPE

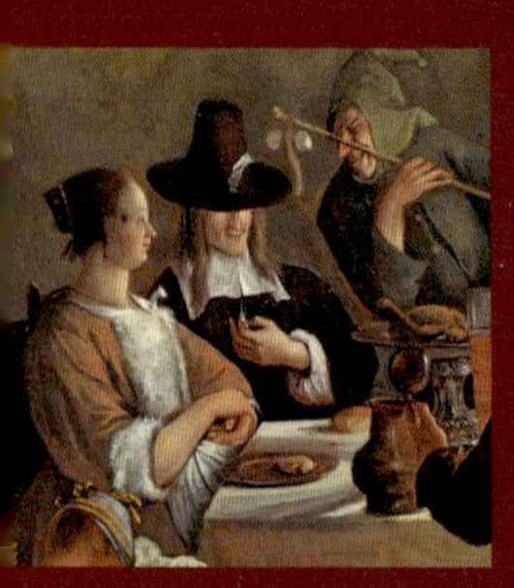
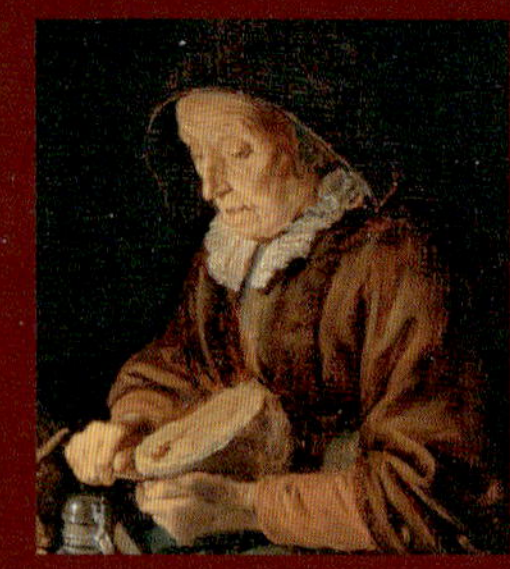
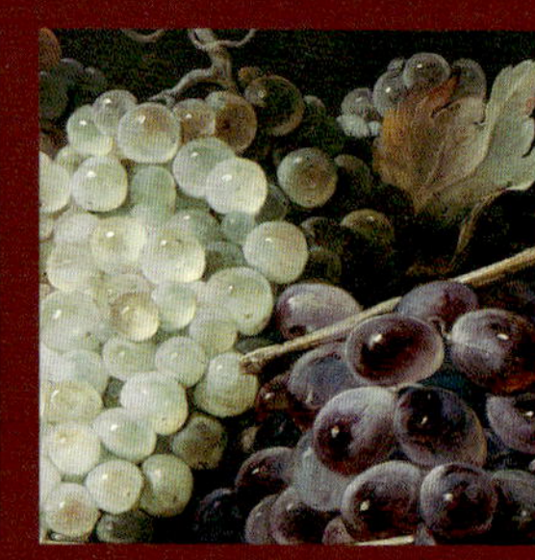
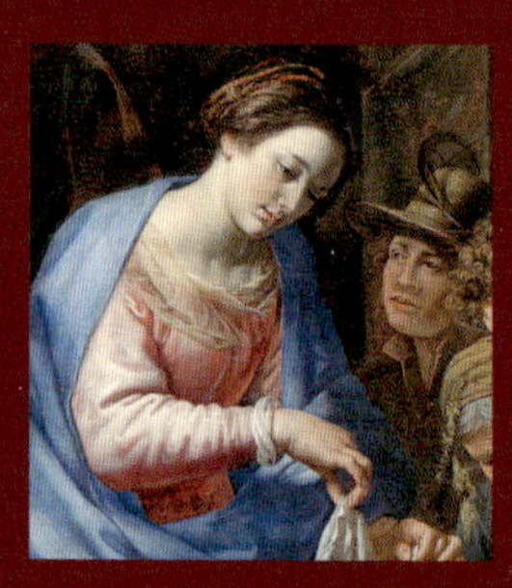
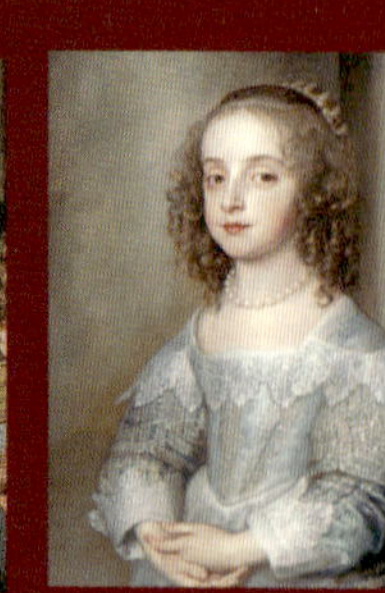

The Seventeenth Century in Northern Europe

In 1648, the division of the Netherlands between the Protestant north and the Catholic south was officially recognized. The so-called United Provinces, or Dutch Republic, became independent and Protestant. The south remained under Catholic Hapsburg rule through governors appointed by the king of Spain.

Peter Paul Rubens, who worked for the Hapsburg court but was based in the major arts center of Antwerp, is the towering figure in the story of seventeenth-century Flemish art. Humanist, diplomat, and director of a studio whose artistic output was enormous, he traversed Europe, painting for sovereigns while trying to make peace. In addition, he worked for the Catholic Church, who commissioned altarpieces to replace those destroyed in the religious turmoil of the previous decades. Many Flemish artists of the time either trained or collaborated with Rubens, including Anthony van Dyck, Jacob Jordaens, and Frans Snyders. Even the style of German sculptor Georg Petel would be forever changed after meeting the great Rubens. Other Flemish artists worked in purposeful contrast to Rubens's full-blown, sensuous, dramatic, and learned paintings. Theodoor van Loon's style, for example, reflected the naturalism of Caravaggio, with its strong light effects and large-scale rustic figures.

Caravaggio's influence was also to be found in the work of artists from Utrecht, a city in the center of the Dutch Republic that had a sizable Catholic community with connections to Rome. In the early years of the century, these Utrecht artists were among the few Dutch painters who went to Italy. After their Roman sojourn, they returned north, bringing with them the types of subject matter, dramatic lighting, and large half-length figures pushed close to the picture plane that characterized much of Caravaggio's work.

For the most part, though, the northern Netherlands was Calvinist, and religious imagery was largely banned from churches. Political power was divided between representative assemblies and a hereditary leader—the stadtholders from the House of Orange. Therefore, unlike elsewhere in Europe, artistic commissions did not come primarily from the church or state. Paintings were made mostly for the open market. Because of its might as a naval power, its stature as the world's entrepôt, and its role as a financial innovator, the Dutch Republic had the most robust economy in seventeenth-century Europe, and painting was a commodity like much else. Artists tended to specialize so that they could capture a segment of the art-buying public. Available at all price points, art was made for and enjoyed not only by the wealthy but also by most other levels of society as well.

History painting remained the most respected type of art production. Early in his career, Rembrandt left his native Leiden to study with the renowned history painter Pieter Lastman in Amsterdam. On his return to his hometown, Rembrandt produced paintings and prints using his own face to study emotions as well as his experience in his studio to explore the theme of the artist at work. After a few years, the ambitious young Rembrandt returned to Amsterdam to seek his fame and fortune. He began by executing portrait commissions in Hendrick van Uylenburgh's workshop. Portraiture was an artist's bread and butter, and in the seventeenth century, likenesses were painted that delineated not only a sitter's features, but also implied the subject's social standing and attempted to capture his or her inner character. Once Rembrandt's reputation had been established as the preeminent portraitist in the city, he could concentrate on becoming a history painter.

Whereas landscape and still-life elements could be found in earlier paintings, they now came into their own. Paintings of daily life and, especially still lifes, appeared in the southern Netherlands, but because of market conditions, these and other new types of subject matter were most notably produced in the north. Landscapes, marines, still lifes, architectural and city views, and genre scenes were turned out in numbers never before seen.

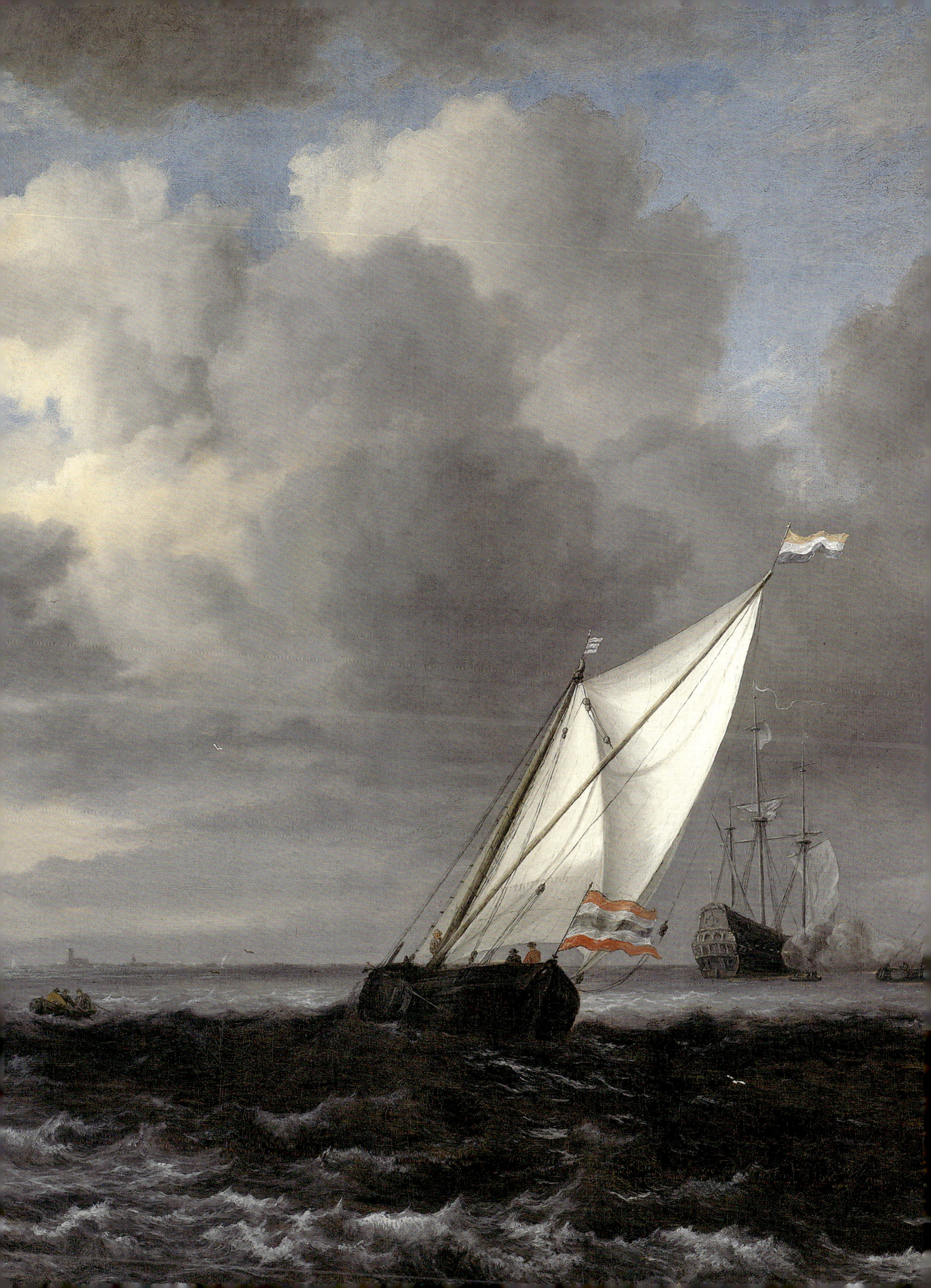

Frans Snyders

Flemish, 1579–1657

Still Life with Fruit, Wanli Porcelain, and Squirrel,
1616

Frans Snyders must have painted this exquisite still life for a wealthy patron of discerning taste. Prices in the seventeenth-century art market in Northern Europe were often influenced by the time it took to complete a work. The extraordinary precision with which Snyders painted this extravagant display of luscious fruits and fine tableware was the product of careful study and meticulous technique. His brushwork is practically invisible. While this is in part due to skill, it is also a function of the copper support; its smooth metallic surface allowed painters to achieve remarkable detail and brilliant color. Copper was, however, more expensive than canvas or panel. At roughly two feet by three feet, this still life would have been extremely costly.

Exceptionally well preserved, the MFA's painting demonstrates trademark characteristics of Snyders's still lifes. He arranged objects deliberately according to juxtapositions of cool and warm tones, light and shadow, and natural and man-made forms. Red strawberries rest in a mounted blue-and-white Wanli bowl, and green and purple grapes are piled atop a silver-gilt tazza. A German stoneware tankard, *façon de Venise* glasses, and an elaborately carved knife are among the luxury goods, objects that appear in other works by Snyders. Not all of the elements are neatly consigned to the composition's center. Those at the edges are cropped, suggesting the assemblage continues beyond the frame.

Snyders was not exclusively a painter of still lifes. In Antwerp, where collaboration between artists was frequent, he often worked with notable painters, contributing, for example, animals, fruits, and flowers to the large canvases of Rubens.

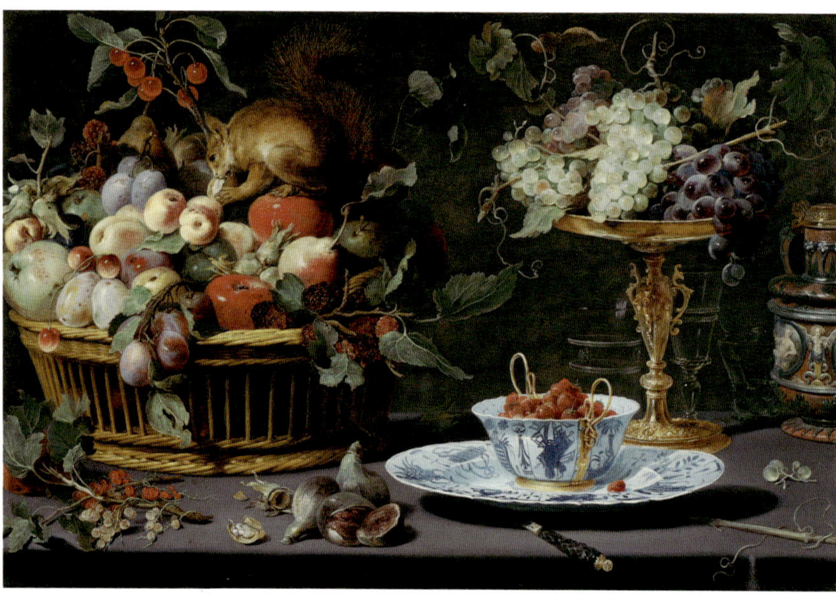

Oil on copper
56 x 84 cm
(22 x 33⅛ in.)
M. and M. Karolik Fund
and Frank Brewer
Bemis Fund 1993.566

Peter Paul Rubens
Flemish, 1577–1640
Mulay Ahmad, about 1609

Over the course of his long career, Peter Paul Rubens copied portraits by other painters. This portrait of Mulay Ahmad, son of King Mulay Hasan of Tunis, is based on a painting by the sixteenth-century Netherlandish artist Jan Cornelisz. Vermeyen. Rubens evidently prized this painted copy, for it was still in his possession at the time of his death some three decades later. The artist likely used the work as inspiration for African and Middle Eastern figures in his history paintings. The Moorish king in two versions of Rubens's *Adoration of the Magi* (now at the Prado Museum, Madrid, and St. John's Church, Malines, Belgium), for example, strongly resembles this portrait's sitter.

Vermeyen probably sketched Mulay Ahmad during his journey to Tunis in 1535 as part of Charles V's crusade against the Turks. In addition to portraying the sitter, the artist recorded the major battles of the Holy Roman Emperor's campaign there, and subsequently transformed his drawings into cartoons for tapestries made to celebrate the triumph of Christianity over the Ottomans.

Rubens may have seen Vermeyen's painting of Mulay Ahmad in the early seventeenth century, although the composition is known today only from Vermeyen's own etching of it. In that print, the prince's head appears disproportionately large, a sign meant to emphasize his importance. Rubens's copy renders Mulay Ahmad with a subtle, reflective expression and more naturalistic proportions, although the artist has elongated the face, torso, and limbs to create a regal, dignified image. The turban and tunic—executed in the artist's exuberant brushwork—reflect Rubens's delight in describing exotic garb, an interest manifest in his 1613/14 sketchbook of costumes. The portrait also highlights Rubens's ability to capture the coloristic nuances of black skin tones.

Oil on panel
99.7 x 71.5 cm (39¼ x 28⅛ in.)
M. Theresa B. Hopkins Fund 40.2

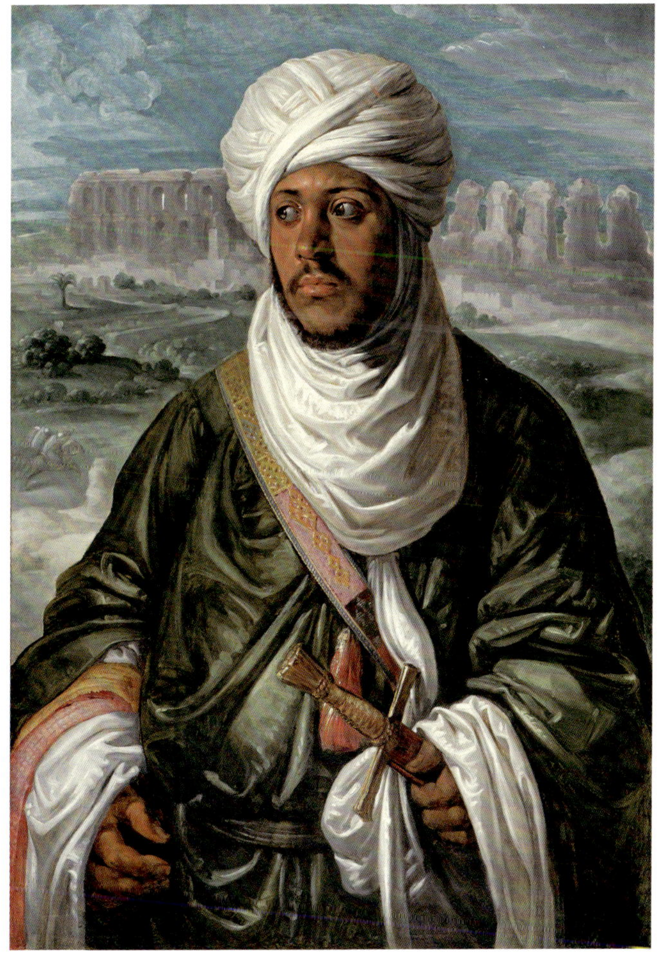

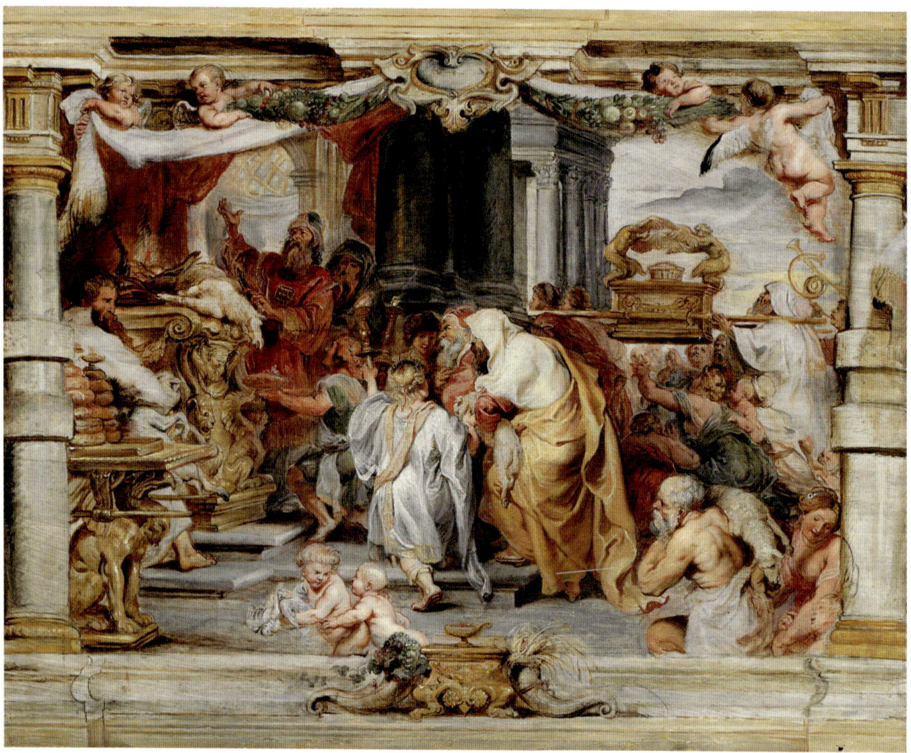

Peter Paul Rubens
Flemish, 1577–1640
The Sacrifice of the Old Covenant, about 1626

Peter Paul Rubens painted this highly finished oil sketch, or *modello*, in preparation for an extensive set of tapestries commissioned by the archduchess Isabella for a chapel in Madrid's Convent of Las Descalzas Reales. After her husband's death in 1621, Isabella took up the habit of the Poor Clares, the Catholic religious order, remaining dedicated to this convent where she had studied as a child. Upon her approval, Rubens and his workshop enlarged the sketches to full-size cartoons that served as a guide for weavers in Brussels. The tapestries generated remain in the convent's collection to this day.

The Triumph of the Eucharist, as the tapestry series is known, celebrates the consecration of bread and wine, one of the seven sacraments of the Catholic Church. For this *modello*, Rubens orchestrated a complex assembly of figures to evoke an Old Testament scene of sacrifice, foreshadowing Christ's sacrifice for humankind. In the center foreground, a low-footed table flanked by cornucopias of grapes (wine) and wheat (bread) represents the Eucharist, which replaced such sacrificial ceremonies in the New Testament. While the scene does not appear to depict a particular biblical passage, the extent to which Rubens adhered to details described in the Bible—the Ark of the Covenant as gilded acacia wood, with two cherubs facing each other, their wings touching, and the table of shewbread at left, also of gilded acacia wood, with a rim around its edge and poles attached—evinces his careful reading of the texts.

Ingeniously, the scenes he depicted for the tapestries are themselves illusionistic tapestries set in architectural frames. Here, across the top, cherubs carry the feigned tapestry from a central cartouche to columns at each side, around which the fabric wraps. The sketch also shows signs of Rubens's creative process. He drew the woman at lower right but colored only the portion of her body included in the feigned tapestry. He made further adjustments to the positions of the cornucopias and the cherubs' heads. This small work reflects the artist's virtuosity in coloristically uniting an elaborate composition and describing a myriad of details with an economic and sure touch.

Oil on panel
70.5 x 87.6 cm (27¾ x 34½ in.)
Gift of William A. Coolidge 1985.839

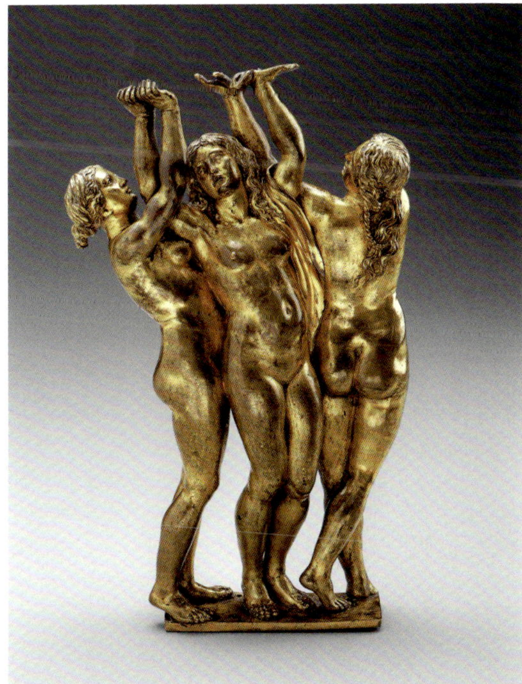

Georg Petel
German, about 1601–1634
The Three Graces, about 1624

Born in Bavaria, Georg Petel traveled extensively during his short life and career. Early visits to Antwerp and Rome exposed him to two major artists of the Baroque period, Rubens and Bernini. While in Antwerp in 1624, Petel most certainly saw Rubens's *Three Graces*, painted around 1620–21, now in the Paintings Gallery at the Academy of Fine Arts Vienna. Petel's sculpture of the same subject, in relief, closely follows Rubens's painting. The translation of the painted form into a sculpted one allowed Petel to explore the relationship between two-dimensional and three-dimensional designs and representation.

The three female figures, with their voluptuous bodies, show Petel's debt to the Flemish master's style, and their broad faces and substantial forms reflect his training and origins in Germany. Standing on a small platform, the women's curving bodies reach upward. Their entwined arms likely supported another feature, perhaps a basket of fruit or flowers or a shell. A version of this sculpture in ivory, also by Petel, is documented but no longer exists, prompting questions of which version came first. While Petel is best known as a carver of ivory, the high quality and finish of this relief are a testament to his skill in bronze.

Gilded bronze
30.5 x 19.1 x 5.1 cm (12 x 7½ x 2 in.)
Gift of John Goelet in honor of Hanns Swarzenski 1976.842

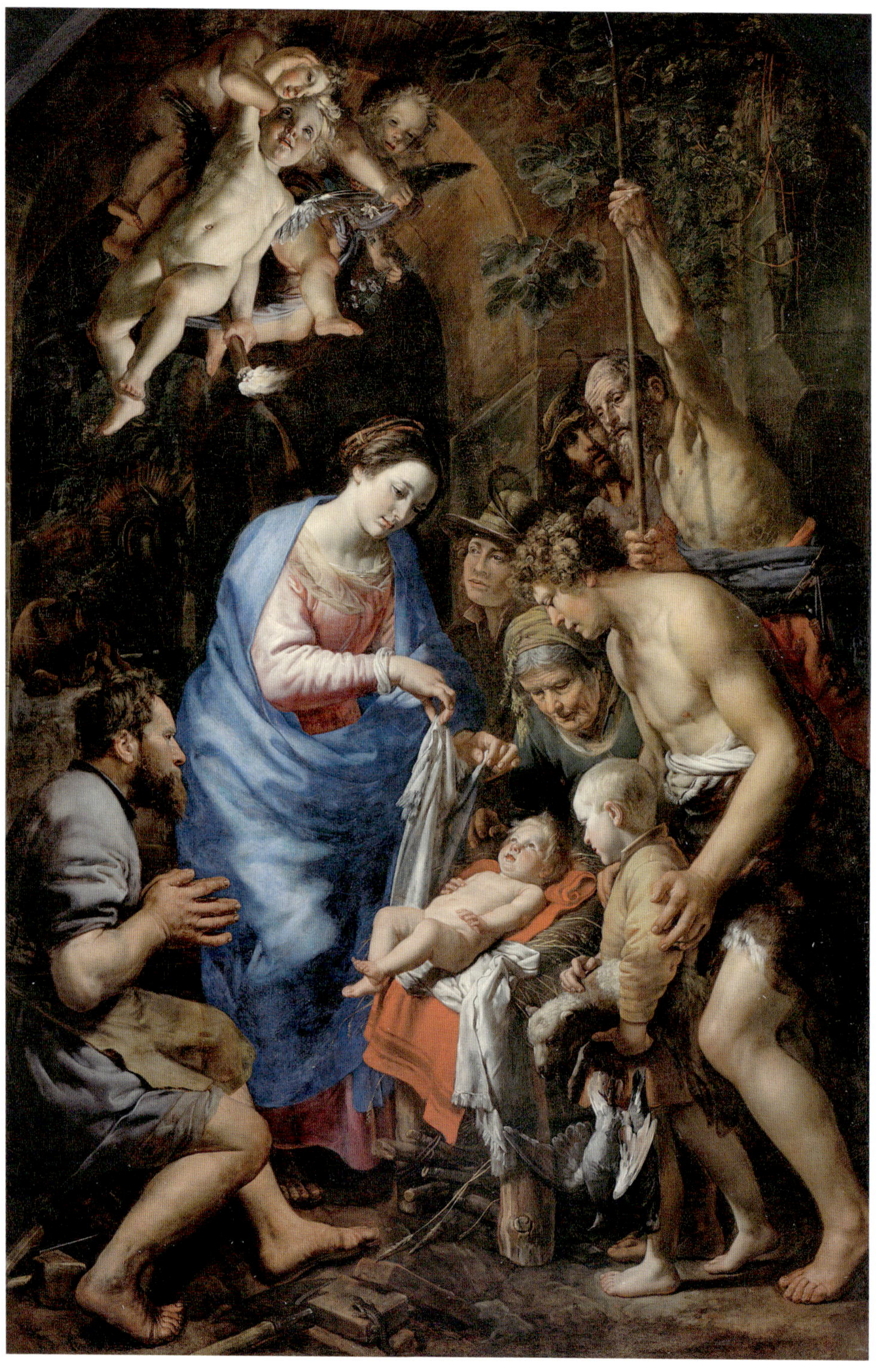

Theodoor van Loon

Flemish, about 1581/82–1667

The Adoration of the Shepherds, 1620s

As court artist to Archduke Albert and Archduchess Isabella, Theodoor van Loon was expected to execute works that would further their mandate as upholders of Hapsburg rule in the southern Netherlands and rigorous defenders of the Catholic faith. In this painting, almost identical to an altarpiece by the artist in the Chapel of the Holy Blood in Bruges, Van Loon relates the biblical event simply and legibly, in a manner intended to stimulate the faithful in their devotion. Reflecting his sojourn in Rome between 1602 and 1608, where he would have seen Caravaggio's new, revolutionary art firsthand, Van Loon's large, firmly modeled figures, engaged in clear and focused actions and imbued with solemn gravity, were perfectly in accord with the dictates of the Council of Trent and the aims of the Catholic Reformation.

The number of depictions of the Adoration of the Shepherds increased in the first decades of the seventeenth century as attention shifted from the Holy Family alone in the stable to the moment when the Christ Child's divine humanity was revealed for the first time. The Virgin Mary's act of lifting the white swaddling cloth from her son recalls the unveiling of the Host during the Mass, and the wheat on which he lies is symbolic of the bread of the Eucharist. Below Joseph's left foot, a lizard, reputedly drawn to light, may allude to Christ as the light of salvation. Mary's dominant role, indicative of the Catholic glorification of the Virgin in the face of Protestant resistance, is reflected in her placement—her action marks the center of the painting—and the fact that her face, salmon-colored dress, and blue cloak are among the most brightly illuminated areas in the composition. Although nothing is known about the commission for this painting, it reflects the Marian devotion so central to the archdukes' piety.

Oil on canvas

250 x 167 cm (98½ x 65¾ in.)

Charles H. Bayley Picture and Painting Fund 2000.1035

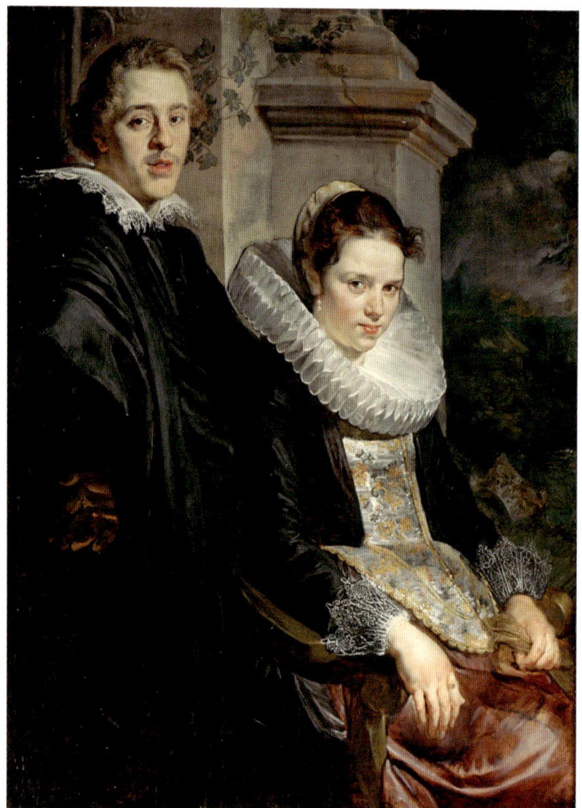

Jacob Jordaens

Flemish, 1593–1678

Portrait of a Young Married Couple, 1621–22

Unlike Rubens and Anthony van Dyck, who worked for royalty and the aristocracy, Jacob Jordaens found his patrons mostly among Antwerp's prosperous middle class. This marriage portrait depicts an affluent young couple dressed in costly and fashionable attire and placed before a bit of stately architecture. Ivy, visible behind the couple, was a common symbol of marriage, implying attachment and affection. Suggestive of his dominant position, the man stands higher than his seated spouse and holds one arm akimbo. The young woman wears a wedding ring on her right index finger, as was the custom among stylish cosmopolitans. In her other hand, she holds a pair of gloves, an expensive possession associated with love and marriage that may have been a wedding present from her husband.

In the first decades of the twentieth century, this painting entered the MFA's collection as a work by Rubens. Jordaens was influenced by Rubens throughout his career and collaborated with the older master on several large projects. Around 1609, shortly after his marriage, Rubens painted a portrait of himself and his wife, Isabella Brant, in a honeysuckle bower, which probably inspired this composition by Jordaens.

Oil on panel

124.5 x 92.4 cm (49 x 36⅜ in.)

Robert Dawson Evans Collection 17.3232

Anthony van Dyck
Flemish, 1599–1641
Princess Mary, Daughter of Charles I, about 1637

Anthony van Dyck was the premier portraitist of the seventeenth century not only in his native Flanders but also among the upper classes of Italy, the Netherlands, and England. After his first visit to London in the winter of 1620–21, he returned in the spring of 1632 at the invitation of King Charles I, who appointed the artist "Principal Painter in Ordinary to their Majesties." The style, refinement, and grace of Van Dyck's portraits provided a striking contrast to the strict conventions and hard execution of earlier British portraiture.

Van Dyck painted the single figure of Princess Mary, eldest daughter of Charles I and his wife, Henrietta Maria, several times between 1637 and 1641. This painting is thought to be the earliest of the series. The poised young princess stands with hands at her waist, one hand cradling the other, echoing the pose Van Dyck used in his earlier portrait of Queen Henrietta Maria (now at the Metropolitan Museum of Art). Bravura brushwork depicts the sheen of the girl's blue satin dress, the intricate details of the silver braid along the hem of the garment, and the fine lace on the cuffs, collar, and apron. Leading strings attached to her gown emphasize her youth, belied by her noble bearing. The gold textile behind the princess appears in a number of Van Dyck's portraits, suggesting it was a studio prop. An autograph version of this painting is at Hampton Court. It has so far been impossible to determine which was the painting Charles I referred to in 1647 as "the Originall of My eldest Daughter (it hangs in this chamber of the board next to the Chimney)."

Oil on canvas
132.1 x 106.3 cm (52 x 41⅞ in.)
Given in memory of Governor Alvan T. Fuller by the Fuller Foundation 61.391

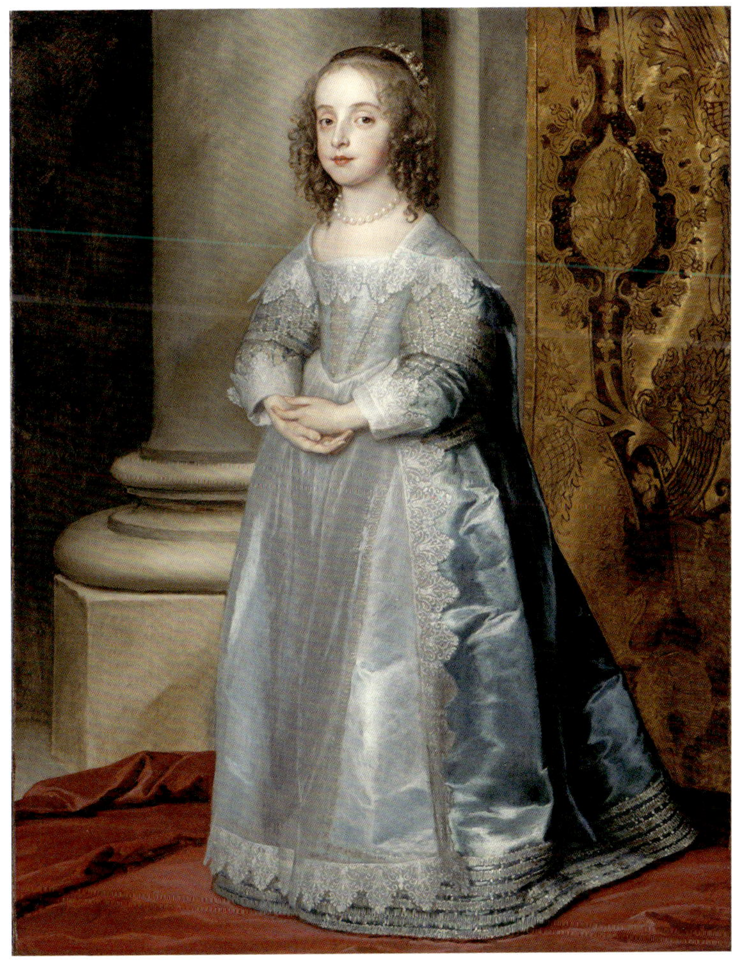

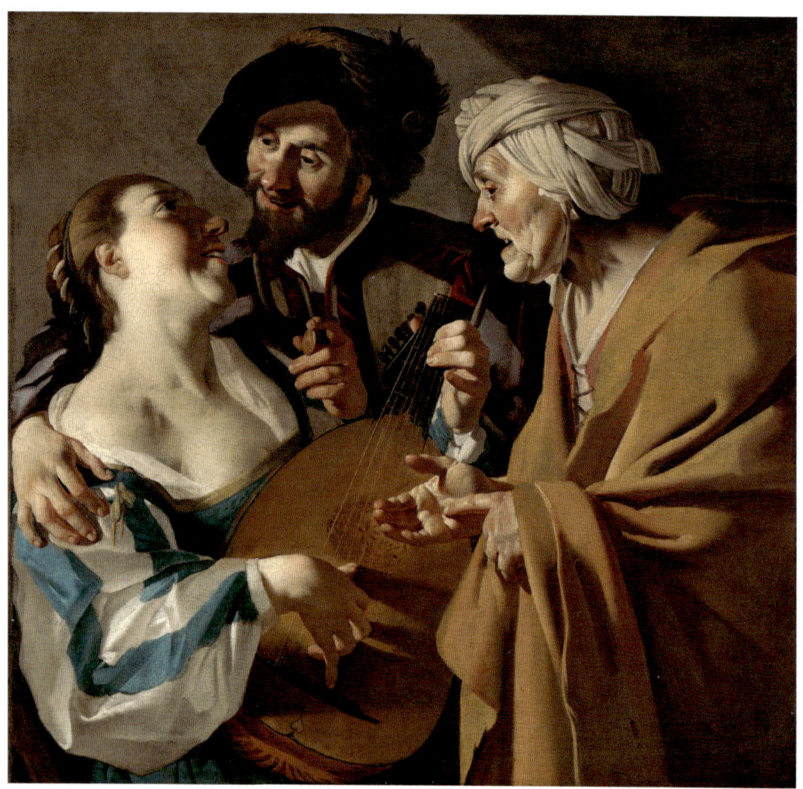

Dirck van Baburen
Dutch, 1590 to 1595–1624
The Procuress, 1622

In Dirck van Baburen's *The Procuress*, an amorous client solicits a voluptuous young woman while a turbaned procuress demands the coin he proffers. Brothel scenes emerged in Netherlandish art in the sixteenth century, notably in depictions of the biblical parable of the Prodigal Son squandering his fortune. A century later, genre painters dispensed with any religious connotation, accentuating instead the more titillating aspects. Van Baburen's young woman, with her marked décolletage and flirtatious smile, strums a lute. Such a figure could embody wantonness and frivolity, in addition to invoking the popular, and tamer, association between music and love.

The bright palette, theatrical garb, and overall vitality of the composition have little to do with the miserable conditions of seventeenth-century brothels. Instead, the figures' animated gestures and almost caricatured appearances suggest an affinity to the staged farces favored by the Dutch elite. Comic in nature, these performances often featured prostitutes, carousers, and peasants behaving raucously.

Van Baburen turned to genre painting upon his return from Italy to the Netherlands around 1620. Like other artists from Utrecht, he had made a pilgrimage to Rome, where he was inspired by the art of Caravaggio and his followers. Van Baburen's half-length figures, placed close to the picture plane and solidly modeled using strong contrasts of light and shadow, are hallmarks of this Caravaggesque influence. This painting, or a replica of it, was owned by Johannes Vermeer's mother-in-law. Vermeer painted it in the background of two of his works: *Lady Seated at a Virginal* (National Gallery, London) and *The Concert* (stolen from the Isabella Stewart Gardner Museum, Boston, in 1990).

Oil on canvas
101.6 x 107.6 cm (40 x 42⅜ in.)
M. Theresa B. Hopkins Fund 50.2721

Pieter Lastman

Dutch, 1583–1633

***Wedding Night of Tobias and Sarah*, 1611**

One of the most important artists working in Amsterdam at the beginning of the seventeenth century, Pieter Lastman produced small, multifigured history paintings. He sojourned in Italy from 1602 to 1607. While in Rome he saw not only the boldly modeled forms and strong light effects in Caravaggio's work but also the grandly conceived copper paintings of monumental figures on a small scale by the German artist Adam Elsheimer. On his return to the Netherlands, Lastman combined these influences with his own predilection for depicting the dramatic climax of a narrative.

Lastman was drawn to the apocryphal story of Tobit and his family. This painting depicts the wedding night of Tobit's son, Tobias, and his wife, Sarah, in faraway Media. Each of Sarah's seven previous husbands had been killed by a demon before the union could be consummated. Lastman seizes on the pivotal moment of the story: on the instruction of the angel Raphael, who had accompanied Tobias on his journey, the boy burns the liver and heart of a fish to drive away the demon, freeing Sarah from the curse. Lastman shows the angel dramatically wrestling with the demon, who rises from the smoke of the fire.

The substantial figures (albeit on a small scale) described by careful contrasts of light and shade, the vivid colors, and the profusion of details that help set the scene—for example, the scattered flowers on the floor and the veil by the candle signaling the couple's recent marriage—are all characteristic of Lastman's work. Many years later, Lastman's most celebrated pupil, Rembrandt, would eliminate all particulars and depict a close-up of a woman in bed in a composition that likely derived from this painting.

Oil on panel

41.2 x 57.8 cm (16¼ x 22¾ in.)

Juliana Cheney Edwards Collection 62.985

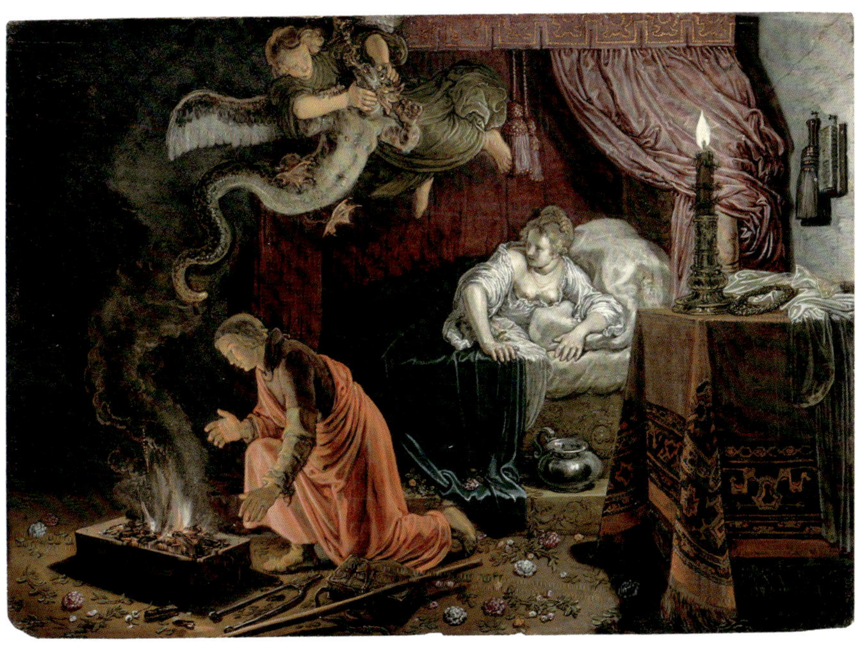

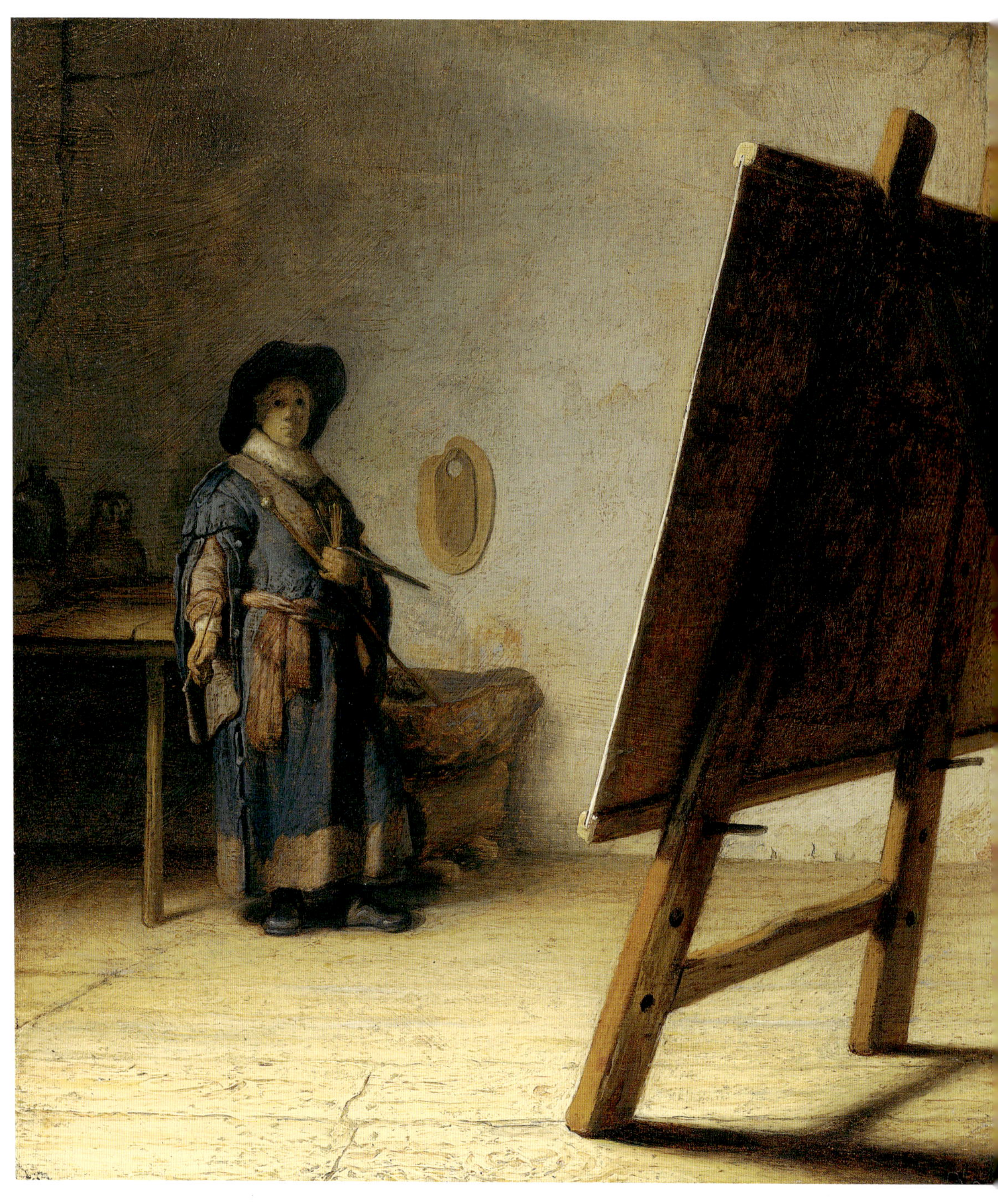

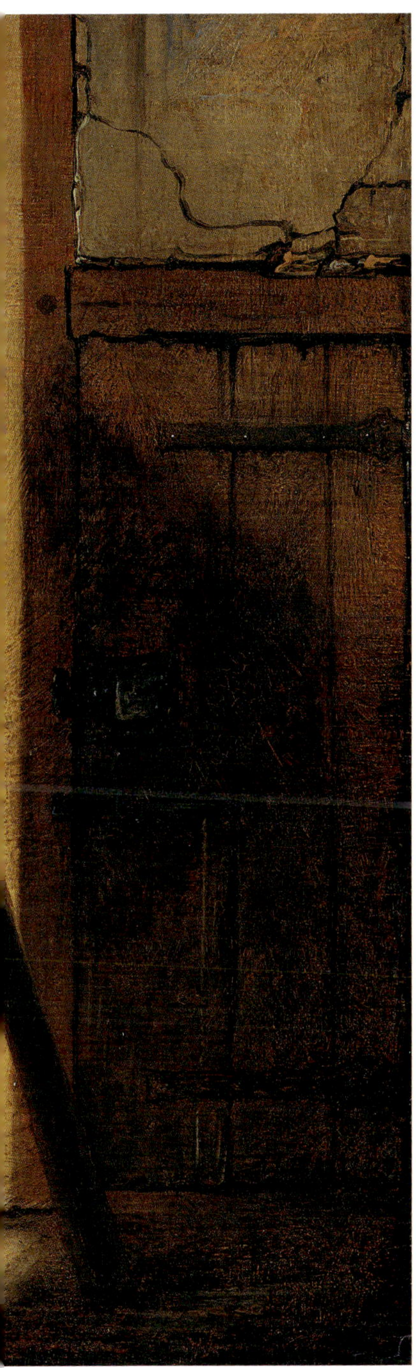

Rembrandt Harmensz. van Rijn

Dutch, 1606–1669

Artist in His Studio, about 1628

In this early work by Rembrandt, a young artist stands in shadow at a distance from a large, brightly lit panel viewed from the back. This artist is clothed in a rather fanciful oversize tabard against the chill of a damp studio with walls of peeling plaster. He holds brushes and a palette; another palette hangs on the back wall. Behind him are vials and jars for his painting oils and varnishes, and next to him is a stone for grinding pigments. The crossbar of the easel holding the panel shows wear from its use as a footrest, implying that the artist usually sits while painting, though no chair is visible. This detail is telling: the artist is not in the process of executing a work of art, so what is he doing? Given the discrepancy in size between figure and panel, and thanks to the strong contrast in lighting, Rembrandt dramatizes the daunting experience of artistic creation.

The painting perfectly represents the hallmarks of the Dutch master's early style, with its strong chiaroscuro, harmonious use of a limited color palette, and evocative descriptions of surfaces and materials. Whether or not the artist depicted is meant as a self-portrait, the image is certainly based on Rembrandt's working conditions at the time. Many contemporary paintings of studio scenes include accoutrements and props that hold symbolic associations or serve practical functions. By contrast, Rembrandt has stripped the space to include only what is necessary to identify it as an artist's workplace. His focus is on the painter's process. Some argue that the artist in the work is conceptualizing his composition. Seventeenth-century art theoreticians praised invention above improvisation or methodical practice. Others wonder whether he has just finished painting and has stepped back to assess his work. It is arguably this ambiguity that makes the image so captivating.

Oil on panel

24.8 x 31.7 cm (9¾ x 12½ in.)

Zoe Oliver Sherman Collection given in memory of Lillie Oliver Poor

38.1838

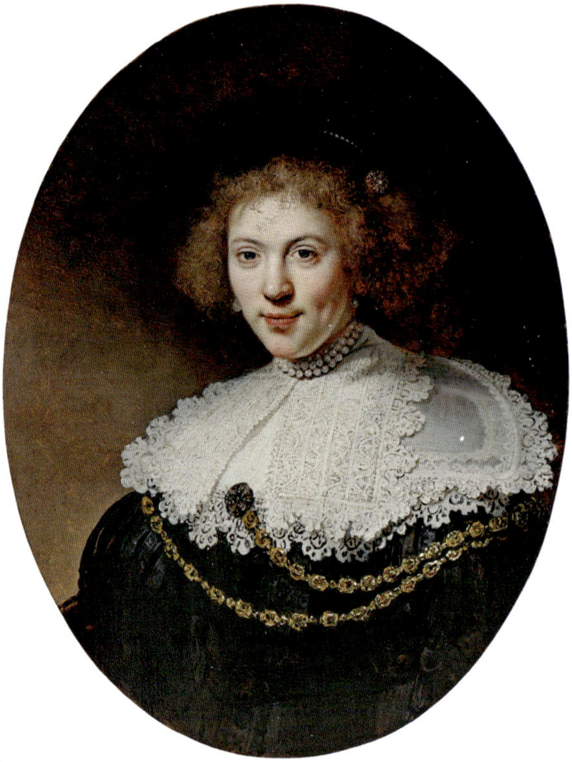

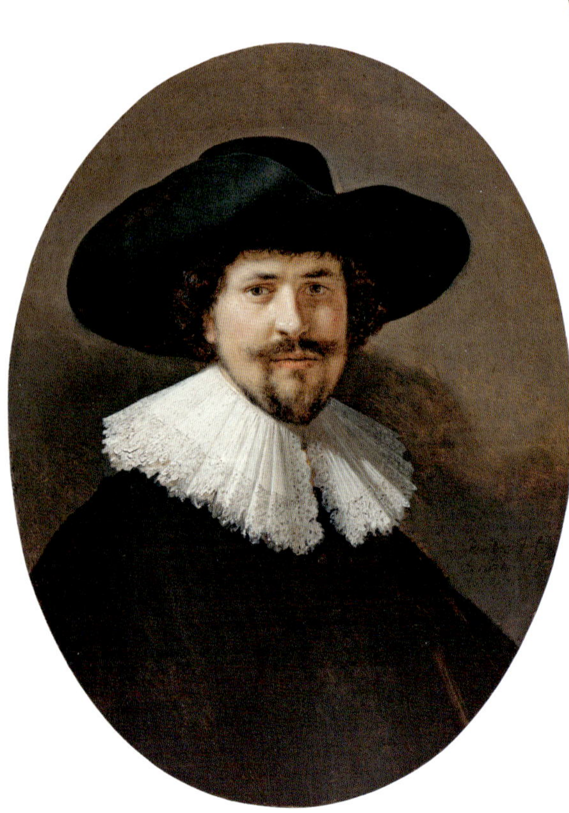

Rembrandt Harmensz. van Rijn

Dutch, 1606–1669

***Portrait of a Man Wearing a Black Hat*, 1634**

Oil on panel

69.9 x 53 cm (27½ x 20⅞ in.)

Gift of Mrs. Frederick L. Ames, in the name of Frederick L. Ames 93.1475

***Portrait of a Woman Wearing a Gold Chain*, 1634**

Oil on panel

69.5 x 53 cm (27⅜ 20⅞ in.)

Gift of Mrs. Frederick L. Ames, in the name of Frederick L. Ames 93.1474

Rembrandt painted these oval portraits shortly after he moved from his native Leiden to Amsterdam. In the thriving capital, the young artist worked with the successful art dealer Hendrick Uylenburgh, who likely secured many commissions for him from the city's well-to-do. The year 1634, inscribed at right on each panel, was perhaps Rembrandt's busiest; it has been estimated that he produced one painting per month during this time.

These oval pendants, a popular shape for paintings in the 1630s, were likely commissioned to commemorate the marriage of this young couple. The bust-length portrait format was among the least expensive and fastest to produce, not only because of the relatively small size of the painting but also because the artist did not need to paint the sitters' hands. Nevertheless, the woman's intricate brocade dress, elaborate lace collar, heavy gold chain, and precious pearls signal her wealth and social status. Unusually, the artist lavished more attention on the woman's portrait than on the man's, perhaps an indication that it was her family who paid for these fashionable images.

Rembrandt excelled at conveying sympathetic likenesses and capturing individual personalities. The woman's smile and dimple are memorable in this regard. Furthermore, the artist was a remarkable handler of paint, able to vary thickness, color, and brushwork to capture differences in materials and textures. He suggested degrees of transparency and translucency in the female sitter's lace collar through tonal juxtapositions and different opacities of paint, and emphasized its decoration with a flick of his brush. He left a small channel of the warm ground layer exposed on her throat, creating the impression of reflected light under her chin. Daringly, he scratched into the wet paint with the butt end of his brush to produce the effect of scattered light on her curls.

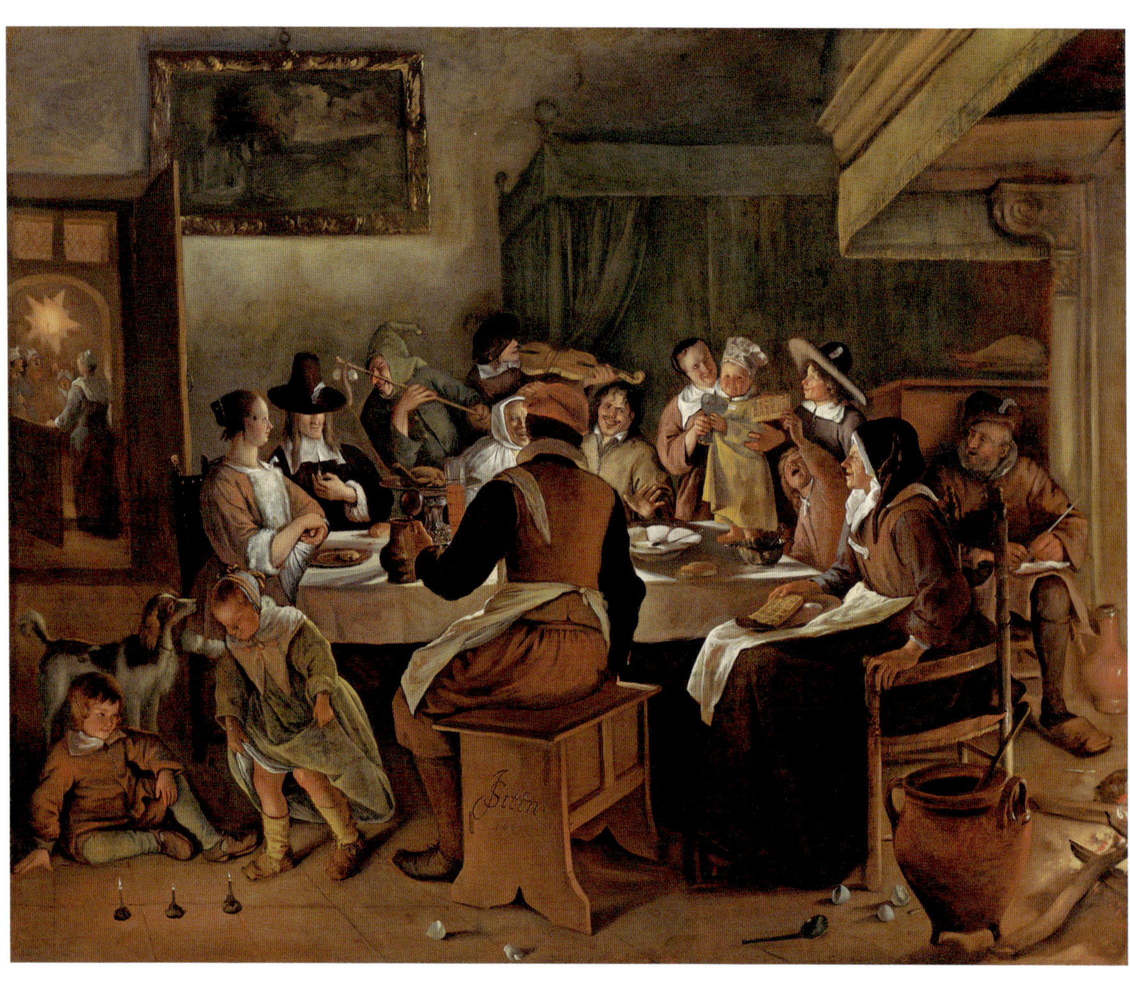

Jan Havicksz. Steen

Dutch, 1626–1679

Twelfth-Night Feast, 1662

Twelfth Night, or the Feast of the Epiphany, was traditionally celebrated in the Netherlands on January 6. It commemorates the Magi's journey in search of the baby Jesus. The Dutch Reformed Church discouraged public celebrations of the holiday, prompting Catholics like Jan Steen to gather in inns or at home to eat and carouse. For the festivities, a king was chosen by finding a bean in a specially prepared cake or by drawing lots; lottery also determined the roles of the members of his court. In Steen's depiction, these paper lots are pinned to the celebrants' clothing and hats. Unusually, the king here is the youngest child, who wears a paper crown and, with the help of his mother, holds a *roemer*, or wine glass. Once the assembled company shouts, "The king drinks!," the participants would redouble their merriment. Steen, an accomplished storyteller, was brilliant at capturing the animated gestures, smiling faces, and revelry that make the celebration palpable.

Although the artist painted this feast numerous times, this is the only instance of him showing the action by artificial light. The figure in the foreground, with his back to the viewer, blocks a candle on the table; the fire at right and the three candles at lower left illuminate the figures on the periphery. In the background, a maid opens the door to a group of singers wearing paper crowns and carrying the "star" that led the three kings to the Christ Child. To capture the nocturnal lighting, Steen expertly used a limited palette of earth colors relieved by patches of bright white.

Oil on canvas

131.1 x 164.5 cm (51⅝ x 64¾ in.)

1951 Purchase Fund 54.102

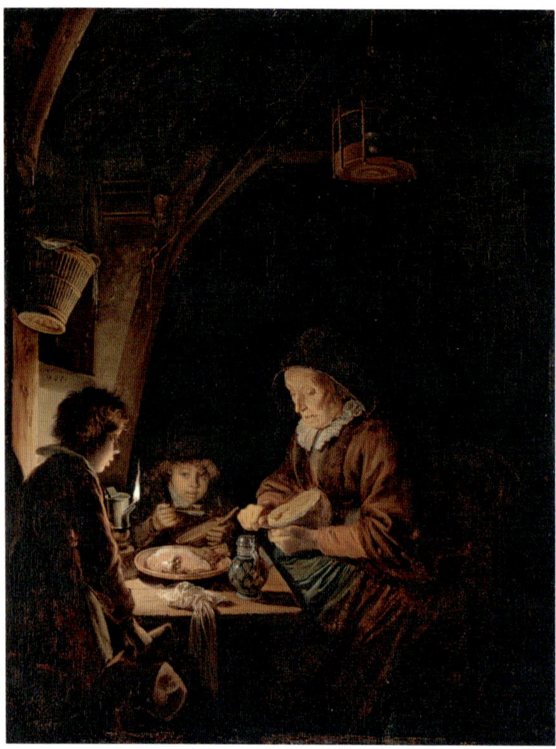

Gerrit Dou
Dutch, 1613–1675
Old Woman Cutting Bread, about 1655

Gerrit Dou, Rembrandt's first pupil, spent his entire career in his native Leiden, where he developed a meticulously detailed type of painting called *fijnschilderij* (fine painting). As early as 1641, the Dutch art theorist Philips Angel held Dou up as a paradigm to the other artists in the city. Angel noted that despite its apparently careful execution, Dou's brushwork actually exhibited a "curious looseness" that kept his paintings from appearing stiff and lifeless. The artist's mostly small-scale panels feature a profusion of expertly painted materials and textures. In *Old Woman Cutting Bread*, he displays sensitive attention to detail in the earthenware jug that reflects the candle's flame, the cloth rag hanging off the simple wooden table, the wicker basket, the old woman's wrinkles, and the tin oil lamp. Dou was also lauded for his ability to capture the effects of artificial light. This work demonstrates how he closely observed the glow of candlelight on the figures' faces and the effect of the warm light reaching into the dark interior.

Seventeenth-century images of women were often connected to the idea of domestic virtue. Among women's responsibilities were the education of the young and providing nourishment, subjects often depicted by painters and printmakers. Mealtime was an occasion for children not only to receive sustenance but also to learn important lessons in civility and appropriate behavior. The boy in the foreground, hat in hand, awaits his slice of bread; the other pauses while eating to look out at the viewer.

Dou's style astounded contemporary viewers and attracted a large number of pupils and followers. Consequently, he enjoyed a privileged position as one of the highest-paid seventeenth-century Dutch painters. Despite its commonplace subject and setting, *Old Woman Cutting Bread* belonged to the Elector Palatine Johann Wilhelm II in the late seventeenth century and was inherited by Ludwig I, King of Bavaria, in the nineteenth century.

Oil on panel
28 x 22 cm (11 x 8⅝ in.)
Henry H. and Zoe Oliver Sherman Fund 2003.71

Frans Hals
Dutch, 1581 to 1585–1666
Portrait of a Man, about 1665

Throughout the seventeenth century, art theorists discussed two distinct styles of painting: one characterized by a smooth, neat application of paint, the other by rougher, looser paint handling. Paintings in the first style invited scrutiny from up close and delighted viewers with their infinite detail. Rough painting, on the other hand, could only truly be appreciated from afar and stimulated not just the eye but also the mind. Frans Hals's portraits, characterized in 1662 by the Flemish biographer Cornelis de Bie as "very rough and bold, nimbly touched and well composed, pleasing and ingenious, and when seen from a distance seem to lack nothing but life itself," epitomize the latter.

The foremost artist working in the city of Haarlem, Hals was in his eighties when he painted this portrait. The disjointed brushwork, with slashes of white standing in for collar and cuffs and broad, curved strokes of various browns for the sitter's hair, gives the appearance of spontaneity, immediacy, and liveliness. It might seem almost abstract had Hals not so ingeniously employed it to suggest material, volume, and a moment in time. Movement is further implied by the position of the sitter's hand and the angle of his body, while depth is suggested by the man's shadow cast on the back wall.

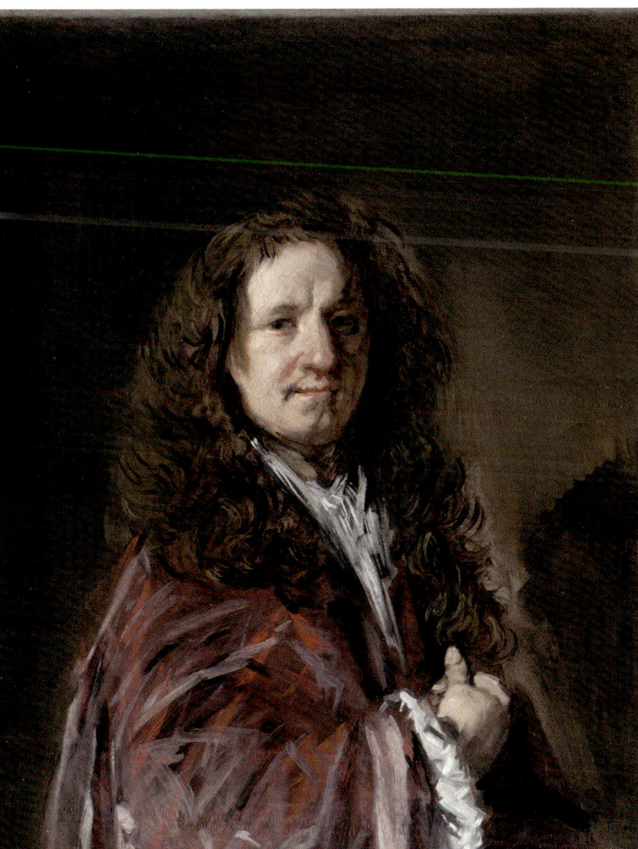

The dashing sitter wears a *Japonse rok*, a Japanese-style silk housecoat modeled on the kimono, which was worn indoors in Holland by well-to-do men. In the late seventeenth century, Dutch fashion also began to reflect the influence of French taste. The man's long hair is likely an expensive, full-bottomed wig, popular at the court of King Louis XIV. Both housecoat and wig would have indicated the subject's high status, proof that Hals attracted wealthy clients even in the last years of his life.

Oil on canvas
85.8 x 67 cm (33¾ x 26⅜ in.)
Gift of Mrs. Antonie Lilienfeld in memory of Dr. Leon Lilienfeld 66.1054

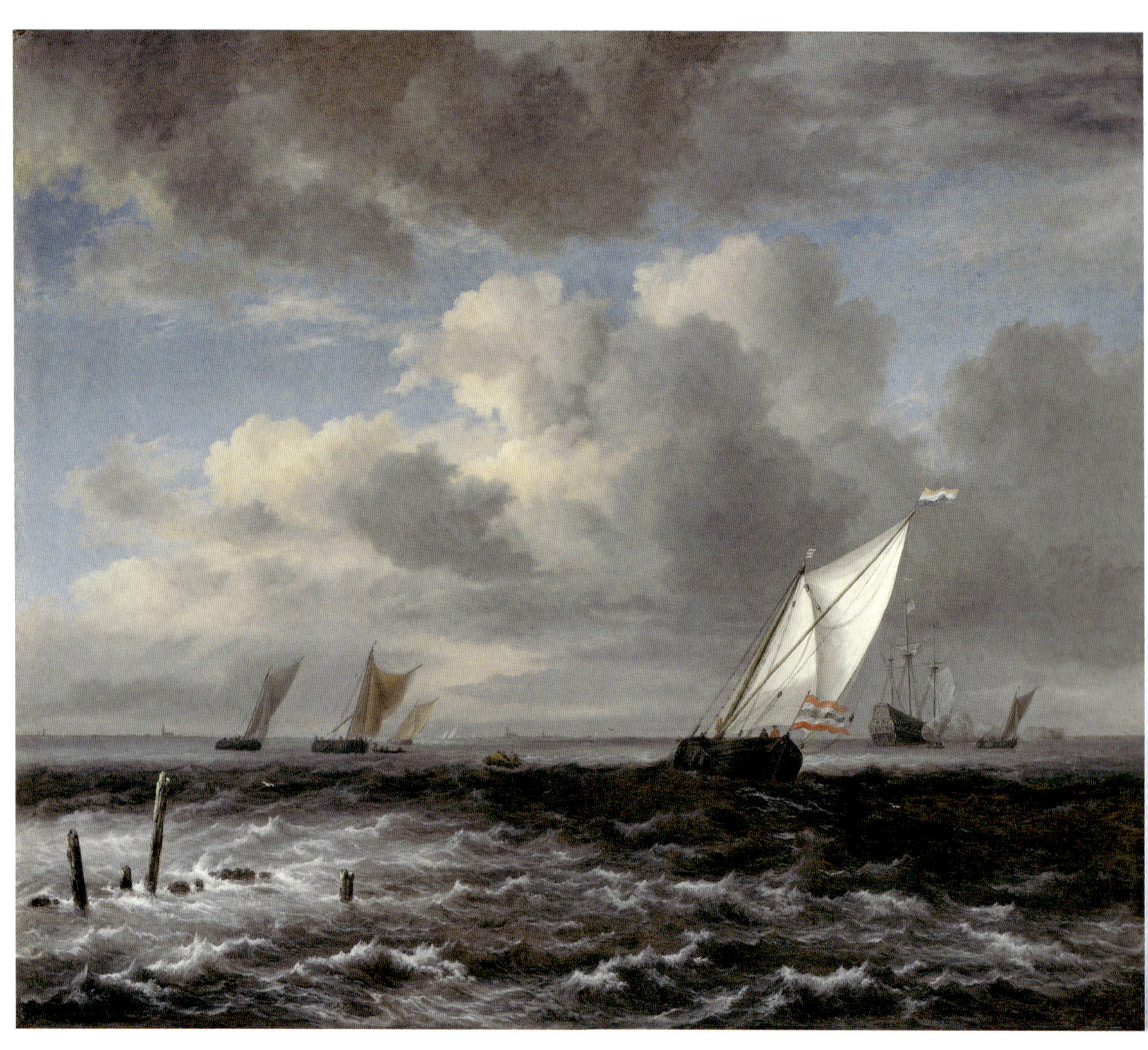

Jacob Isaacksz. van Ruisdael

Dutch, 1628/29–1682

Rough Sea, about 1670

Jacob van Ruisdael, arguably the most important seventeenth-century Dutch landscape painter, also produced a small number of seascapes. This painting, in which the majestic sky takes up nearly three-quarters of the pictorial space, is among the last of his marines.

Water was all-important to the Dutch, who in the seventeenth century were a major maritime and mercantile power. Their nation was a world leader in shipbuilding and its attendant industries. Vessels designed for maximum cargo space allowed for the more efficient transport of people and goods along both domestic and far-flung trade routes. Armed warships provided protection for the merchant fleet on their transoceanic voyages as well as for the herring boats harvesting valuable food for local consumption and export.

Catching the light in the foreground is a flag-studded *wijdschip*, a Dutch cargo and passenger vessel. In the distance at right, a warship with its foresheet unfurled fires a salute to a nearby boat; at left are other vessels of various sizes. The spires of a city are visible on the horizon beyond the white-capped waves. While it has been suggested that the view is of Het IJ, an estuary on the northeastern side of Amsterdam, it is unlikely that Ruisdael painted this view on the spot. With its soaring skies, tonal harmonies, and dramatic contrasts of light and shade, the true subject of the painting is the dynamic, rapidly changing weather patterns of the sea or, more broadly, the variable moods of nature.

Oil on canvas

107 x 125.8 cm (42 1/8 x 49 1/2 in.)

William Francis Warden Fund 57.4

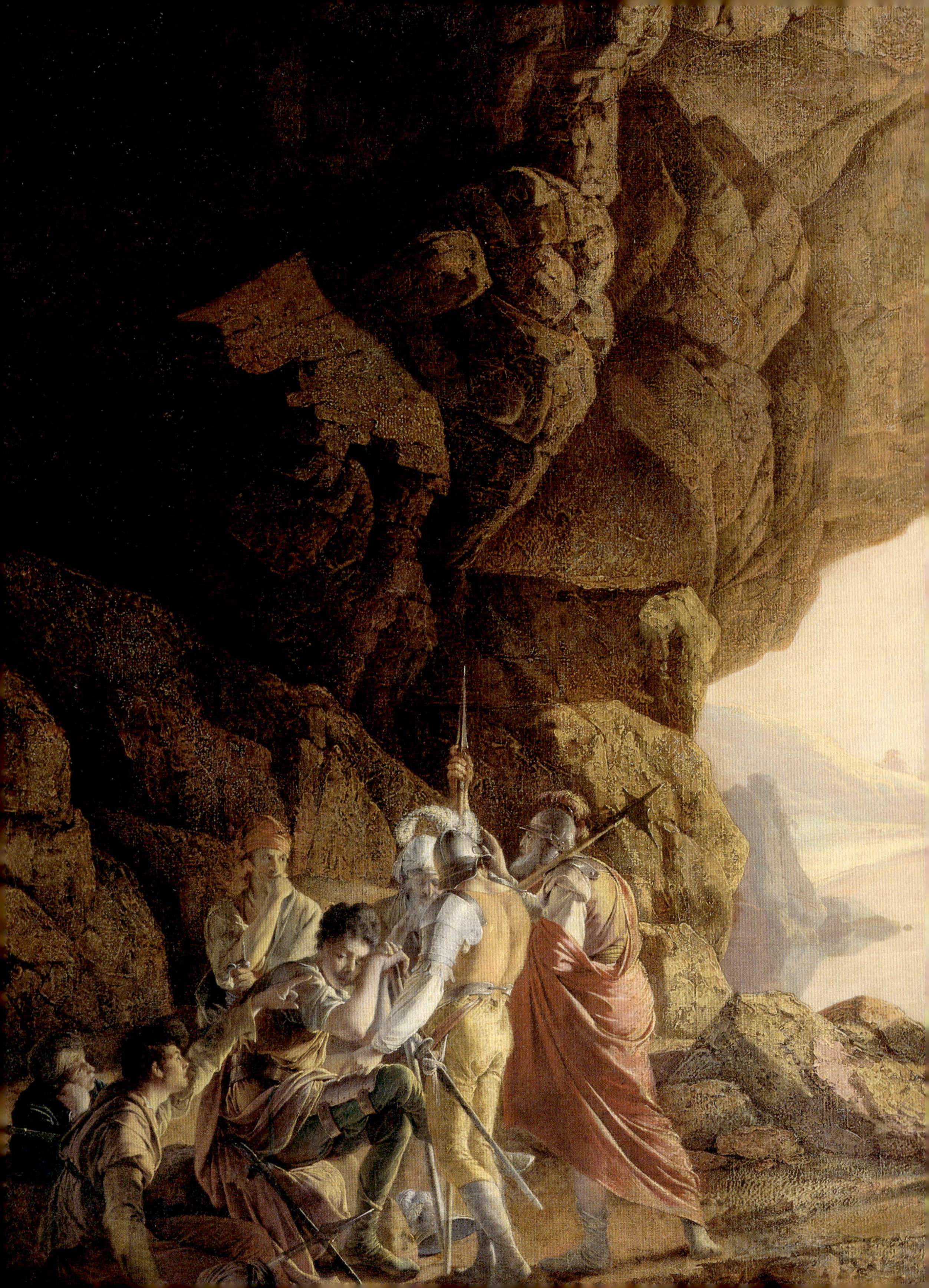

6 THE EIGHTEENTH CENTURY

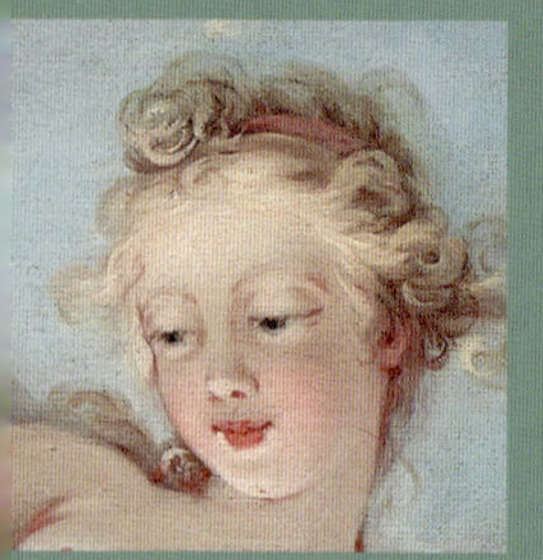
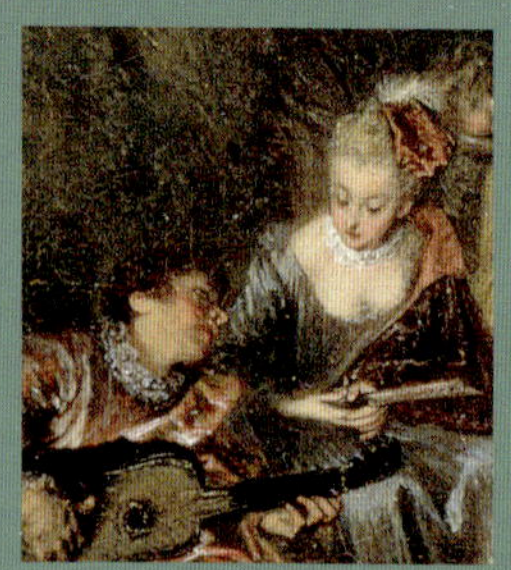
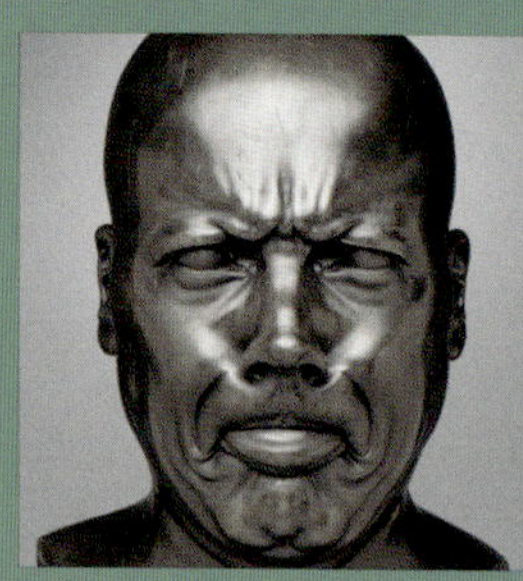
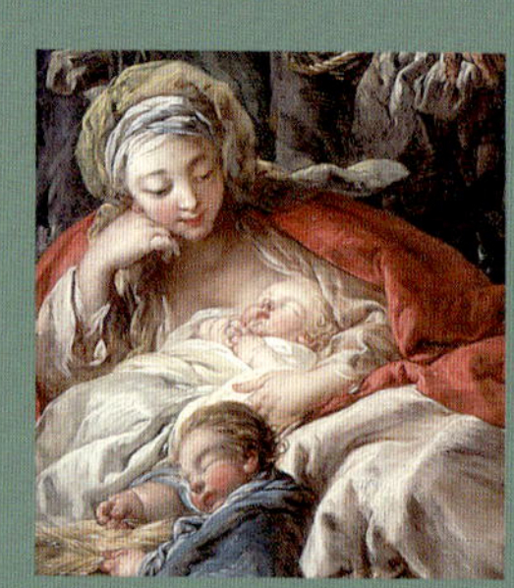
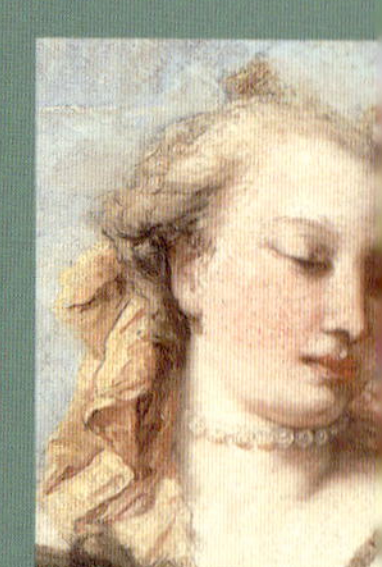

The Eighteenth Century

While every historical period features political and cultural change, some witness far more upheaval than others. When the eighteenth century began, it seemed as if European life was fundamentally unalterable. Monarchies held sway across the continent, with King Louis XIV of France fifty-six years into his reign. Italian cities, particularly Rome and Venice, were arguably the centers of the art world. The Christian church, whether Catholic or Protestant, permeated everyday life. An artist could have a flourishing career producing only religious subjects. The Enlightenment, stressing the importance of rational thought and scientific inquiry, was barely a murmur.

By the century's close, the Age of Reason had achieved nothing less than the transformation of political and social thinking. Extraordinary growth in scientific knowledge led to a new confidence in science itself and an assumption that progress was human destiny. New attitudes toward individual liberty, the church, and governance were manifest in the wrenching changes of the American War of Independence (begun in 1775), the French Revolution (begun in 1789), and Napoleon's conquest of Italy (begun in 1796), events traditionally thought to mark the culmination of the Enlightenment. These explosive events were interconnected. The proclamation of universal liberty of the American Declaration of Independence (1776) powerfully shaped the Declaration of the Rights of Man and of the Citizen (1789) in France, and the subsequent toppling of the monarchy created a power vacuum that the young Napoleon filled within a decade. The movement to abolish slavery in Europe and the Americas grew over the course of the century from a fringe belief to a widely held truth. The church's hold on the laity became substantially weaker, as thinkers asserted a faith in reason, rather than organized religion, as the basis for determining morality and conduct. In sum, a century that started very much as a continuation of the Renaissance ended in something recognizable as the foundation of the modern world.

These shifts affected what art was made, where it was made, and who made it. As the church lost its grip on institutions and individuals, art became correspondingly secular, prioritizing profane delight rather than religious devotion. Artists made fewer religious works or eschewed such subjects altogether. For the first time outside the Netherlands, art on secular topics flourished across Europe, and even predominated. Genre scenes, capturing moments from daily life, and portraits of sitters who were neither noble nor wealthy were produced in large numbers, reflecting growing markets. Put another way, the range of subjects in this chapter is not found across Europe in earlier sections of this book.

European culture became more cosmopolitan. This was a century of increasingly international artists, with many on the move. More than before, artists traveled in search of work, a fresh start, or for their own education. The traditional pattern of Italian artists seeking employment abroad continued; Canaletto worked in England for nearly a decade, and some of Tiepolo's grandest commissions occurred in Germany and Spain. Now, however, it became common for non-Italian artists, from Pajou to Wright of Derby to Goya, to undertake extended sojourns in Italy. This paralleled the thriving institution of the Grand Tour, the often years' long voyage for Northern European aristocrats through Italy that served as the capstone of a fine education. Reaching its apogee in the eighteenth century, the Grand Tour fostered new kinds of patrons—tourists eager to acquire luxury souvenirs—and fueled certain subjects, particularly views of Italian cities, and paintings and sculptures that evoked ancient Rome. The restless travels of so many artists and clients helped unify the continent, which is one reason why this chapter, unlike some previous ones, is not subdivided between northern and southern Europe.

Finally, the century's changes also reflected broad shifts in taste. The preference at the turn of the century for the extreme grandeur of the Late Baroque, seen in the sculpture of Lemoyne, was replaced by the 1730s with the Rococo. This was simultaneously an abundantly decorated and more intimate style, exemplified by painters Boucher and Fragonard. They were favorites of the consort of Louis XV of France, Jeanne Antoinette Poisson (known as Madame de Pompadour), and the style came to epitomize the excesses of late-stage absolutism. Rococo taste prized asymmetrical forms drawn from nature, especially shells and vines, expressed in sinuous curves. In the 1760s, critics began to deride the Rococo as frivolous. A new style, taking inspiration from classical Greece and Rome, soon became pervasive, encouraged by the order and rationalism of the new ideals of democratic governance and scientific thinking. Although this new style, called

Neoclassicism, embraced all of the visual and performing arts, it was especially successful in sculpture. Portrait busts, such as those of Houdon, could endow contemporary sitters with the poise and dignity of their ancient predecessors. As in Italian Renaissance more than three centuries earlier, the key to the future lay in the past.

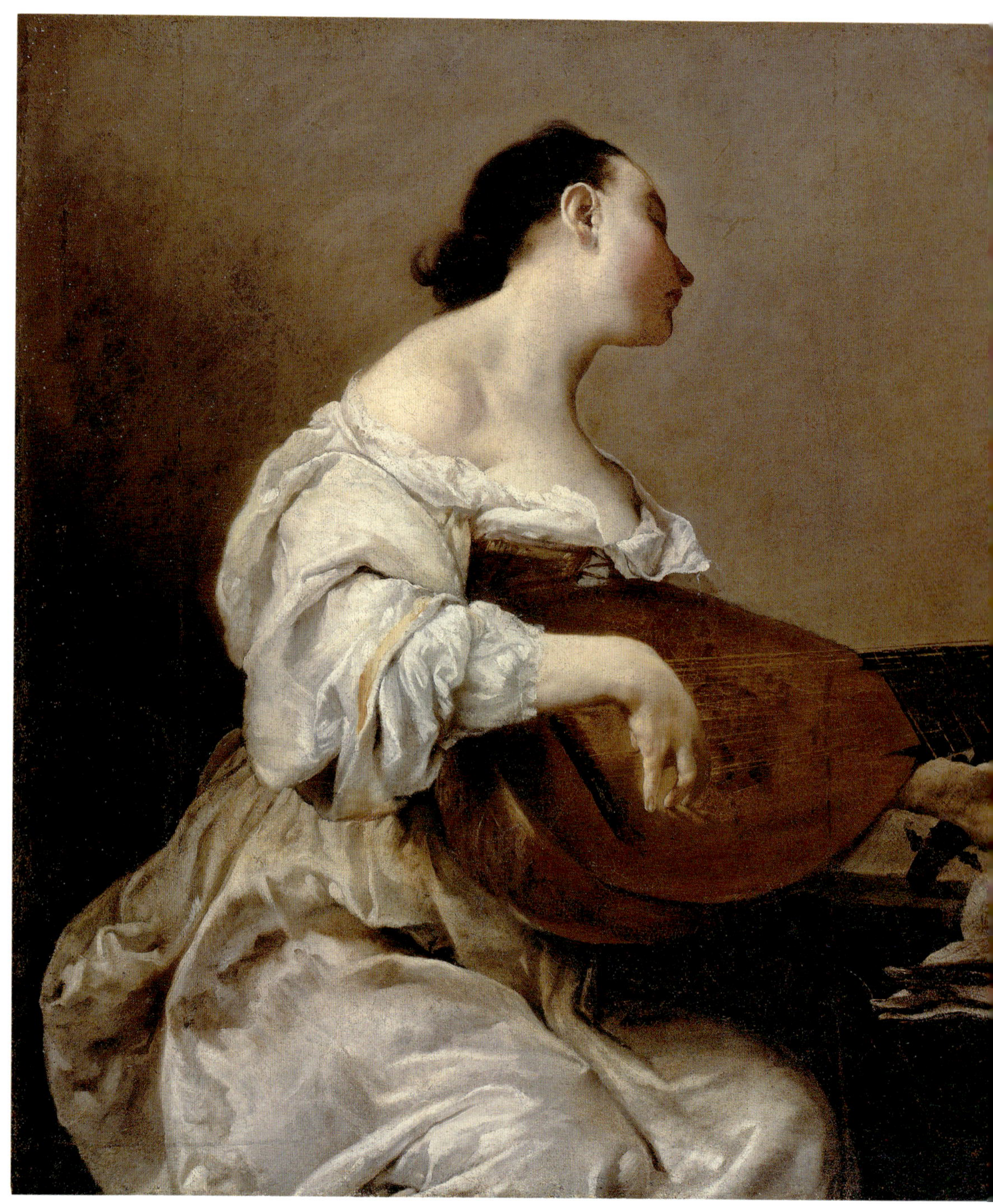

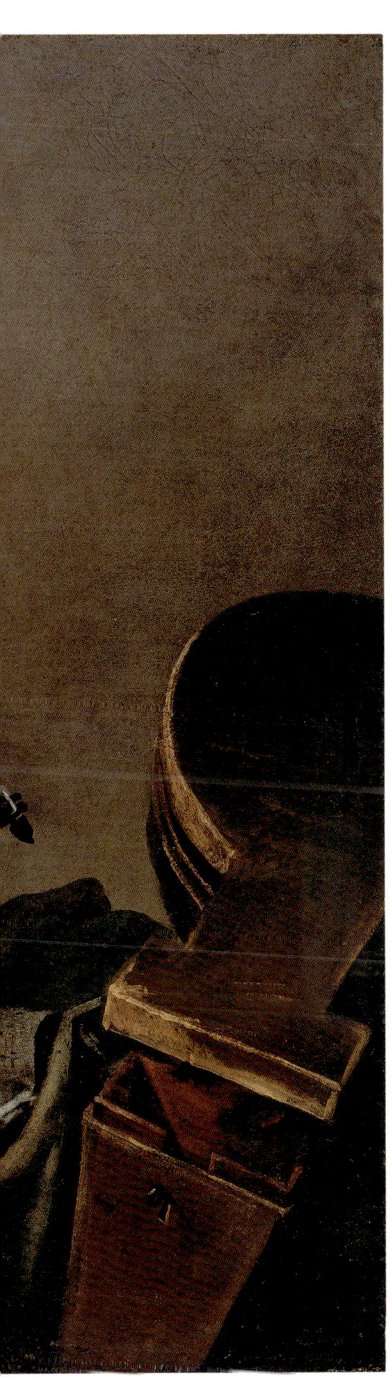

Giuseppe Maria Crespi

Italian (Bolognese), 1665–1747

Woman Tuning a Lute, about 1700–1705

Based in Bologna, Giuseppe Maria Crespi painted religious works, pastoral scenes, and portraits, among other subjects. Today he is especially celebrated for his role in the development of genre painting, or depictions of daily life.

Here, set against a neutral background, an elegantly dressed woman, cheeks flushed, tunes a lute. Her face is turned away from the viewer as she plucks the strings with her right hand and adjusts the pegs with her left. At right, the case for the instrument lies open next to a songbook with crumpled pages. Using a near monochrome palette and delicate light effects, Crespi endows his figure with a human presence and expertly captures the textures of flesh, wood, cloth, and leather.

The subject of lute players first arose in sixteenth-century Venice and gained considerable popularity in the hands of seventeenth-century painters such as Caravaggio and his followers in Italy and Northern Europe. Crespi's eighteenth-century work achieves an unprecedented sense of subtlety and tenderness. Female lute players have been interpreted in a variety of ways: as personifications of the art of music, as allusions to love and courtship, and as everyday examples of women lost in their art.

Oil on canvas

121.3 x 153 cm (47¾ x 60¼ in.)

Charles Potter Kling Fund 69.958

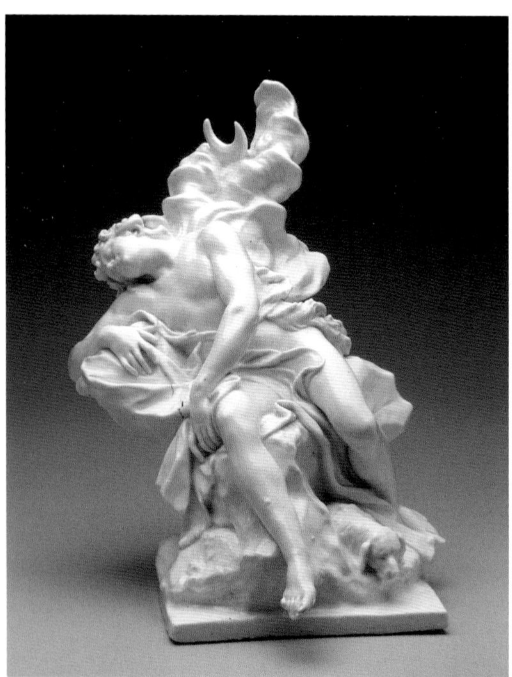

Sleeping Endymion, about 1755-65, Doccia Manufactury (Florence). Glazed hard-paste porcelain, h. 42 cm (16½ in.). Frank B. Bemis Fund, 2002.319

Agostino Cornacchini
Italian (Roman), 1686–1754
Sleeping Endymion, 1716

Agostino Cornacchini's terracotta sculpture of the sleeping shepherd Endymion is an example of a preparatory model for a work intended to be made using a more costly material such as marble or bronze. Just as drawings can provide insight into a painter's creative process of experimentation and invention, clay models offer a glimpse into the sculptor's process. What makes Cornacchini's statue particularly intriguing is that it was signed and dated in the wet clay of the base, indicating that the artist or his patron saw it as a finished work of art. At the very least, this ensured that Cornacchini's composition was recognized as his own.

The sculpture represents a character from *Metamorphoses*, the epic poem by the ancient Roman writer Ovid. Endymion, beloved of Diana, goddess of the moon, was granted eternal youth through eternal slumber by the god Jupiter. He sleeps below a crescent moon symbolizing Diana's protection. The terracotta suffered losses over time, including the crescent moon and Endymion's lower right leg and foot, but these details are seen in versions in other materials, including the Doccia porcelain example in the MFA's collection (left). The delicate modeling of Endymion's head and flesh, the charming dog at his feet, and the details of costume and foliage exemplify the freshness and immediacy of the terracotta medium.

Terracotta
33.7 x 27 x 32 cm (13¼ x 10⅝ x 12⅝ in.)
H. E. Bolles Fund 56.141

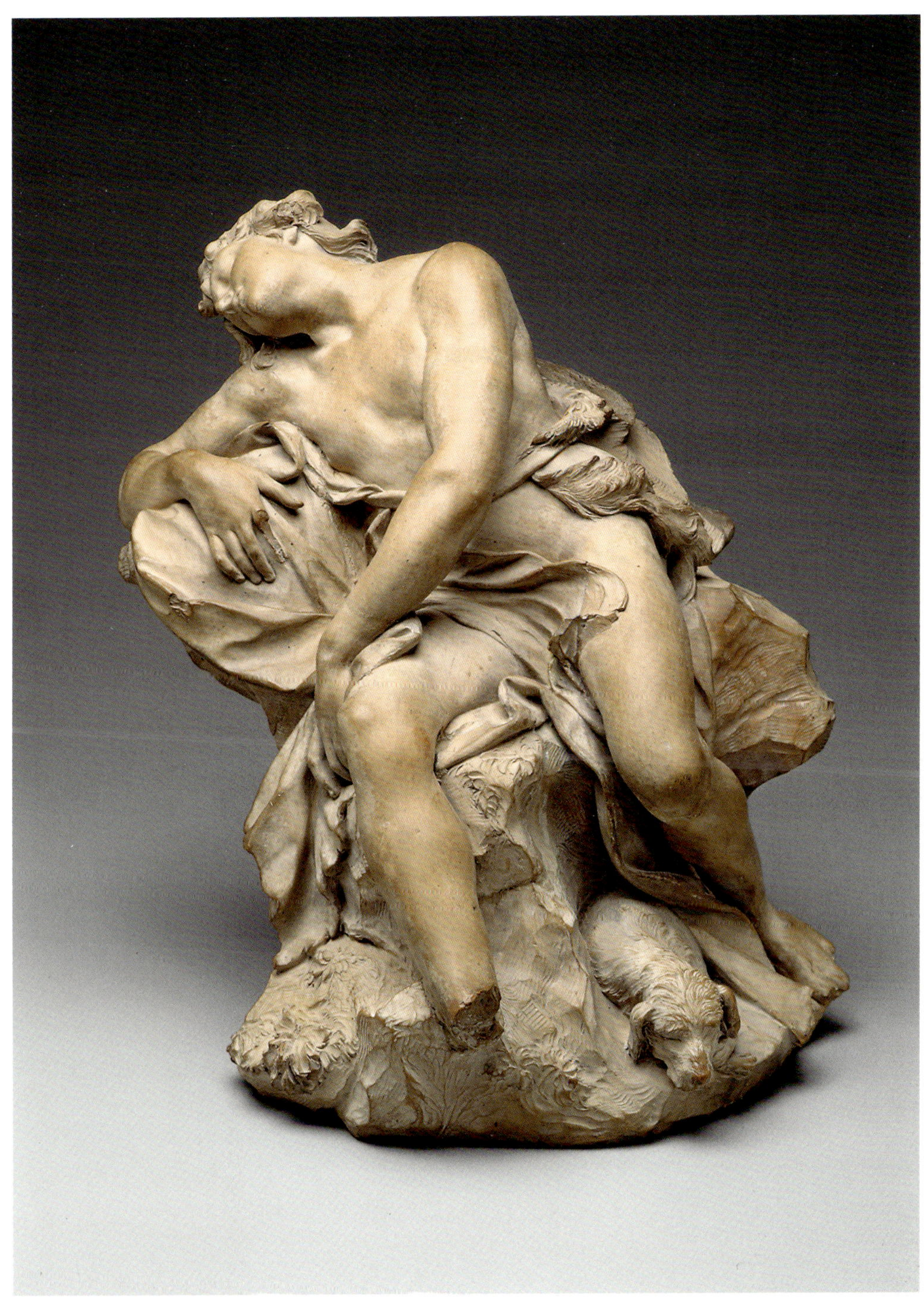

Giuseppe Piamontini
Italian (Florentine), 1663–1744
The Massacre of the Innocents, about 1710

The Massacre of the Innocents, an episode from Christ's infancy, was represented throughout the Renaissance and the Baroque period in paintings, sculpture, drawings, and prints. The scene provided an opportunity for artists to explore high drama employing figures in intensely energetic poses, women experiencing unbearable grief, and the bodies of infants strewn on the ground, hidden in their mothers' arms, or seized by Roman soldiers. Giovanni Pisano, Raphael, Rubens, and Poussin all treated this scene, and Giuseppe Piamontini holds his own among these artistic giants.

Piamontini does not shy away from the horrifying violence of the incident. His bronze relief displays the variety of figures and emotions that made for an exciting narrative scene characteristic of High Baroque art. Set in a vaulted space that uses perspective to convey depth, the work is a masterpiece. It is the culmination of a bronze casting tradition in Florence that reaches back to the famous doors of the Baptistery of San Giovanni known as the Gates of Paradise, made in the fifteenth century by Lorenzo Ghiberti. Made in monochrome bronze, beautifully detailed and polished, Piamontini's relief embodies a technical virtuosity that somewhat mitigates the painful impact of the scene's inhumanity.

Bronze
66.7 x 83.8 cm (26¼ x 33 in.)
John H. and Ernestine A. Payne Fund, European Decorative Arts Curator's Fund, and museum purchase with funds donated by Randolph Fuller and John Goelet 1974.606

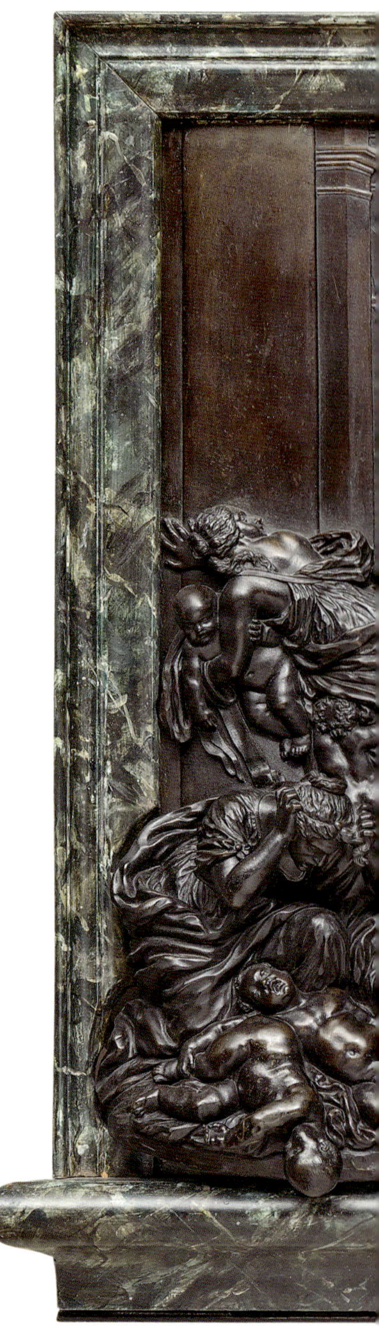

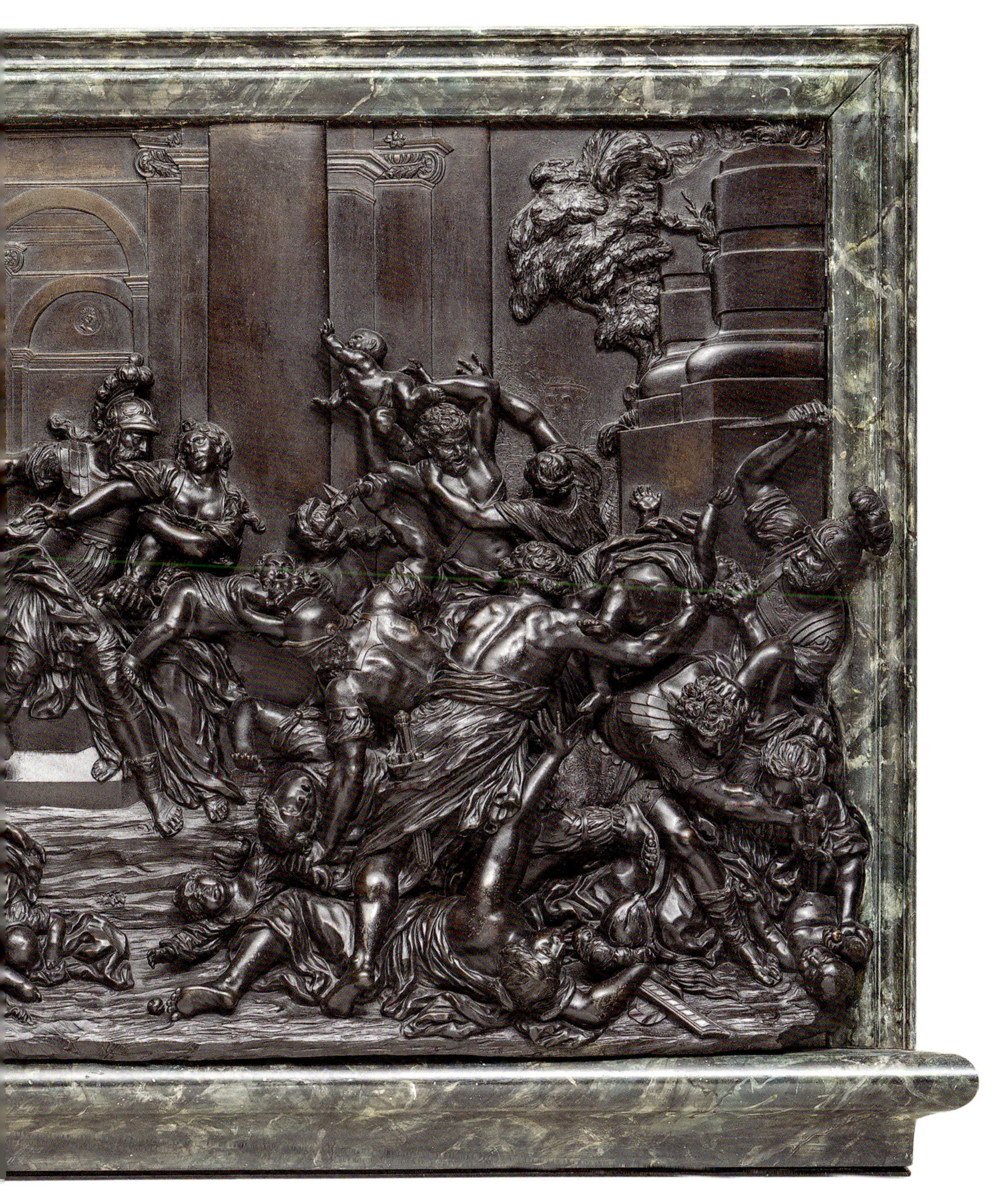

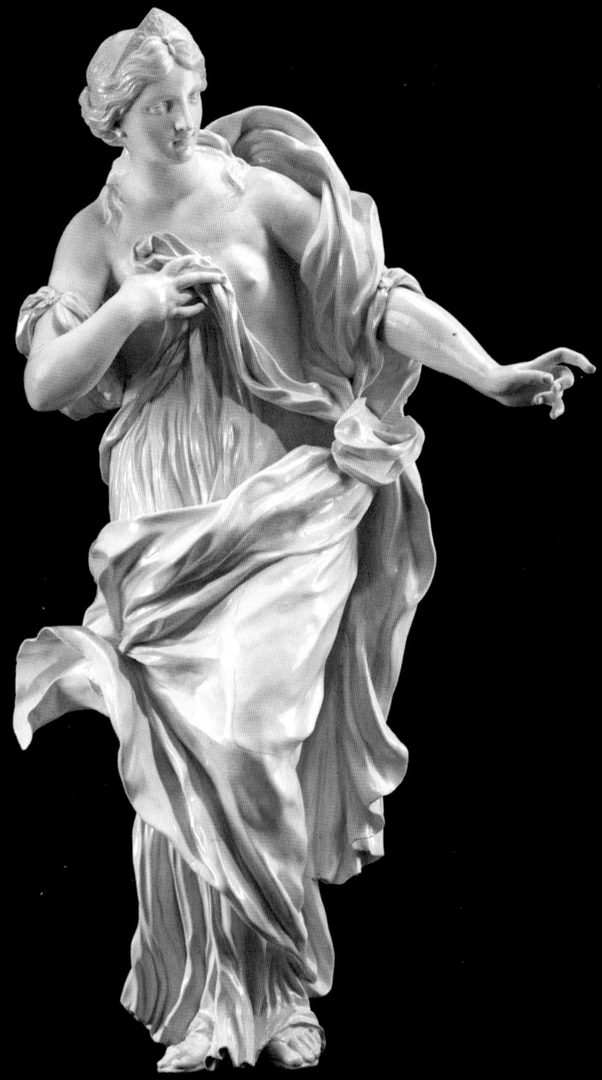

Doccia Manufactory (Florence)
Juno, about 1745–55
After a model by **Giuseppe Piamontini**
Italian (Florentine), 1663–1744

Swirling drapery envelops a standing figure. Seeing one breast bared, the viewer might think this is Venus, the ancient Roman goddess of love. Documentary and visual evidence confirm that it is instead Juno, consort to Jupiter, the king of the gods. Juno is usually represented fully dressed and standing as the goddess of marriage and protector of justice. The sense of wind whipping through the drapery and the whiteness of the material suggest that Juno is presented here as representative of the element of air, one of several aspects of her complex character. Together, the grace of her pose, with extended arm and modest yet revealing gesture; the flow of her drapery; and the lovely, even quality of her features make this statue a brilliant example of Florentine High Baroque sculpture.

Made in three pieces, this work is also a virtuoso example of the porcelain statuary made for Count Carlo Ginori in the third quarter of the eighteenth century at the Doccia manufactory in Sesto Fiorentino, outside Florence. Ginori dreamed of establishing a museum of large-scale porcelain works representing the greatest examples of ancient, Renaissance, and modern sculpture, which could be reproduced for paying clients. The challenges of casting such large figures, even in pieces, meant the endeavor would ultimately fail. This figure of Juno is based on a model made by the eighteenth-century Florentine sculptor Giuseppe Piamontini, known for his works in marble and bronze. Intended to be paired with a figure of Jupiter, this Juno is one of only a handful of large-scale Doccia sculptures known today. It is possible that many did not survive; however, it is more likely that very few were ever produced, given the cost and challenges of manufacture.

Glazed hard-paste porcelain
H. 38½ in. (97.79 cm)
Partial gift in memory of I. W. Colburn by Frances H. Colburn, Clarissa Colburn Hunnewell, and Oliver C. Colburn, and museum purchase with funds from the John Lowell Gardner Fund, John H. and Ernestine A. Payne Fund, Russell B. and Andrée Beauchamp Stearns Fund, Otis Norcross Fund, and Tamara Petrosian Davis Fund 2008.1414

Christ at the Column, about 1700
Italian

When the MFA purchased this sculpture in 1889, it was attributed to Bernini, the greatest Baroque sculptor. The piece was acquired from a famous collection in Florence and is likely Italian, probably made in the decades around 1700. The artist who carved it, the patron who commissioned it, and the location for which it was made remain unknown.

The sculpture shows Jesus tied to a half column, nude except for the drapery that covers his hips and twists through his legs and behind his back. His hands are bound to a ring at the top of the column; a whip lies at his feet. This is a distillation of the narrative of Christ's Flagellation, which he endured before his crucifixion. The work exemplifies how the inclusion of significant objects can stand in for a larger story that would be hard to convey in a figural sculpture. The half column refers to a relic housed at the Church of Santa Prassede in Rome that is believed to be a fragment of the column to which Jesus was bound, and the whip brings the Flagellation vividly to mind. Both subtly guide viewers to imagine the scene for themselves. Stressing sorrow over pain, this *Christ at the Column* is a contemplative image made to inspire prayer and empathy.

Marble
88.9 x 33 x 39.4 cm (35 x 13 x 15½ in.)
Museum purchase with funds donated by contribution
89.507

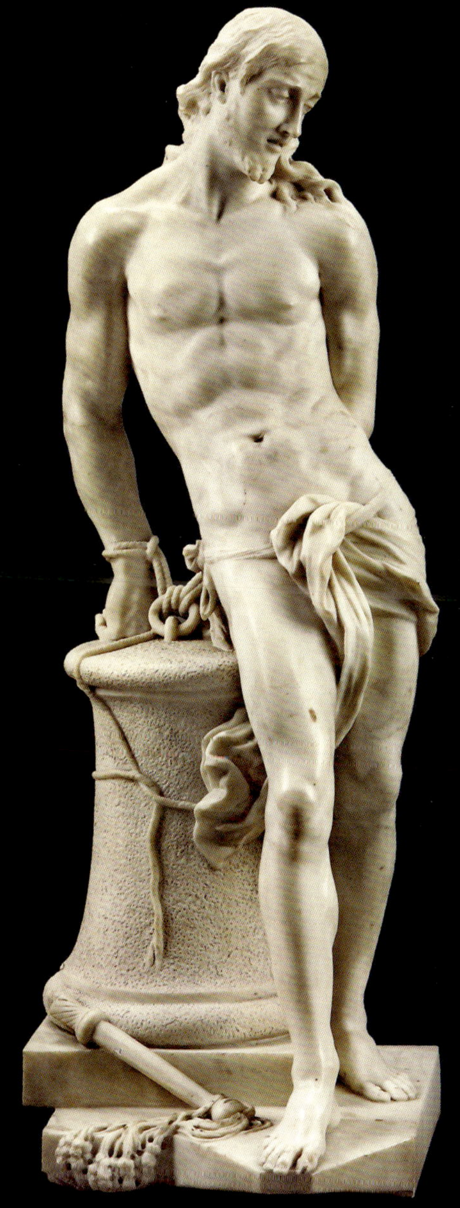

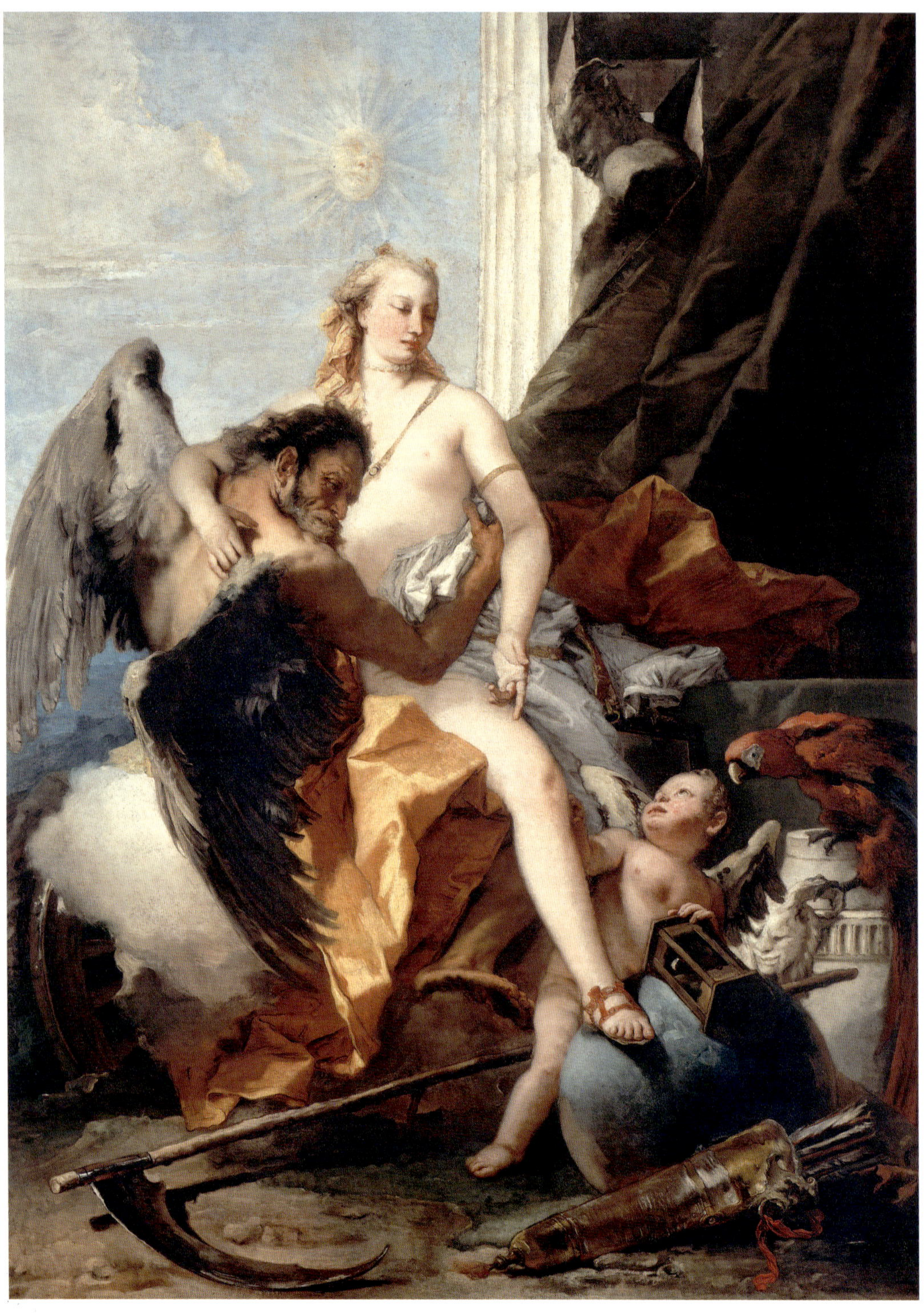

Giovanni Battista Tiepolo

Italian (Venetian), 1696–1770

Time Unveiling Truth, about 1758

Giovanni Battista Tiepolo's command of the Grand Manner—the depiction of monumental figures from classical and Christian texts in a lofty, theatrical style—earned him an international reputation as a master of large decorations. Whether in fresco or on canvas, Tiepolo's works graced the walls and ceilings of palaces and churches in his native Venice. This canvas was probably commissioned by Giovanni Girolamo Orti for his family's palazzo in Verona on the Venetian *terrafirma*. Here, Tiepolo revisits a favorite subject, that of time, chosen perhaps to credit his client's wisdom.

Time, shown partially in shadow, appears as a grizzled old man with a rough beard and cumbersome gray wings. His scythe lies on the ground. Seated on a chariot, he undresses the beautiful woman personifying Truth, her expression proud and unruffled. Her emblem, the sun, illuminates her body, the face of the cupid below, and the hourglass, another attribute of Time, which the cupid balances on a globe of the world. The broader message is that with time, truth comes to light, while lies and the ephemeral appeal of earthly things disappear. Despite the plethora of symbols, Tiepolo enlivens what might have been a dry topic with an erotic undertone and unmistakable grandeur.

At the end of the eighteenth century, the Spanish artist Francisco Goya y Lucientes explored the same concept in a small painting (see p. 191), almost the nocturnal counterpart of the brilliantly lit Tiepolo work here. Whereas the Italian artist employed a bright palette and heroic characters, Goya, by contrast, infused his work with a gloomy, even sinister, sensibility.

Oil on canvas

231.1 x 167 cm (91 x 65¾ in.)

Charles Potter Kling Fund 61.1200

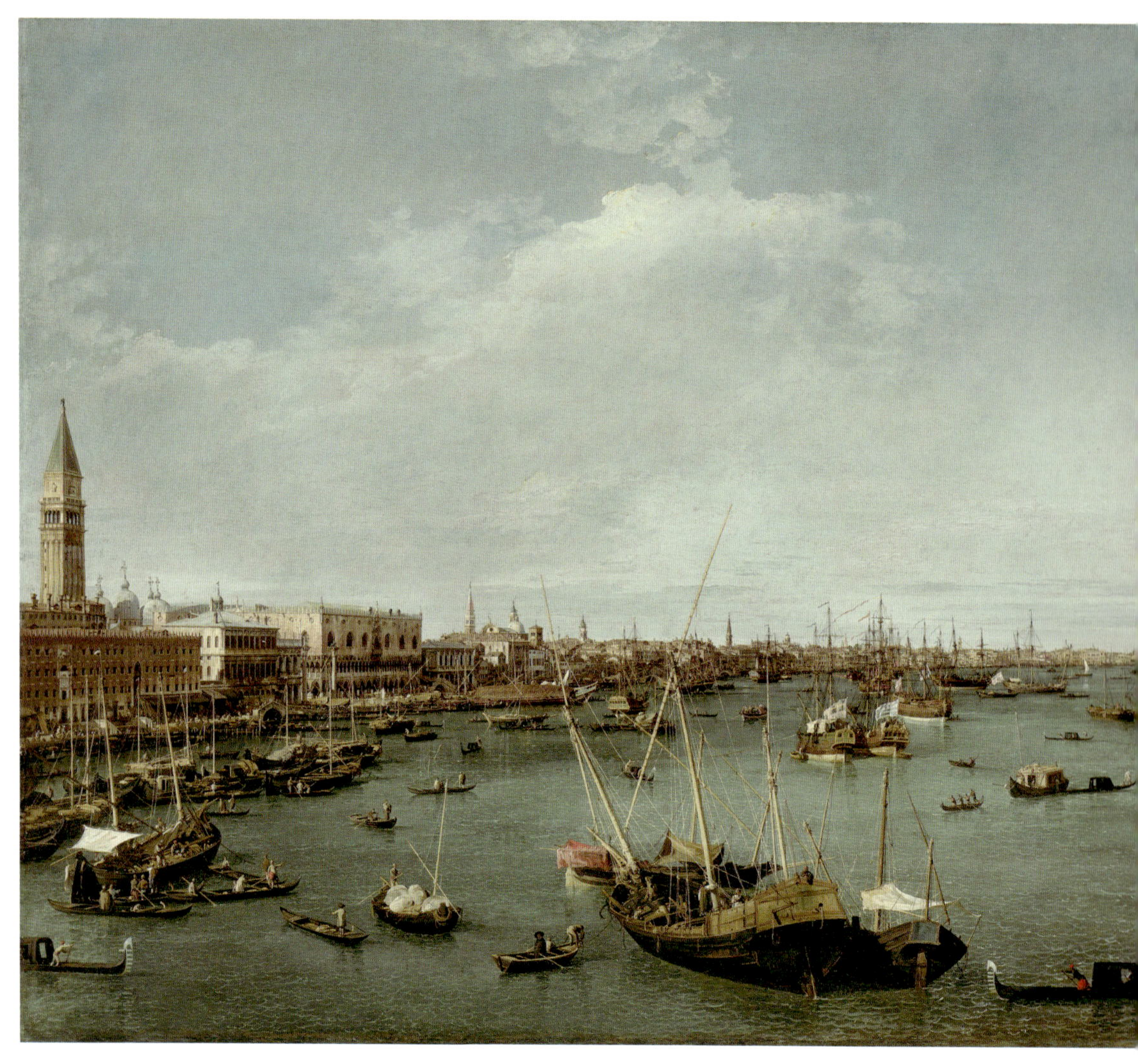

Oil on canvas

124.5 x 204.5 cm (49 x 80½ in.)

Abbott Lawrence Fund, Seth K. Sweetser Fund, and Charles Edward French Fund 39.290

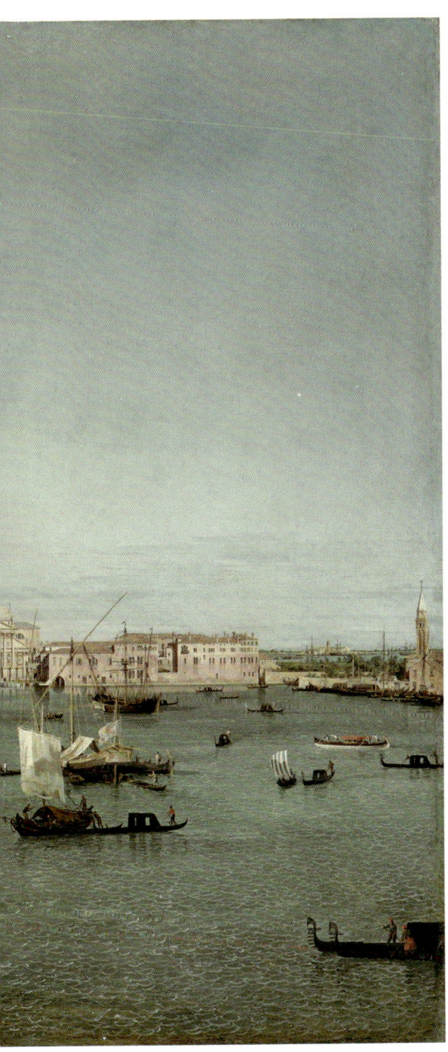

Canaletto (Giovanni Antonio Canal)
Italian (Venetian), 1697–1768
Bacino di San Marco, Venice, about 1738

Canaletto was famous for the amount of detail he introduced to his *vedute*, or view paintings, of Venice. For example, in this sweeping depiction of the Bay of St. Mark, a few minuscule touches of paint convey scaffolding on the white bell tower of the Church of Sant'Antonin, left of the painting's center. Documents reveal its construction ended in 1738, allowing an approximate date for the painting. With Canaletto, however, precision does not necessarily equal accuracy. The viewpoint is imaginary, as no building enjoys this particular vista, and the scope encompasses far more than a person can see at once. Positions of individual monuments, such as some of the other bell towers and particularly the white Church of San Giorgio Maggiore at right of center, have been shifted for a more pleasing effect. In this, Canaletto understood that his audience cared more about overall impression than cartographic truth.

Starting in the late 1600s, travelers from Northern Europe, particularly Great Britain, would complete their education by embarking on a Grand Tour that encompassed important cities, ruins, and literary sites in Southern Europe, and especially in Italy. While the end point was often Rome or Naples, these voyages almost invariably included Venice, a city whose watery setting makes it unlike any other in the world. In the eighteenth century, Venice was past its prime as a military and economic force, yet it remained a cultural powerhouse famed for its opera houses, art collections, and talented artists working in a range of media. View paintings of Venice made ideal souvenirs, and Canaletto was the most sought-after practitioner.

This canvas, the finest Canaletto in North America, hung for years at Castle Howard, the country estate of the Earls of Carlisle in Yorkshire, England. By the early twentieth century, the family owned as many as sixteen paintings by Canaletto. The sale of this one to the MFA in 1939 was fortuitous; the following year, a fire at Castle Howard destroyed many works of art, including several by Canaletto.

Francesco Guardi

Italian (Venetian), 1712–1793

Procession of Gondolas in the Bacino di San Marco, about 1782

Like Canaletto, born fifteen years earlier, Francesco Guardi specialized in painting *vedute* of his native Venice, but his approach differed from that of his predecessor. Whereas Canaletto presented his subjects in sharp focus and crisp detail, Guardi used loose, gestural brushwork to evoke a hazy and atmospheric Venice. The disparity speaks to Guardi's predilection for the depiction of motion and the transience of clouds and reflections. By contrast, Canaletto impresses with his apparent topographical accuracy.

Guardi was particularly interested in ceremonial subjects. This procession of gondolas entering the Bacino di San Marco, or Bay of St. Mark, probably represents the arrival of a foreign dignitary and his retinue in three gilded vessels. They are followed by a flotilla of black gondolas, while in the background three anchored warships offer a cannon salute, evidenced by the smoke billowing over the water. On grounds of style, the painting seems to date to the early 1780s. The esteemed visitor may be Pope Pius VI, who came to Venice in 1782.

Canaletto depicted the same teeming harbor some forty years earlier, capturing not a ceremony but rather the buzz of a regular day. He approached the scene from a different angle, one that focused on the monuments and government buildings around Piazza San Marco. San Giorgio Maggiore, the island church shown at left in Guardi's work, appears toward the right in Canaletto's painting.

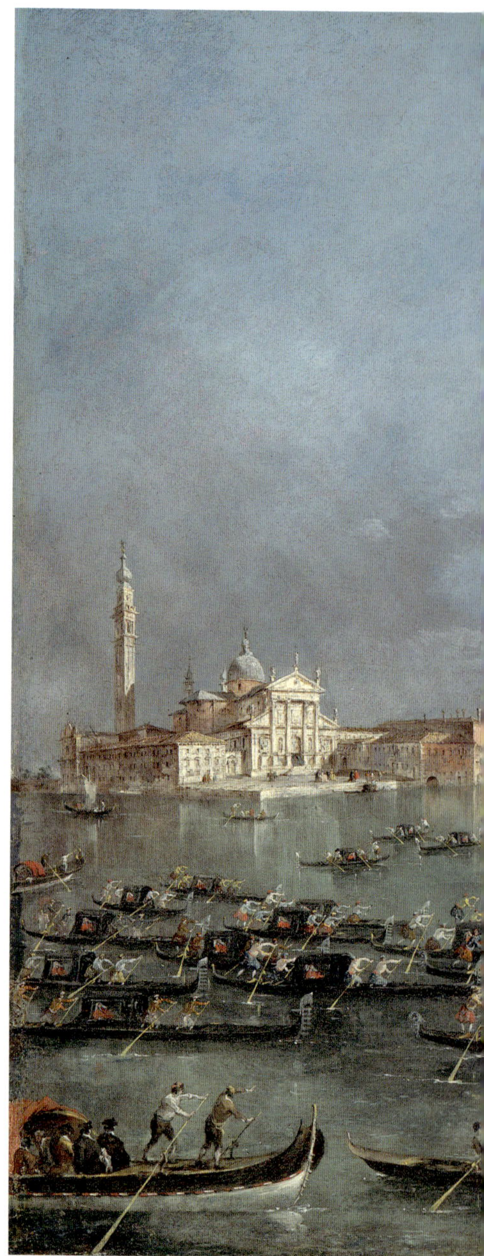

Oil on canvas

98.1 x 138.1 cm (38⅝ x 54⅜ in.)

Picture Fund 11.1451

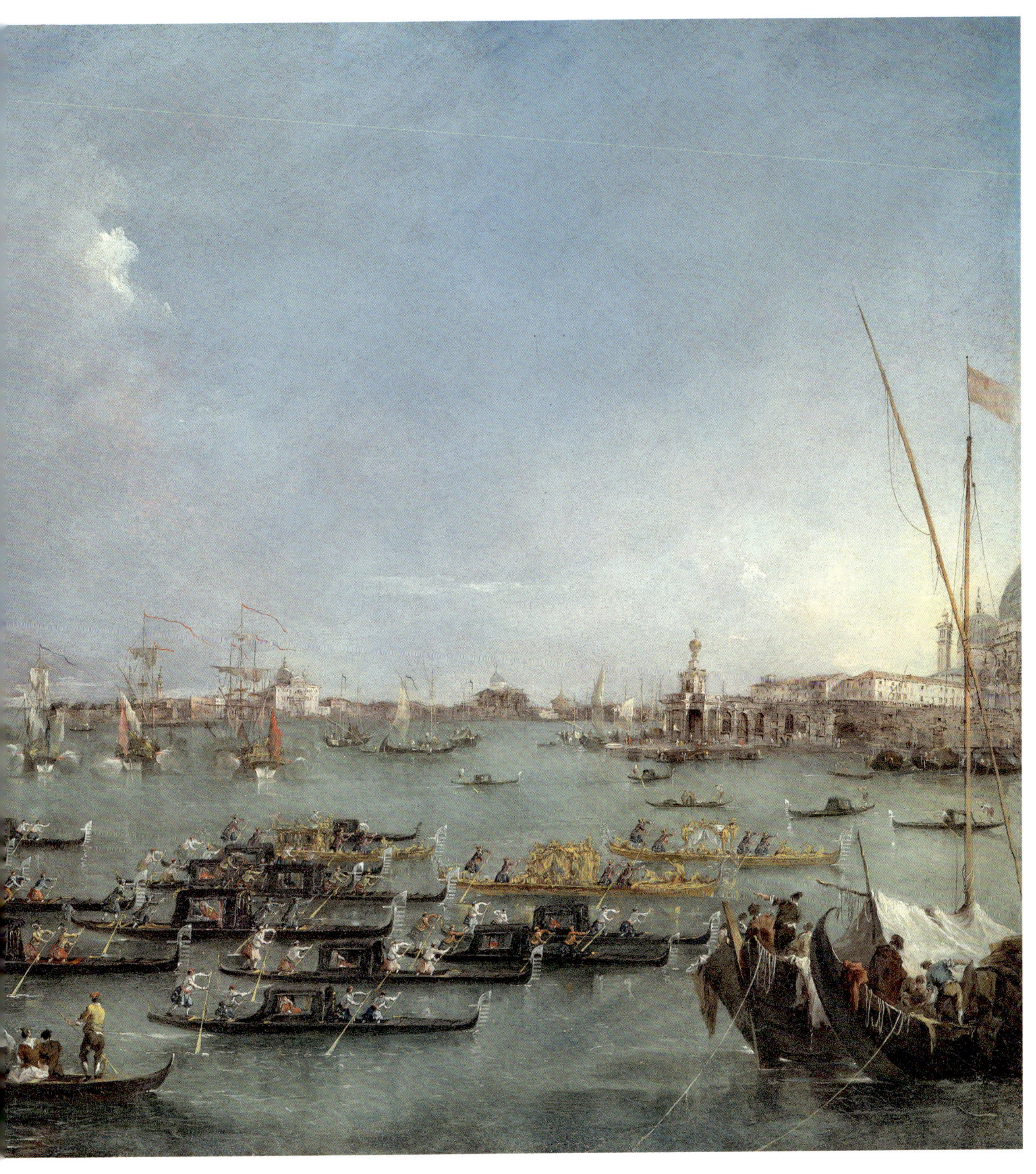

Giovanni Paolo Pannini

Italian (Roman), 1691–1765

Picture Gallery with Views of Modern Rome, 1757

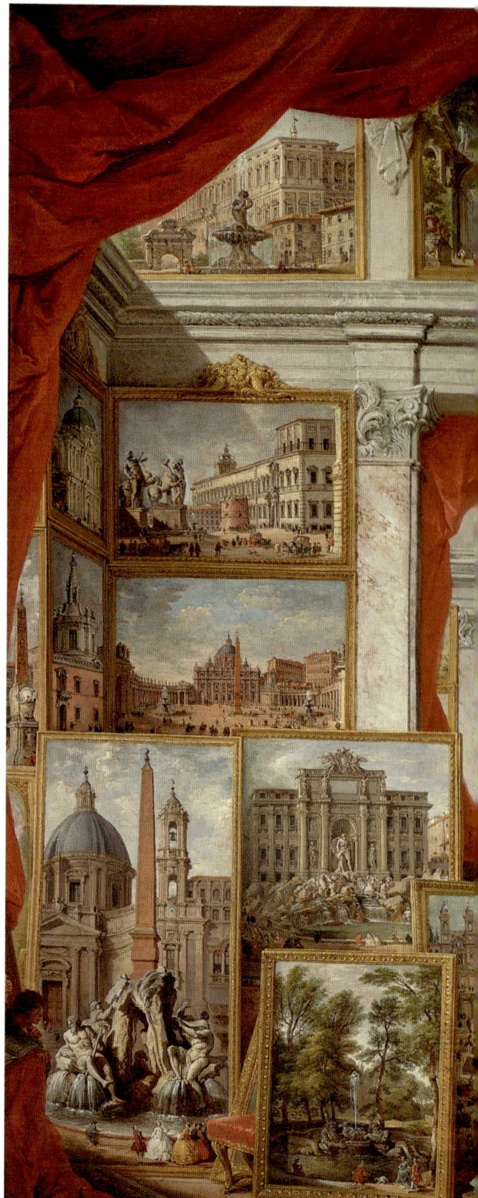

During the eighteenth century, many Northern Europeans participated in the Grand Tour, a journey culminating in Italy that completed a young man's education. Giovanni Paolo Pannini and other Italian artists such as Canaletto catered to these Grand Tourists by painting souvenir views of Italy's famous monuments. As seen in this example, Pannini also sometimes depicted imaginary galleries stacked to the ceiling with paintings. This work was part of a set commissioned by the Duc de Choiseul, French ambassador to the Vatican.

The practice of painting a picture gallery can be traced to seventeenth-century Flemish depictions of private art collections. Calling on his experience as a stage designer, Pannini transformed the genre by creating impossibly grandiose spaces featuring classical architecture. Seated at bottom center is the duke himself, surrounded by other connoisseurs and young artists. The walls of the church-like space are filled with imaginary framed paintings of Rome's most celebrated sites, including St. Peter's Basilica, the Trevi Fountain, and the Spanish Steps, as well as sculptures by Michelangelo and Gian Lorenzo Bernini, Rome's most esteemed modern sculptors.

Considered in conjunction with its similarly titled pendant, *Picture Gallery with Views of Ancient Rome*, this painting offers not only an extravagant souvenir of the duke's time in Rome but also an assertion of the accomplishments of modern artists, which rivaled the extraordinary achievements of their classical predecessors.

Oil on canvas

170.2 x 244.5 cm (67 x 96¼ in.)

Charles Potter Kling Fund 1975.805

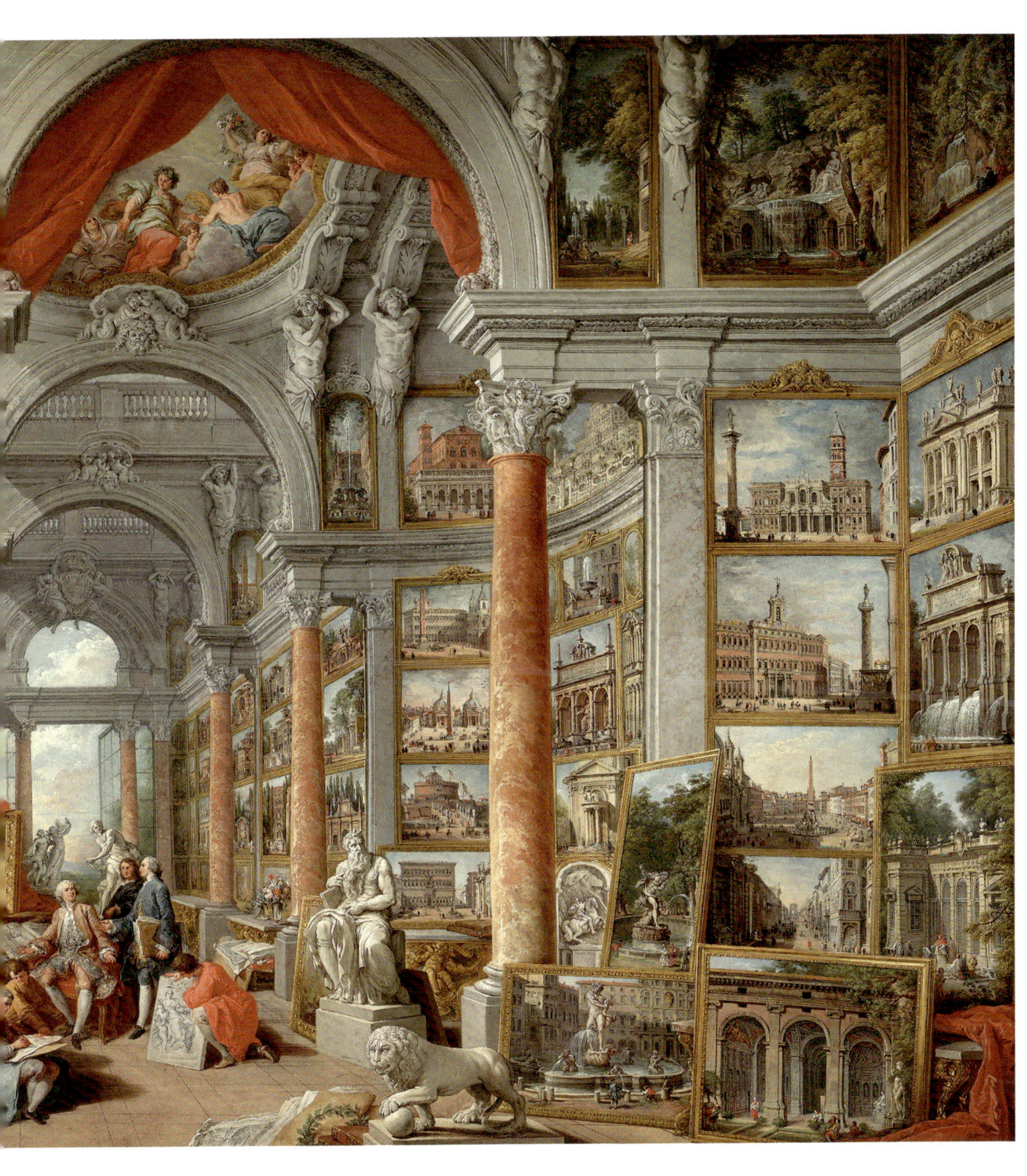

Pierre Etienne Monnot

French, 1657–1733

The Holy Families, probably 1700–1710

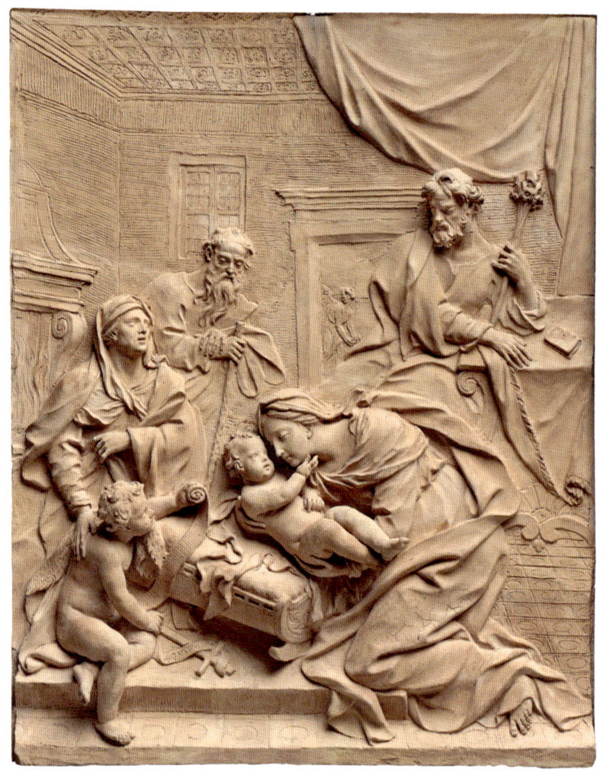

Terracotta

71.4 x 56.8 cm (28⅛ x 22⅜ in.)

Gift of Randolph J. Fuller 1987.212

This terracotta relief was created as a model for a sculpture to be carved in marble. A preparatory work such as this displays the touch of the artist in the clay, which is part of what makes such models so appealing in their own right. Pierre Etienne Monnot lived and worked in Rome, and an inventory of works in his studio conducted after his death lists this relief and notes that it was to be given to the executor of his will. This bequest makes it clear that Monnot himself recognized the quality and value of the piece as a work of art in its own right and provides a rare insight into the life of a sculptor in eighteenth-century Rome.

A quality of intimacy characterizes the scene itself. Set in a cozy domestic setting furnished with fireplace, table, and baby's cradle at center, it focuses on the tender embrace between mother and child. Mary, kneeling, sweeps the baby into her arms; he reaches for her and grasps her chin in his tiny hand, a common human gesture of love and affection. Joseph looks on from behind, holding the flowering branch that identifies him. Also gathered around the baby is his extended family, with his young cousin John the Baptist exuberantly reaching toward Mary and Jesus. John's mother, Elizabeth, and father, Zacharias, complete the loving circle, which conceptually includes the viewer of the relief. The work was likely conceived as a private devotional object and has a specificity of setting and emotion that can be compared to painted scenes of similar subjects.

Antoine Watteau
French, 1684–1721
La Perspective (View through the Trees in the Park of Pierre Crozat), about 1715

One of the most celebrated French artists of the early eighteenth century, Antoine Watteau invented a new type of painting called *fête galante*, which depicts aristocratic figures in open-air settings flirting and engaging in conversation. Watteau's gracefully rendered gatherings owe a debt to seventeenth-century Flemish painting, in particular Rubens's depictions of gardens of love, as well as earlier Venetian paintings of Arcadian gatherings by Titian and Giorgione.

This is a rare *fête galante* with an identifiable setting. The eighteenth-century French art dealer and connoisseur Pierre-Jean Mariette first described the building seen in the distance as the Château de Montmorency, the country estate of Pierre Crozat, a Parisian financier and art collector and one of Watteau's most important patrons. Here, Watteau depicts the building as it appeared after Crozat had it partly demolished and turned into a garden pavilion.

Despite the inclusion of an actual landmark, *La Perspective* is an artifice, a dreamlike world evocative of the theater. The fashionably dressed figures are arranged like actors on a stage, with the pavilion and allée of trees serving as a backdrop. Although the couples in the painting appear to convey different stages of love, from initial conversation to joint music-making, Watteau left the narrative deliberately open-ended.

Oil on canvas
46.7 x 55.3 cm (18⅜ x 21¾ in.)
Maria Antoinette Evans Fund 23.573

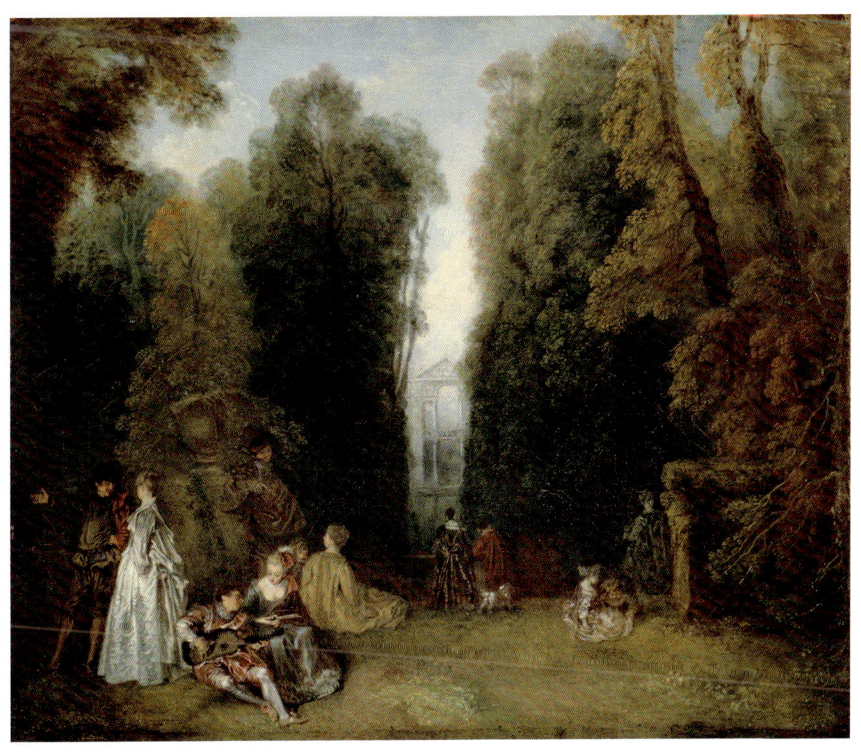

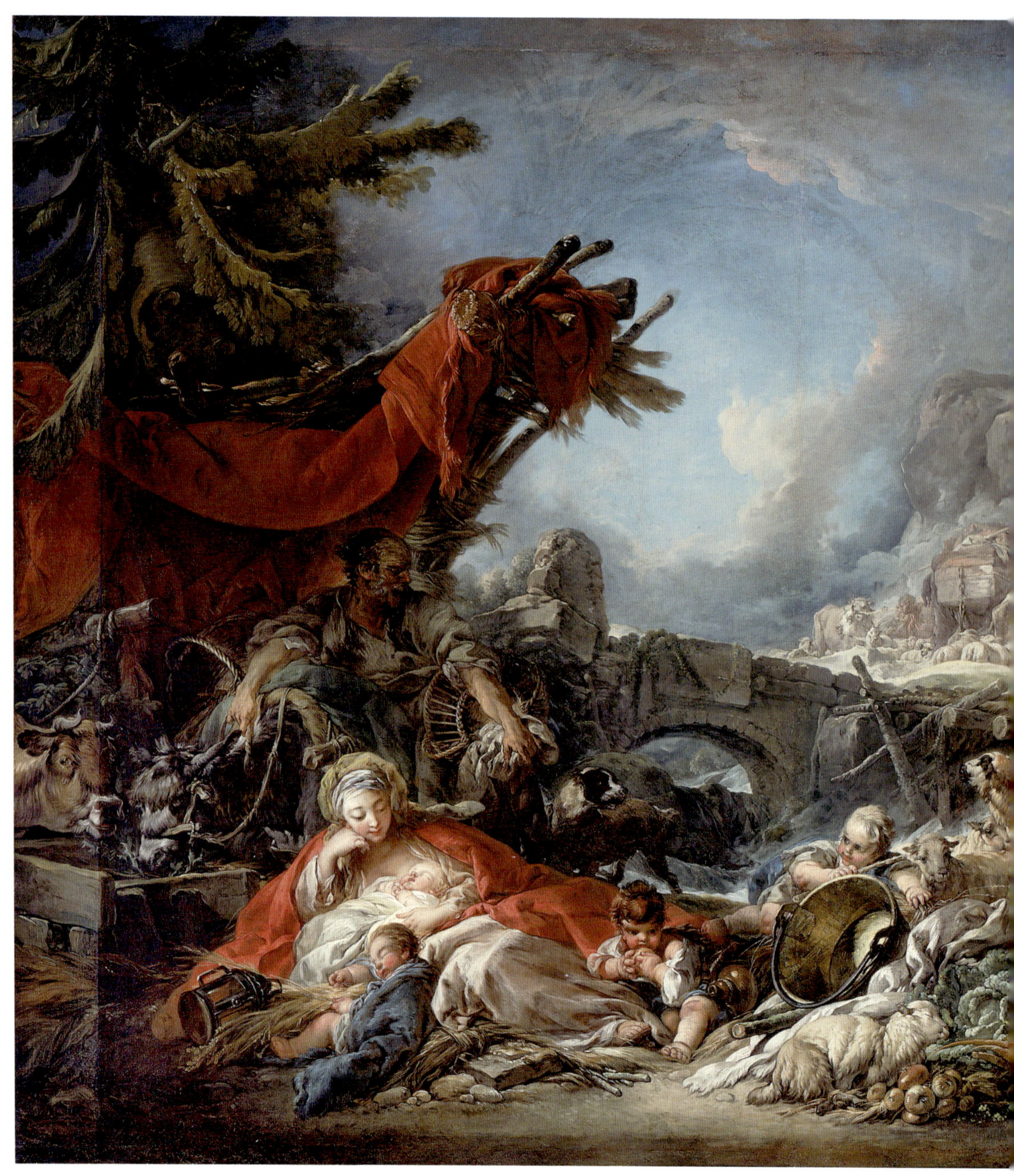

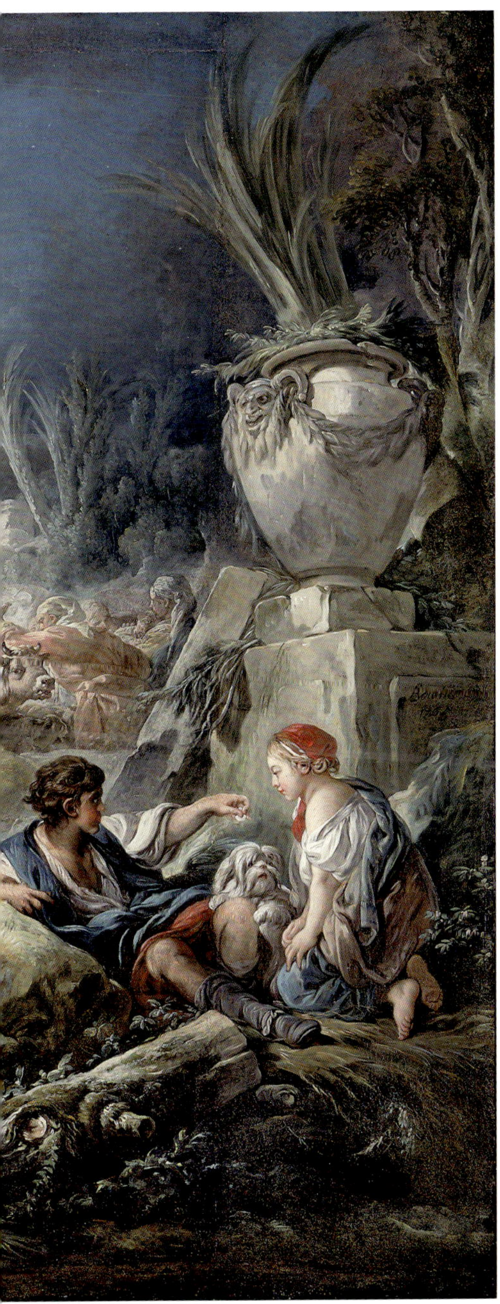

François Boucher
French, 1703–1770
Halt at the Spring, 1765

François Boucher's extraordinary skill with a paintbrush brought forth new worlds of bright, frothy colors and idyllic sensibilities, making him the most fashionable artist in eighteenth-century France. He was also prolific and versatile, producing portraits, landscapes, and mythological paintings as well as designs for tapestries, porcelain, and theater costumes and sets.

Halt at the Spring features a subject that Boucher addressed throughout his career and across many media: a pastoral scene populated by picturesque country folk. At left, a sweet-faced young woman looks lovingly at a chubby baby asleep on her chest, while a gruff older man protectively keeps watch behind her. This painting began life as a smaller canvas depicting the religious scene of the Rest on the Flight into Egypt, and these three figures were originally Mary, Joseph, and the infant Christ. In the early 1760s, the canvas was enlarged and reworked into the bucolic fantasy here, with myriad animals, still-life details, and sweeping clouds above. The philosopher and art critic Denis Diderot celebrated this picture in his review of the Salon of 1761: "What colors! What variety! What richness of objects and of ideas!... One senses how absurd it all is; but nevertheless one cannot leave the painting. It grips you."

This work was given to the MFA in 1871 along with a companion piece, *Return from Market*. Together, they were the first European paintings to enter the Museum's collection.

Oil on canvas
208.6 x 289.9 cm (82⅛ x 114⅛ in.)
Gift of the heirs of Peter Parker 71.2

Jean-Honoré Fragonard

French, 1732–1806

Aurora Triumphing over Night, about 1755–56

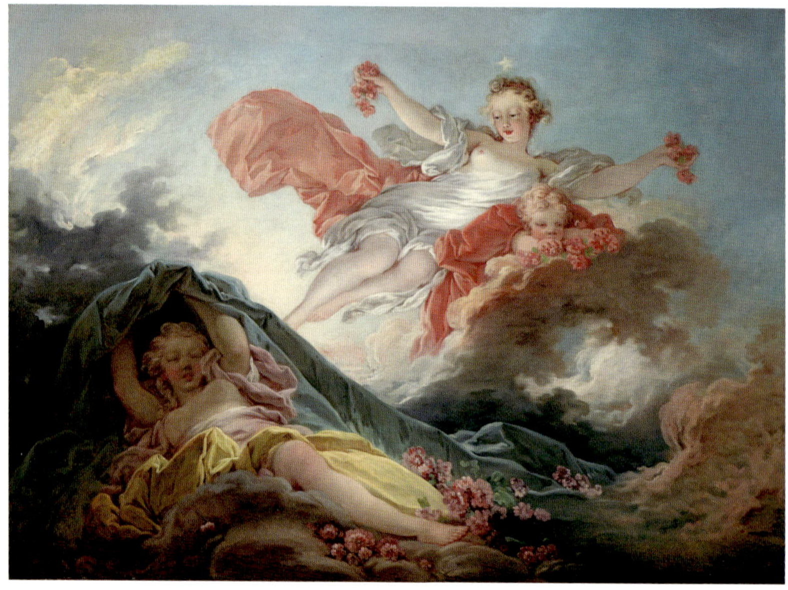

Aurora, goddess of the dawn, held aloft on clouds and accompanied by a drowsy putto, sprinkles flowers over the recumbent figure of Night, who lethargically lifts a blue mantle. As the goddess who brings light to the world each day, Aurora has long been associated with enlightenment and poetic inspiration as well as daybreak. The morning star is seen above her head.

Painted by a young Jean-Honoré Fragonard, this work resembles that of François Boucher, to whom he had been apprenticed. The now rectangular canvas was originally rounded at the corners and scalloped along the top and bottom, details typical of the Rococo, a lavishly ornamental style of art, architecture, and design that swept Europe in the eighteenth century. Its raking viewpoint, with figures presented as seen from below, confirms that the painting would have been installed high on a wall, likely over a door. To its original viewers, the subject would have been recognizable at a glance. The painting's luminous colors, elegant combination of light and shadow, and sensual brushwork would complement the flickering play of light on the gilded and mirrored surfaces in the pastel interior of a Rococo room.

The pendant to this painting (now in the National Gallery of Art, Washington, DC) depicts the goddess Diana, skyborne and ringed by the moon, admiring the slumbering shepherd Endymion. By the time Fragonard painted these, there existed a tradition of pairing the two narratives in French decorative programs, since Aurora personified Morning and Diana, Night. Both works may have been part of a larger design scheme highlighting the times of day or something more personal to the client.

Oil on canvas

95.3 x 131.4 cm (37½ x 51¾ in.)

Museum purchase with funds by exchange by contribution, and by exchange from a Gift of Laurence K. and Lorna J. Marshall 2013.62

Jean-Louis Lemoyne

French, 1665–1755

Jacques-Rolland Moreau, 1712

Although a previous misinterpretation of the inscription and date led to an incorrect identification, this dignified and monumental figure is now rightly determined to be Jacques-Rolland Moreau, a counselor to King Louis XIV and a high treasurer for war. Jean-Louis Lemoyne also sculpted a pendant bust of Moreau's wife, Elisabeth Le Detz, one of the only female portraits he is known to have made. Like other sculptors of the day, he worked in a range of media, including marble, terracotta, and wood.

Belonging to a dynasty of artists that included both his brother and his son, Lemoyne was educated at the Academy of Fine Arts in Paris. Although he was awarded the prestigious Prix de Rome in 1687, an annual prize awarded to French artists that enabled them to travel to Rome to see firsthand the sculpture and architecture of antiquity, Lemoyne did not travel to Italy and instead settled in Bordeaux for a number of years. Between 1703 and 1710, Lemoyne worked for the court of Louis XIV on decorative elements for the gardens of Versailles and would have had the opportunity to see works by Bernini, the leading sculptor of the Italian Baroque style. This bust's grandeur and animation, seen especially in the flowing, luxurious wig, reflect that influence.

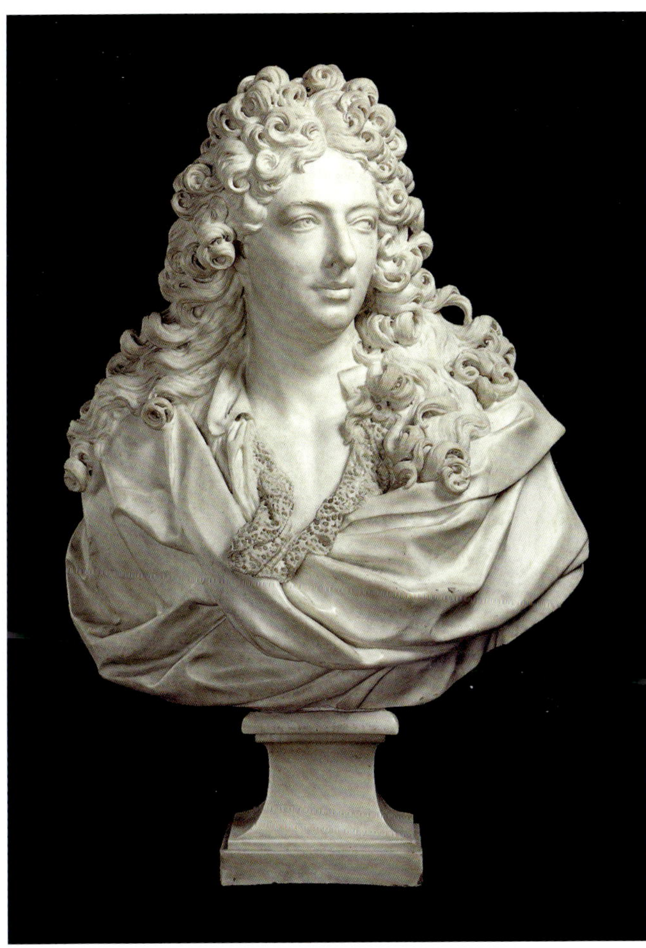

Marble

92.7 x 62.5 x 37.5 cm (36½ x 24⅝ x 14¾ in.)

Frank B. Bemis Fund, William Francis Warden Fund, and Museum purchase with funds bequeathed by Genevieve Gray Young in memory of Patience Young and Patience Gray Young

1998.395

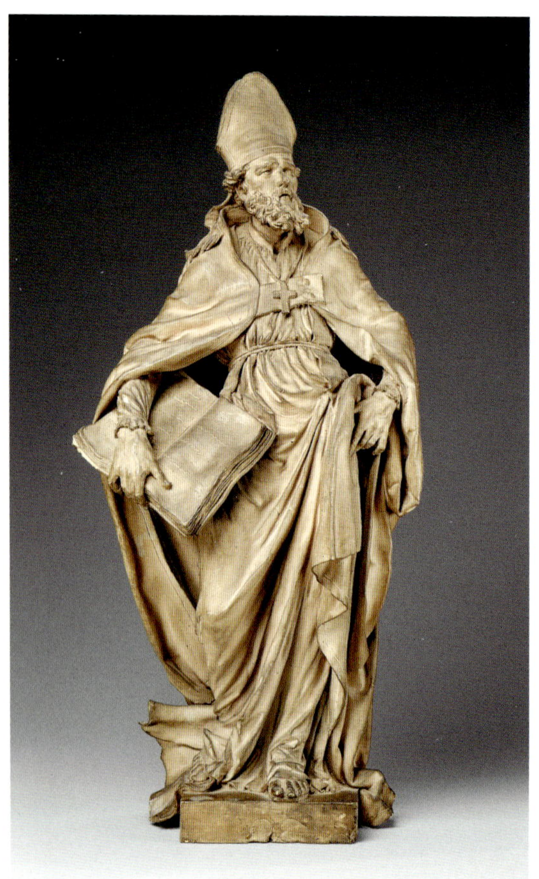

Joseph Chinard

French, 1756–1813

Saint Augustine, 1781

Joseph Chinard is best known for his elegant, exquisitely finished terracotta sculptures, which were usually created not as models for statues in other materials but as works of art in their own right. This statuette of Saint Augustine is signed and dated by Chinard, a clear indication that the artist considered it a completed work. Made for a private chapel in his hometown of Lyon, it is among the earliest of Chinard's works and displays his extraordinary abilities as a modeler in clay.

Augustine, an early Christian saint who was born in Roman North Africa and became bishop of Hippo, was one of the most important theologians and writers of the Christian tradition. Here, he is shown wearing a miter and holding open a large book with his right hand. His voluminous cope is held by a clasp decorated with a cross. He turns his head to the side, seemingly immersed in thought, and perhaps is about to speak. Chinard evokes the style of Roman Baroque sculpture, characterized by a sense of motion and animation enhanced by ample drapery. The statue was paired with one of the apostle Paul, another early Christian saint who, like Augustine, experienced a life-changing moment of spiritual conversion.

Terracotta

64 x 31 x 20 cm (25 ¼ x 12 ¼ x 7 ⅞ in.)

Frank B. Bemis Fund and Mary S. and Edward J. Holmes Fund 1997.17

Augustin Pajou
French, 1730–1809
Bust of Madame Sedaine, 1781

Augustin Pajou captured the intelligence and poise of Madame Sedaine, née Suzanne Charlotte Sériny (1739–1826), in this impressive and stately portrait bust. Madame Sedaine was the wife of the poet Michel-Jean Sedaine, of whom Pajou had sculpted a portrait six years prior. She was said to have been a great wit; indeed, Pajou conveys an obvious amiable quality in this attentive and insightful portrait.

A pupil of the French sculptor Jean-Baptiste Lemoyne, Pajou was a popular figure at the court of Versailles with both Louis XV and Louis XVI, as well as with Louis XV's last official mistress, Madame du Barry. He is perhaps best known for his royal and court portraits, though he also produced monumental sculpture and small decorative groups. In addition, he was active as a wood carver, providing gilded panels for the opera house at Versailles.

Pajou was particularly proficient in working with terracotta. To create this sculpture, he employed the technique of press molding, in which soft clay is pushed into a mold—usually made of plaster of Paris—to create the overall form and shape. The molded form is then finished off with a thin layer of liquid clay to which the artist adds the finishing touches and finer details. As opposed to freely modeling the clay, this method afforded the work more stability when firing. This is one of the earliest examples of Pajou's use of the press-molding technique.

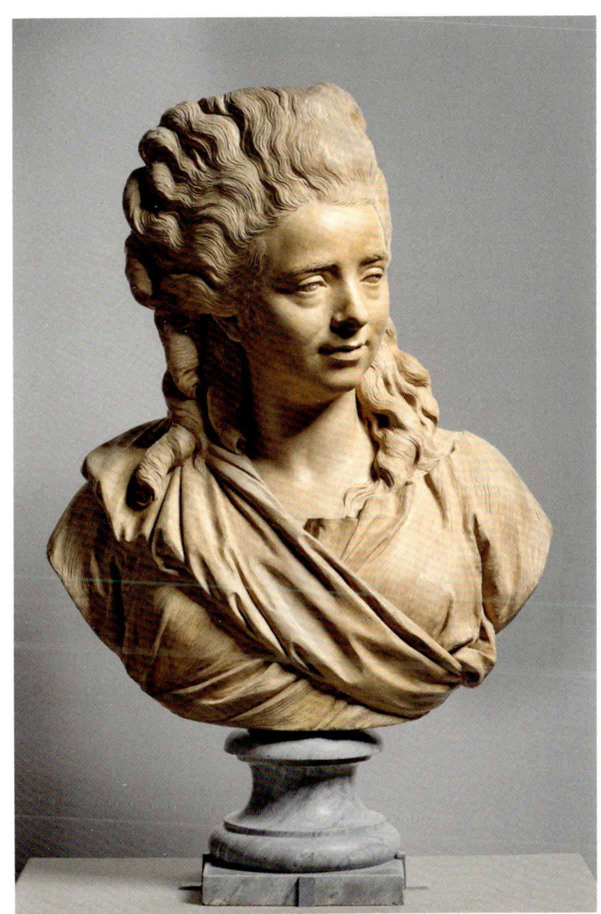

Terracotta
76.8 x 52 x 23 cm (30 ¼ x 20 ½ x 9 in.)
Bequest of Forsyth Wickes—The Forsyth Wickes Collection
65.2220

Jean-Baptiste Greuze
French, 1725–1805
The White Hat, about 1780

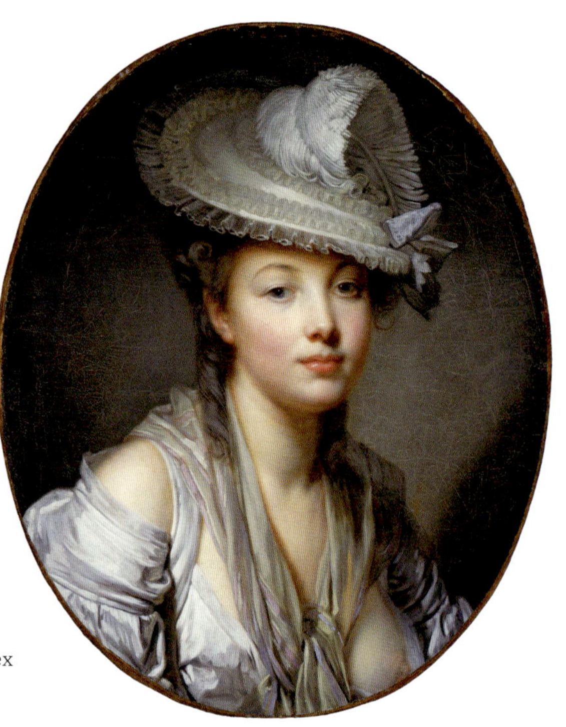

Jean-Baptiste Greuze is known for his paintings of sentiment, be they bourgeois domestic dramas or images of lone female figures such as this one. Both types of works were intended to appeal to the viewer's emotions as well as to the mind and the eye. Enlightenment thinkers, including Denis Diderot and Jean-Jacques Rousseau, praised the practice of sentiment, as it entailed intuition and conscience in addition to sensitivity to sensory perception and emotion. It did not require extreme facial expressions or theatrical gestures but could be appreciated through careful contemplation of quiet, complex emotional states and situations.

In *The White Hat*, Greuze has created a work of simple complexity. This unidentified woman, likely a model or the product of the artist's imagination, appears at once innocent and alluring. Her slightly downcast gaze is countered by her glistening, moist lips and subtle smile. She blushes hot against the cool palette of white and purple fabrics whose lush paint handling contrasts with the delicate detailing of her face and hat. Her state of deshabille, or undress—note the loose garments and exposed breast—was popularized by Marie-Antoinette, queen of France, who in the 1780s began wearing white muslin dresses that did not require restrictive underpinnings. This more "natural" alternative to rigidly corseted gowns was initially scandalous but quickly gained favor.

Oil on canvas
56.8 x 46.4 cm (22⅜ x 18¼ in.)
Gift of Jessie H. Wilkinson—Jessie H. Wilkinson Fund, Grant Walker Fund, Seth K. Sweetser Fund, and Abbott Lawrence Fund 1975.808

Allan Ramsay
Scottish, 1713–1784
Portrait of Horace Walpole's Nieces: The Honorable Laura Keppel and Charlotte, Lady Huntingtower, 1765

Allan Ramsay was among the foremost portraitists of his era in England and honored as painter to King George III in 1761. He was particularly praised for the delicacy of his brushwork and for his depictions of women. This characteristic double portrait, commissioned by the writer, aesthete, and politician Horace Walpole, depicts two of his favorite nieces and was displayed in his Gothic Revival villa known as Strawberry Hill.

Laura, in profile, and her youngest sister, Charlotte, in three-quarter view, posed for Ramsay on separate occasions; the artist, in fact, painted their heads on individual canvases that were later sewn onto the larger support. Laura looks up from her stitching, and Charlotte maintains a finger in the pages of a book as though interrupted while reading. This conversation-piece format lends the portrait an air of intimacy despite its classicizing stillness. Ramsay's sensitive handling of the sisters' distinctive features, and his finesse in rendering the luminous fabrics and intricate lace of their garments, further softens the composition's formal restraint. The artist achieved a subtle balance of decorum and tenderness perfectly suited to his commission.

Oil on canvas
156.2 x 137.2 cm (61½ x 54 in.)
Bequest of Eleanor B. Winthrop in memory of Nathaniel T. Winthrop 2009.2783

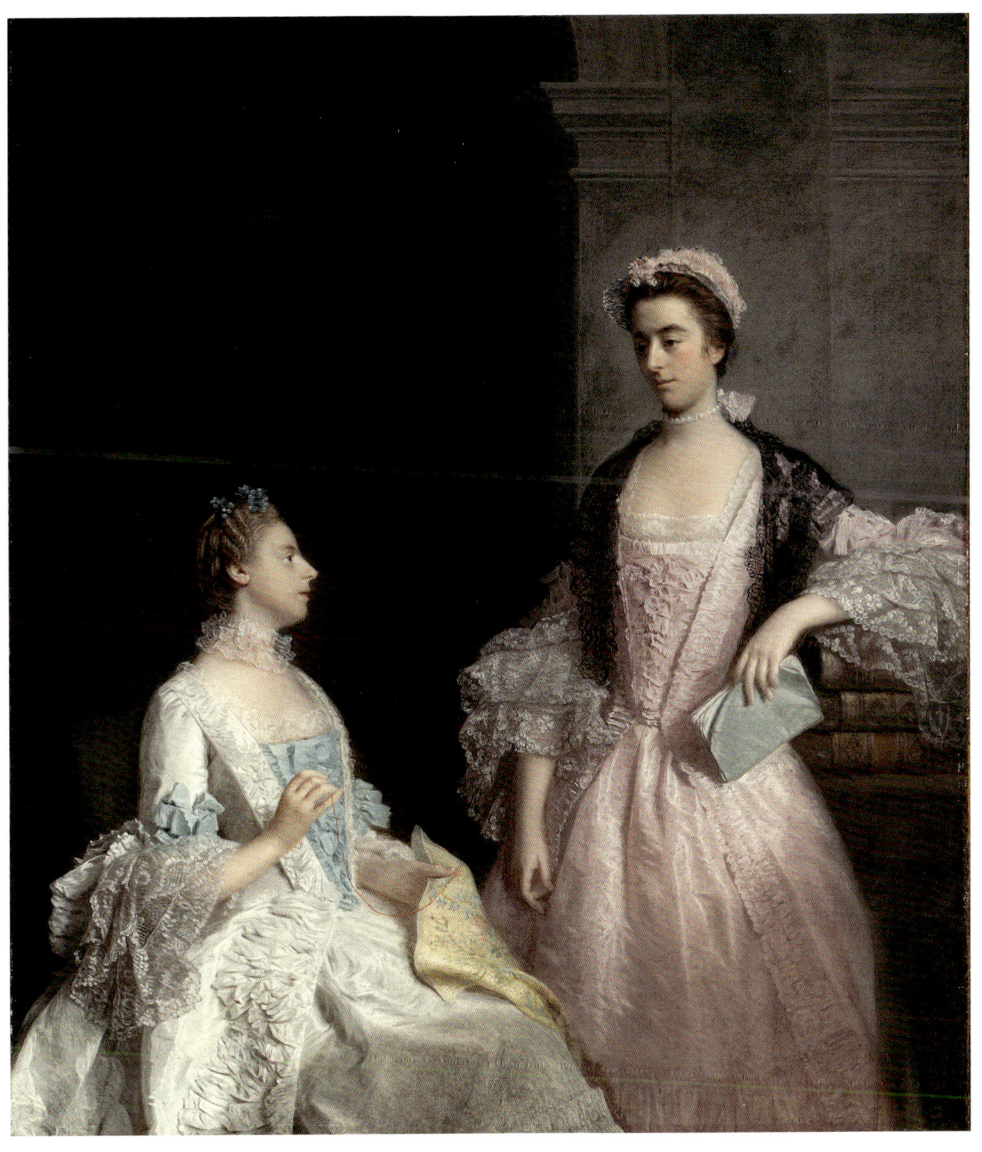

Thomas Gainsborough
English, 1727–1788
Haymaker and Sleeping Girl, about 1788

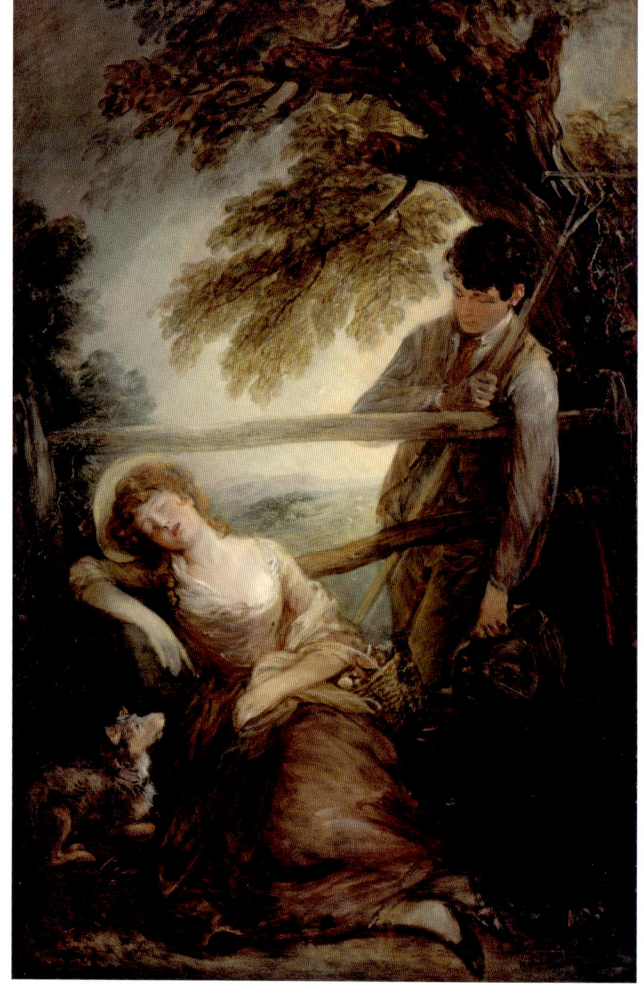

Along with Sir Joshua Reynolds, Thomas Gainsborough was the preeminent portraitist in eighteenth-century England. Gainsborough specialized in placing his subjects in verdant landscapes, endowing them with effortless elegance.

Though portraiture paid the bills, Gainsborough preferred landscape painting, as it gave greater license to his imagination. He spent many evenings devising tabletop dioramas that were the starting point for his painted topographies. Not fully satisfied, in the 1780s he conceived a new style of painting, one he felt would serve as his lasting contribution to art. Coined by Reynolds as "fancy pictures," these works are monumental genre paintings on the scale of full-length portraits, employing the characteristic feathery brushwork of Gainsborough's finest landscapes. As a group, they frequently convey poignant moods.

Here, two figures dominate a rural setting. At left, a girl leans against a fence, sleeping soundly. A boy stands at right, on the other side of the fence, gazing down at her. Although superficially a depiction of youthful lust, the painting offers a profound meditation on desires unfulfilled. The young woman's fair skin, delicate clothing, and proper shoes indicate she is not a country girl. By contrast, the youth is dressed for farming, as evidenced by the hay in his hat and on his rake. Pausing in his labors, he is separated from her not only by the rails of the fence but also by the gulf in social class. At any moment the terrier beside her may bark, waking her and ending the young man's daydream.

Gainsborough rarely made preparatory drawings for his paintings; however, the existence of a sheet for this composition at the British Museum in London reveals how carefully he planned this work. Gainsborough Dupont, nephew and apprentice of the painter, chose this canvas when he was offered any painting in his uncle's studio.

Oil on canvas
227.3 x 149.9 cm (89½ x 59 in.)
M. Theresa B. Hopkins Fund and Seth K. Sweetser Fund
53.2553

John Michael Rysbrack
English (born in Flanders), 1694–1770
Allegorical figure of Historia, 1744

John Michael Rysbrack left his hometown of Antwerp in Flanders around 1720 and moved to London with his older brother the painter Pieter Andreas Rysbrack. He went on to become one of the most prolific sculptors of the early eighteenth century, active in monumental sculpture, portrait busts, and architectural elements. The younger Rysbrack was also a skilled draftsman, and it is known from a surviving presentation drawing that this terracotta sculpture relates to a proposed funerary monument for John Campbell, 2nd Duke of Argyll. Rysbrack had earlier executed portrait busts of the Duke and Duchess of Argyll, and he obviously had hopes of receiving the more important commission for the major monument in Westminster Abbey.

This terracotta *modello* of the allegorical figure of History (*Historia*) would have been presented to the clients along with finished drawings of the proposed monument. Only six terracotta models by Rysbrack survive today, all in museum collections. Unfortunately for Rysbrack, the important commission for the Argyll tomb went to his artistic rival the Frenchman Louis François Roubilliac. This loss in 1745 began a downward turn in Rysbrack's popularity.

Notably for an artist active in England at the time, Rysbrack never traveled to Rome. Even without this experience, he was the rare sculptor in England whose work was of the same caliber as that of artists in continental Europe. His portrait busts in marble were particularly popular in the 1730s, when there was a preference for sculpted portraits over painted ones. Rysbrack worked first in clay, usually from life, then skipped straight to the marble version, never using plaster casts.

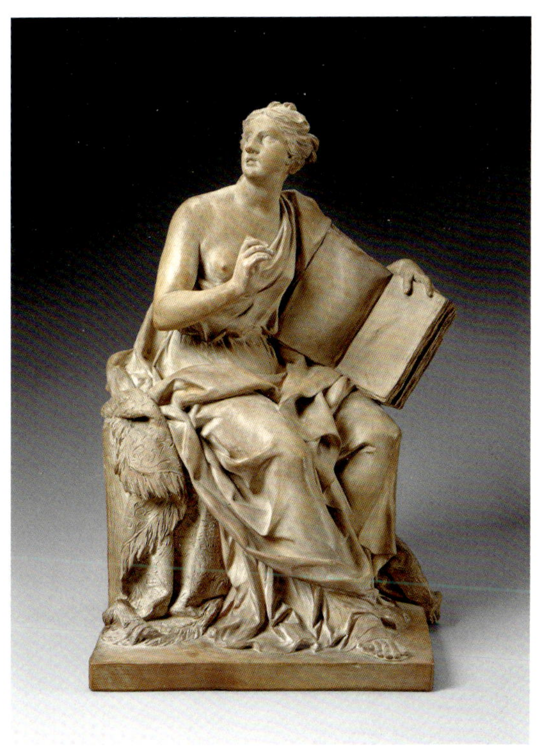

Terracotta
48 x 30.5 x 26.4 cm (18⅞ x 12 x 10⅜ in.)
Mary S. and Edward Jackson Holmes Fund 1997.142

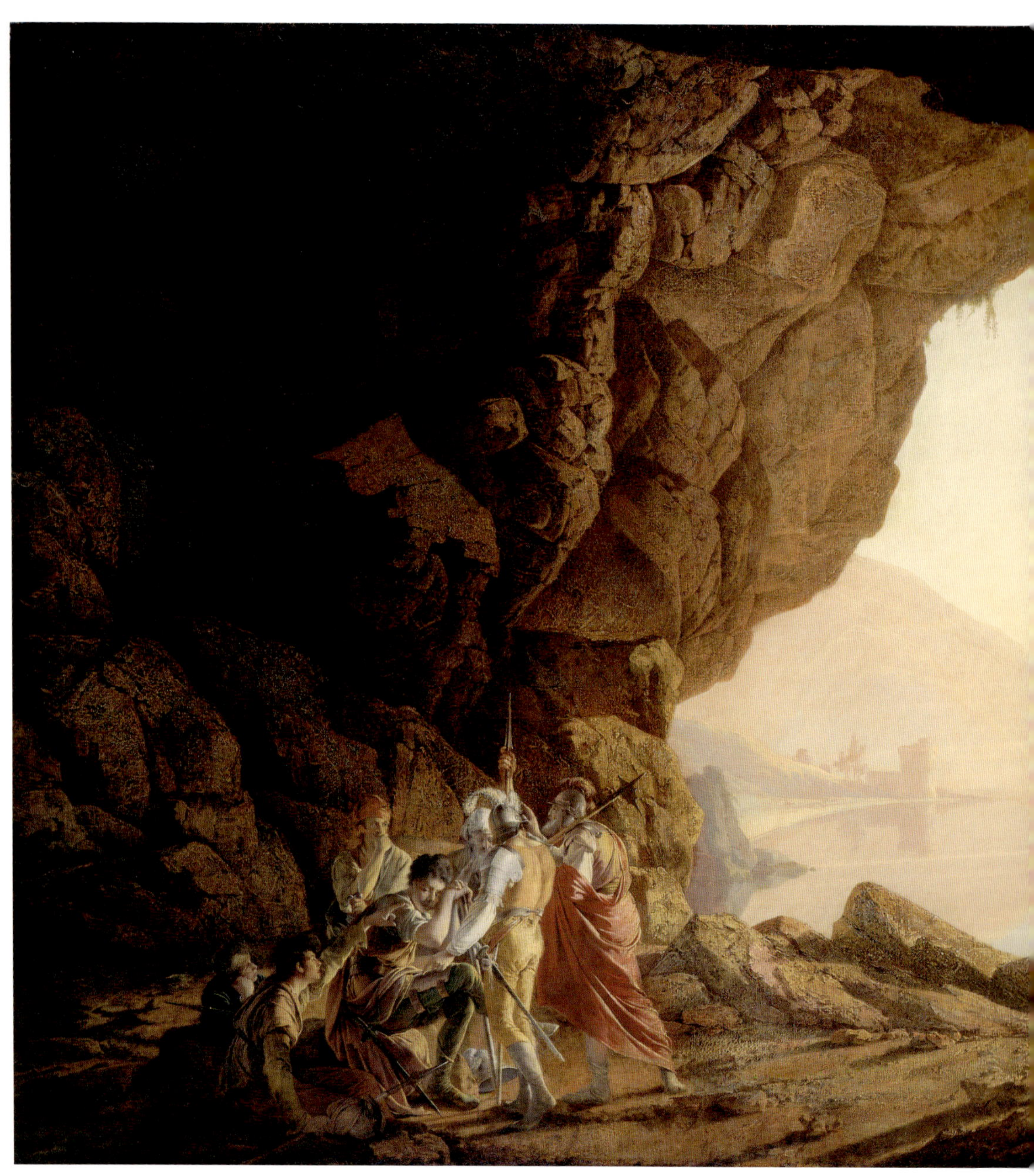

Oil on canvas

121.9 x 172.7 cm (48 x 68 in.)

Charles H. Bayley Picture and Painting Fund and other Funds, by exchange 1990.95

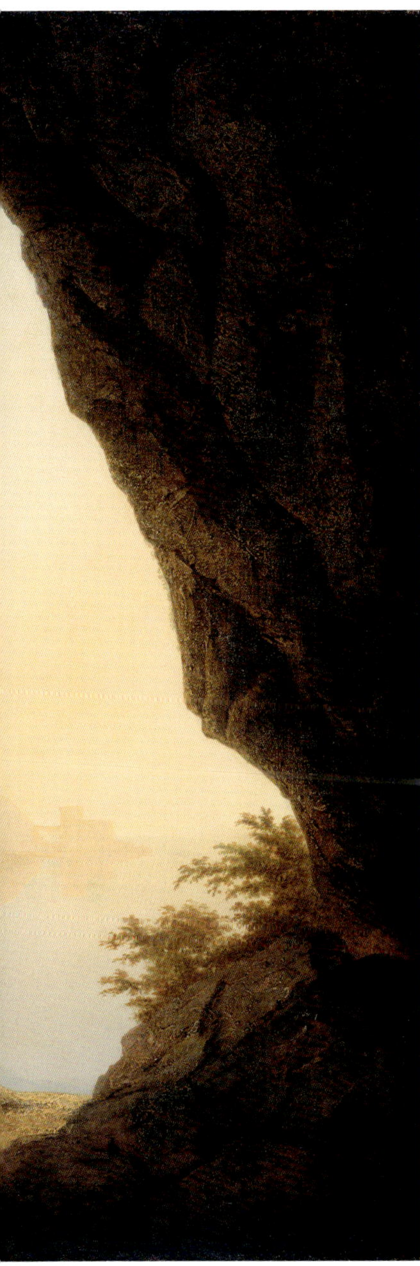

Joseph Wright of Derby
English, 1734–1797
Grotto by the Seaside in the Kingdom of Naples with Banditti, Sunset, 1778

Joseph Wright of Derby was celebrated during his lifetime and to this day for his rendering of light, whether in an indoor genre scene depicting a scientific experiment of the Lunar Society, or as here, in a dramatic landscape. In 1774, during a yearlong stay in Italy, he studied Roman ruins and visited the Neapolitan coast and the Gulf of Salerno, making detailed drawings of the grottoes he observed. This painting is based on such a drawing but takes the composition further by adding bandits. The narrative remains unknown despite the bandits' theatrical gestures and distinctive garments. Wright of Derby may have borrowed the figures from works he admired by the seventeenth-century Italian artist Salvator Rosa, which begins to explain the awkward inconsistencies of scale given that the seated men, were they to stand, would tower over the others. Outside the grotto, the hazy glow of sunset over the placid water highlights the rocks and fissures of the cave's mouth and contrasts with the tenebrous interior just beyond the men. Their troubled expressions and animated gestures possibly relate to the approaching nightfall.

This painting was first exhibited at the Royal Academy in London in 1778. Two years later, the artist showed another painting, based on a coastal drawing from Italy titled *A Cavern with the Figure of Julia Banished Thither by Her Grandfather Augustus*. These two grotto scenes were purchased by Joshua Cockshutt in 1780 and remained together for more than two hundred years. Whether they were actually pendants or became so only through history, their subjects are often interpreted jointly, with the suggestion that the bandits in one painting delivered the exiled adulteress, depicted in the other, to her fate.

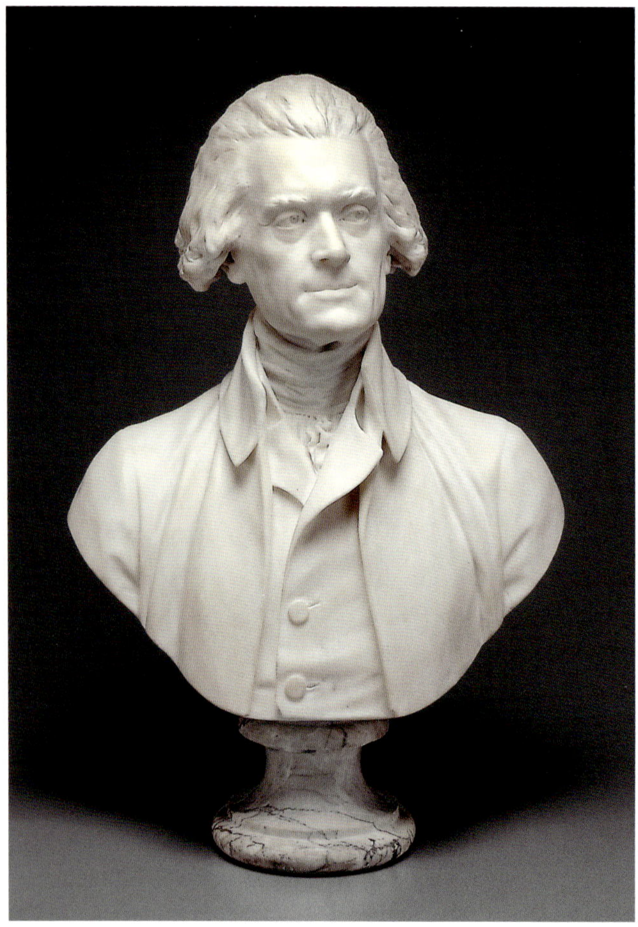

Jean-Antoine Houdon
French, 1741–1828
Thomas Jefferson, 1789

This likeness of Thomas Jefferson is well known, as it was the basis for his depiction on the nickel. Stately and dignified, the future president of the United States is expertly captured by Jean-Antoine Houdon. This is actually Houdon's second version of the bust, as the first was accidentally broken at Monticello, Jefferson's estate. The original was executed in Paris in 1789 while Jefferson was acting minister to France for the newly established United States.

Jefferson arrived in Paris when the new artistic movement of Neoclassicism was growing increasingly popular. Drawn to this style by his love of ancient cultures and antiquities, Jefferson found in Houdon the ideal artist, describing him as "perhaps the foremost artist in the world." In 1761, Houdon had won the prestigious Prix de Rome, the annual prize awarded to French artists that enabled them to travel to Rome. Houdon's knowledge of antique sculpture is evident in his ability to bring forth from hard marble a sense of the vitality of a living, breathing figure without losing solidity.

Despite receiving official sanction of his work from the French Royal Academy of Painting and Sculpture, Houdon did not receive many commissions for large-scale monumental sculpture. Instead, he relied on the numerous private patrons who appreciated his insightful portraits. His portrayals of young children, including his own daughter Sabine, are much admired.

Marble
56.5 x 48 x 26 cm (22¼ x 18⅞ x 10¼ in.)
George Nixon Black Fund 34.129

Jean-Antoine Houdon
French, 1741–1828
John Paul Jones, 1780

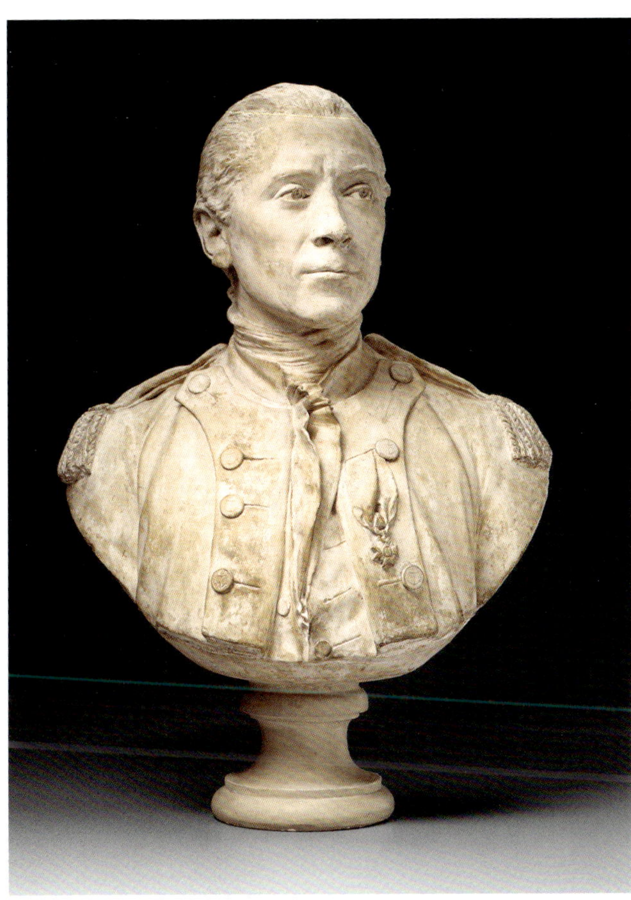

Plaster
71.1 x 47 x 33 cm (28 x 18½ x 13 in.)
Gift of Charles H. Taylor, Jr. 31.874

Jean-Antoine Houdon was the leading French sculptor of the late eighteenth century, known for his portrait busts that feature a keen naturalism and references to ancient sculpture. This bust depicts the naval hero John Paul Jones. Born in Scotland in 1747, he is best known for his famous victory in 1779 while commanding the warship *Bonhomme Richard* against the British during the American Revolution. The original marble version of this bust was commissioned in 1780 by the Paris Masonic Lodge of the Nine Sisters to commemorate the naval officer's victory.

In the portrait, Jones is shown wearing the uniform of an admiral and a cross presented to him by King Louis XVI. His eyes look into the distance with intense vitality, determination, and wistfulness. The bust was exhibited at the Salon of 1781, and Jones apparently was so pleased with his likeness that he commissioned twenty versions in plaster—including this work—to give to friends and acquaintances. Jones himself presented this version of the bust to Thomas Jefferson. Despite the distinguished portrayal, Jones remained a polarizing figure during his life and died in relative obscurity in Paris in 1792.

In 1785, at the behest of Thomas Jefferson, American ambassador to France at the time, Houdon visited the newly formed United States to create a portrait sculpture of George Washington. Made from a life mask and measurements of Washington himself, the sculpture is an accurate depiction of the future president.

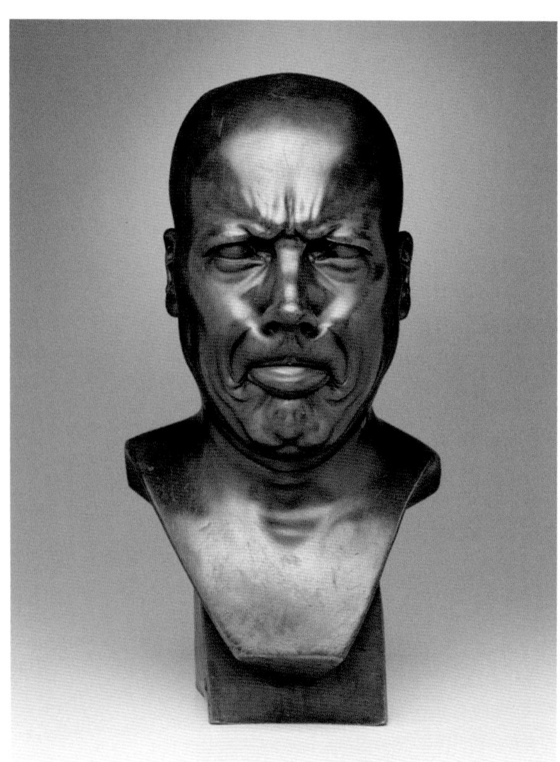

Franz Xaver Messerschmidt

Austrian, 1736–1783

A Hypochondriac, about 1775–80

This highly expressive face is Franz Xaver Messerschmidt's own. The artist distorts his own features by pinching, pushing, and grimacing to create an image that is captivating but disconcerting. This sculpture is part of a series, later called the *Character Heads*, created by the artist in the last decade of his life, when he was suffering from both physical and emotional illnesses. Messerschmidt claimed that through these sculptures, he was attempting to repel a spirit within him who was jealous of his knowledge and artistic skill.

Early in his career, Messerschmidt studied at the Academy of Fine Arts Vienna and trained with his uncle, a Rococo sculptor. He went on to become one of the most unique and unusual artists of his day. After working in Rome, Paris, and London, he received a number of commissions from the Hapsburg court in Vienna. Ultimately, however, he rejected the court life and spent his later years in obscurity in Pressburg (now Bratislava).

The works in the *Character Heads* series reflect contemporary interests in the field of physiognomy, which proposes that the shape of the head and face reflects the character of the person. Shortly after Messerschmidt's death, an exhibition of the *Character Heads* was mounted in Vienna. Forty-nine heads—the series originally numbered more than sixty—were featured. The title *A Hypochondriac* appeared in the exhibition catalogue and has since been assigned to the piece. The MFA's work was the first by this artist to enter an American museum collection, upon the advice of the visionary curator Hanns Swarzenski.

Lead

42.6 x 25 x 23 cm (16¾ x 9⅞ x 9 in.)

William E. Nickerson Fund, No. 2 57.117

Francisco Goya y Lucientes

Spanish, 1746–1828

Time, Truth, and History, about 1797–99 or 1804

Although celebrated in his time as the foremost portrait painter in Spain, Goya's later admirers—including today's—associate him with the unsettling moods that are found in many of his paintings, drawings, and prints. Whether the subject is from the occult, such as a coven of witches, or a learned allegory, as in this small painting, the artist often employed bats, owls, and other winged figures, as well as dramatic contrasts of light and darkness, to evoke a menacing air.

Here Time is rendered as a muscular man, hovering with the aid of expansive wings. These wings create a boundary between the illuminated foreground and the inky darkness of the background. Time grasps an hourglass in his left hand and in his right, the hand of a female nude: the naked Truth, who makes eye contact with the viewer. At the base of the composition, another nude woman sits on a fragmentary column. With a book open on her lap, she is engaged in her writing. Representing History, this woman turns, looking backward. Above this trio, ominous bats and owls emerge from the gloom, drawing the glance of Time.

The subject derives from an adage recorded by the Renaissance scholar Erasmus of Rotterdam (1466–1536). The general concept that the passage of time will reveal the full truth had flourished in the art of the eighteenth century, and was vividly rendered by many painters including Tiepolo (see pp. 166–67). A generation later, Goya augmented the pairing of Time and Truth by including the figure of History, perhaps acknowledging the Enlightenment emphasis on reason and veracity. A decade after this work was created, Goya painted a much larger version (now at the Nationalmuseum in Stockholm), introducing a number of changes.

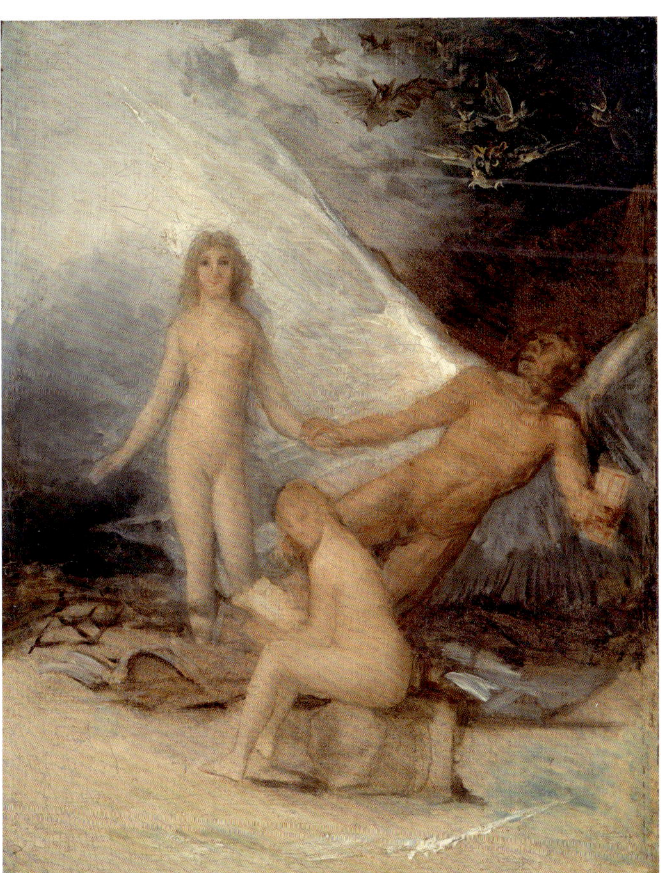

Oil on canvas
41.6 x 32.7 cm (16⅜ x 12⅞ in.)
Gift of Mrs. Horatio Greenough Curtis in memory of Horatio Greenough Curtis
27.1330

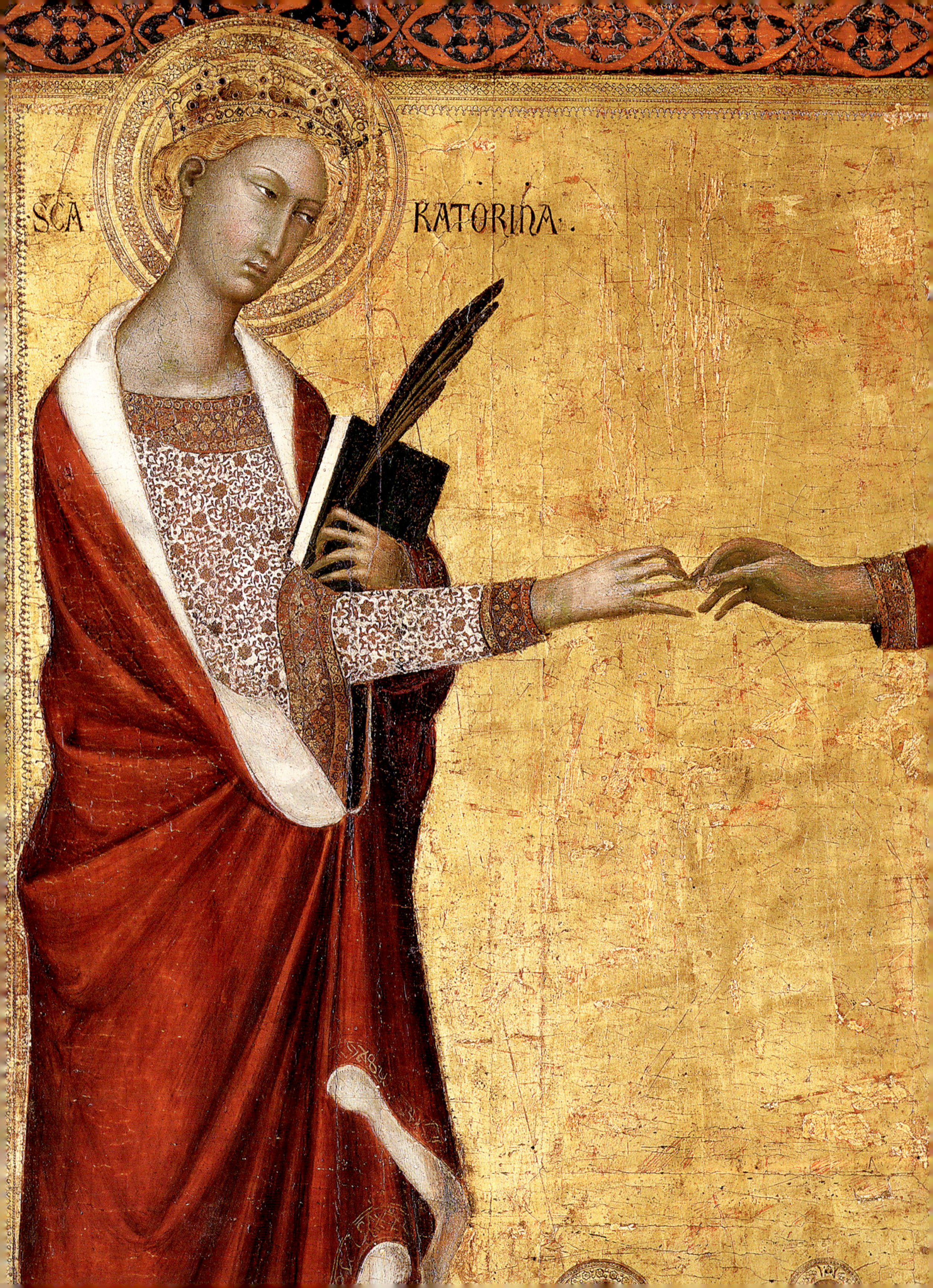
SCA KATORINA.

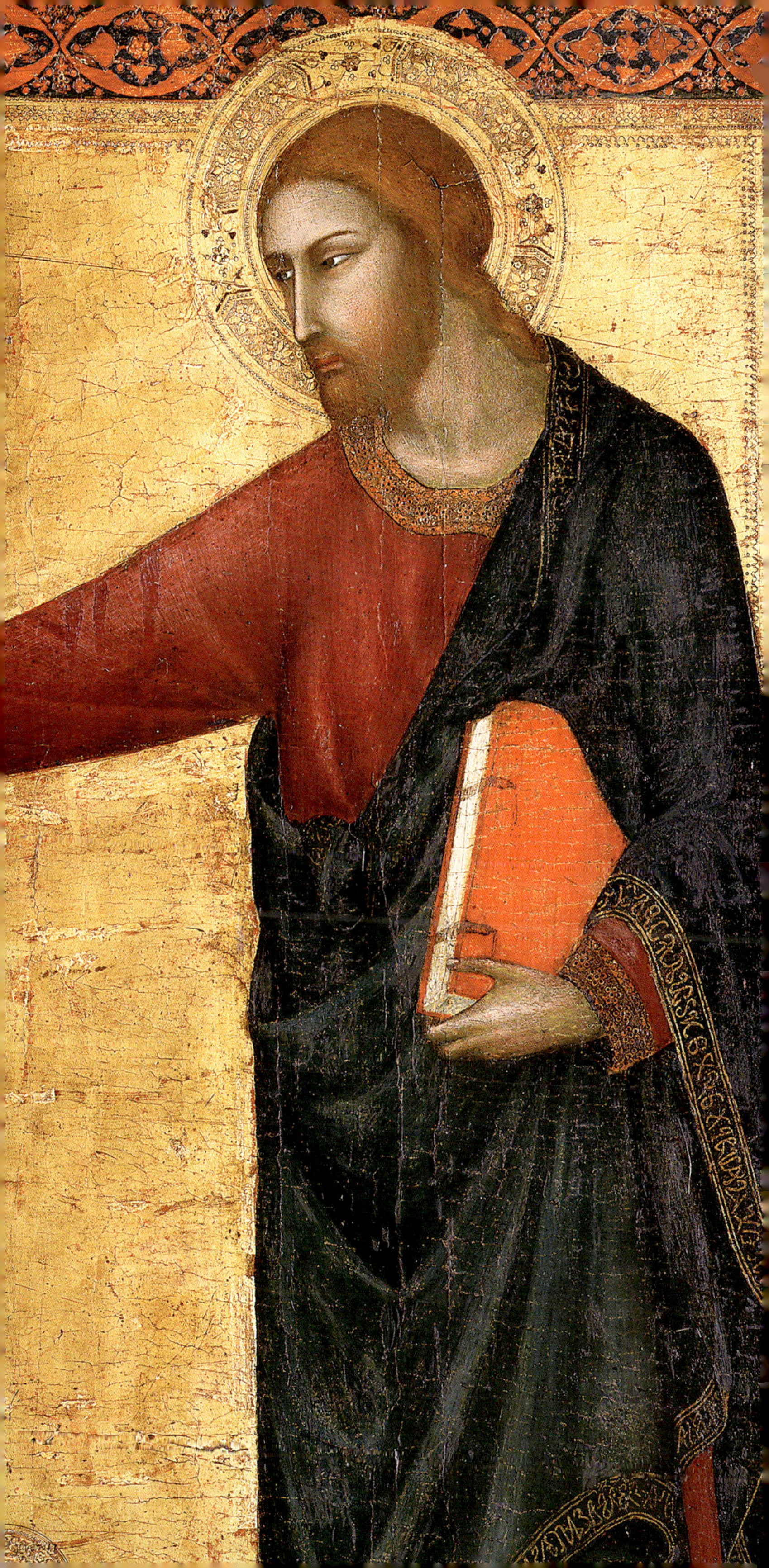

Further Reading

Baer, Ronni, ed. *Class Distinctions: Dutch Painting in the Age of Rembrandt and Vermeer.* Boston: MFA Publications, 2015.

Baer, Ronni. *The Poetry of Everyday Life: Dutch Painting in Boston.* Boston: MFA Publications, 2002.

Bagnoli, Martina, ed. *A Feast for the Senses. Art and Experience in Medieval Europe.* Baltimore: The Walters Art Museum; New Haven: Yale University Press, 2016.

Baxandall, Michael. *The Limewood Sculptors of Renaissance Germany.* New Haven: Yale University Press, 1982.

Baxandall, Michael. *Painting and Experience in Fifteenth-Century Italy.* 2nd ed. New York: Oxford University Press, 1974.

Belting, Hans. *The Image and its Public in the Middle Ages.* New Rochelle, NY: Catarzas, 1990.

Cahn, Walter and Linda Seidel. *Romanesque Sculpture in American Collections 1: New England Museums.* New York: Burt Franklin, 1979.

Cambareri, Marietta. *Della Robbia: Sculpting with Color in Renaissance Florence.* Boston: MFA Publications, 2016.

Fozi, Shirin and Gerhard Lutz, eds. *Christ on the Cross. The Boston Crucifix and the Rise of Monumental Wood Sculpture, 970-1200.* Turnhout: Brepols, 2020.

Gillerman, Dorothy, ed. *Gothic Sculpture in America 1. The New England Museums.* New York: Garland, 1989.

Harbison, Craig. *The Mirror of the Artist: Northern Renaissance Art in its Historical Context.* New York: Harry N. Abrams, 2003.

Haskell, Francis. *Patrons and Painters: A Study in the Relations Between Italian Art and Society in the Age of the Baroque.* 2nd ed. New Haven: Yale University Press, 1980.

Haskell, Francis and Nicholas Penny. *Taste and the Antique. The Lure of Classical Sculpture, 1500-1900.* 2nd ed. New Haven: Yale University Press, 1986.

Ilchman, Frederick, ed. *Titian, Tintoretto, Veronese: Rivals in Renaissance Venice.* Boston: MFA Publications, 2009.

Ilchman, Frederick, Thomas Michie, C.D. Dickerson III, and Esther Bell, eds. *Casanova: The Seduction of Europe.* Boston: MFA Publications, 2017.

Kanter, Laurence B. and Eric Zafran. *Italian Paintings in the Museum of Fine Arts, Boston, I.* Boston: Museum of Fine Arts and Northeastern University Press, 1994.

Paoletti, John T. and Gary M. Radke. *Art in Renaissance Italy.* Upper Saddle River, NJ: Pearson Prentice Hall, 2012.

Penny, Nicholas. *The Materials of Sculpture.* New Haven: Yale University Press, 1993.

Schroth, Sarah and Ronni Baer, eds. *El Greco to Velázquez: Art During the Reign of Philip III.* Boston: MFA Publications, 2008.

Shearman, John. *Mannerism.* New York: Penguin, 1967.

Shearman, John. *Only Connect: Art and the Spectator in the Italian Renaissance.* Princeton: Princeton University Press, 1992.

Snyder, James, Larry Silver and Henry Luttikhuizen. *Northern Renaissance Art.* 2nd ed. Upper Saddle River, NJ: Prentice Hall, 2005.

Sutton, Peter C. *The Age of Rubens.* Boston: Museum of Fine Arts; Ghent: Ludion, 1993.

Westermann, Mariët. *A Worldly Art: The Dutch Republic, 1585-1718.* New Haven: Yale University Press, 2016.

Zafran, Eric. *French Paintings in the Museum of Fine Arts, Boston, I.* Boston: Museum of Fine Arts, 1998.

Index